The Wild and the Domestic

Environmental Arts and Humanities Series

BARNEY NELSON

The Wild and the Domestic

Animal Representation, Ecocriticism,

and Western American Literature

University of Nevada Press ▲▲ Reno & Las Vegas

Environmental Arts and Humanities Series
Series Editor: Scott Slovic

University of Nevada Press,
Reno, Nevada 89557 USA
Copyright © 2000 by
University of Nevada Press

FIRST PRINTING
09 08 07 06 05 04 03 02 01 00
5 4 3 2 1

Library of Congress
Cataloging-in-Publication Data
Nelson, Barney, 1947–
The wild and the domestic; animal
representation, ecocriticism, and western
American literature / Barney Nelson.
    p. cm. — (Environmental arts and
humanities series)
Includes bibliographical references (p.) and
index.
ISBN 0-87417-347-7 (pbk.:alk.paper)
1. Austin, Mary Hunter, 1868–1934—
Criticism and interpretation.   2. Women
and literature—West (U.S.)—History—
20th century.   3. American Literature—
History and criticism.   4. Western
stories—History and criticism.   5. West
(U.S.)—In literature.   6. Animals in
literature.   7. Ecology in literature.
8. Nature in literature.   I. Title.
II. Series.
PS3501.U8 Z68   2000
818'.5209—dc21   99-045814

An earlier version of "The Indigenous Desert Cow" was published as "Edward Abbey's
Cow," in *Coyote in the Maze: Critical Essays on Edward Abbey*, edited by Peter Quigley
(Salt Lake City: University of Utah Press, 1998).

An earlier version of "Hoofed Locusts or Wild Eco-Sheep?" was published as "The Flock:
An Ecocritical Look at Mary Austin's Sheep and John Muir's Hoofed Locusts," in *Exploring
Lost Borders: Critical Essays on Mary Austin*, edited by Melody Graulich and Elizabeth
Klimasmith (University of Nevada Press, 1999).

Portions of the Introduction will be published as "Rustling Thoreau's Cattle: Wildness
and Domesticity in 'Walking'," in *Thoreau's Sense of Place: Essays in American Environmental Writing*, edited by Richard Schneider (forthcoming from the University of Iowa
Press).

For my brother, Richard Edward DeGear

Contents

The Rural Storyteller

Before we can adorn our houses with beautiful objects the walls must be stripped, and our lives must be stripped, and beautiful housekeeping and beautiful living be laid for a foundation: now, a taste for the beautiful is most cultivated out of doors, where there is no house and no housekeeper.
Henry David Thoreau (*Portable Thoreau* 293)

I am a genuine crusty old woman from the rural culture. So I've been stewing about which stories I should tell in order to establish my credibility as one. Should I say that my rural family heritage traces back for fifteen agricultural generations on North American soil, or that I wore black four-buckle overshoes to a one-room country school? Should I tell about the time I won Reserve Grand Champion at the Jackson County, Iowa, 4-H fair or stories from my thirteen years on one of West Texas's grand old ranches, eating from a chuck wagon and moving the remuda? Should I talk about my twenty-seven-year career as a livestock magazine photojournalist, my gardens, or my chickens? Should I tell about my hunting days, my bronc-riding days, or my running-my-own-cattle days? No, none of these stories quite captures the real spirit of my voice. So, I guess I'll just have to talk about washing dishes.

I read a magazine article the other day about a friend who has become somewhat of a legend as a horseman's horseman. I'll call him John to protect his privacy.[1] The article talks about John washing dishes but sort of makes it sound humorous. Washing dishes is not funny.

Back in my undergraduate college days, I had a pretty, blonde, city-raised roommate who had a handsome cowboy on the string. She surprised him one night with a big birthday party, and we fed half the county hamburgers, beans, potato salad, cake, and homemade ice cream. Under the stars, she played her guitar and sang to the guests around a campfire. My unglamorous contribution was cooking and carrying: full plates outside, empty ones inside. After the party, my roommate drove her cowboy back to the ranch, a nice, long romantic drive in the moonlight. I was quite jealous. I didn't have blonde hair, couldn't carry a tune in a bucket, and didn't have a boyfriend. I felt sorry for her later, though, when she burst into our apartment in tears.

"He was mad about something all the way home," she wailed. "He never spoke to me. When he got out, all he said was, 'Who washed the dishes?'"

I should have warned her because I knew he was a traditionalist. Rules are rules. They never had another date. Like I said, washing dishes is not funny.

My mother started me very young. I used to stand on a chair next to her at the sink and dry while she washed. She tried to make a game of it. Her best idea was that if I caught up with her, I could quit and go outside. But if she found a wet glass put away, I had to start all over. She would keep the game interesting by slowing down until I was just about to grab the last fork. Occasionally, she even let me win. So, we giggled and raced, but dried carefully and had a squealing good time. However, the game taught me, at a very young age, that washing dishes is not something a woman does willingly. Long before I had outgrown the chair, her game wasn't fun anymore.

While I dried, my mother also told stories. She showed me the ugly boiling-water scar that covered her arm from her elbow to her wrist. She told me that she and her mother had been washing dishes at this very sink the night a tornado dropped the barn's big hay tongs right outside this window. All the buildings except the house were leveled. Hurt and dying animals screamed for help. While my grandparents ran out into the storm, Mom gave the SOS long ring on the old crank telephone. Within minutes, the yard was full of neighbors. We were still using the same phone; it hung right next to the sink. We still had the same neighbors.

She told me about the hand-worked dishtowel I was using. As a young girl she learned to embroider, and for her hope chest had carefully cross-stitched a dishcloth for each day of the week. When she and my dad married, he promised to help her with the dishes. He used each of her pretty new dishtowels once, then never helped again. Mother and I laughed, but it was not funny. I still have one of those towels.

Young girls growing up in farm and ranch communities always had to wash dishes. It was good training for our tradition-bound future lives. Even in college, when the rural gang had a party, the men might volunteer to cook the meat, but the women washed the dishes. Later, as a young wife who loved horses, washing dishes at ranch get-togethers became very painful for me. After dinner, the men sat out on the back porch and told horse stories while I was stuck in the kitchen with the women washing dishes.

So, the day she was born, I made up my mind that my pretty daughter was going to have a better life. I saw to it that she had little boots and spurs, little leggins, a little saddle and rope, a big ol' hat with a big ol' red-tailed hawk feather, and a good ol' horse named "Boss." She rode with the men and got to be a real good hand, better than her mom. At four she took complete charge of the *tecole* bucket,[2] at six she got fighting mad when another cowboy rode in front of her, at eight she drew her first day wages, at nine she was dragging calves, at eleven she bossed a crew of grown men on a circle. She was the apple of her daddy's eye, the sweetheart of young cowboys from Montana to Texas. While I washed the dishes, I listened to the men out on the back porch telling her their horse stories and saying how much they liked pretty little girls who were good hands.

About this time I met John and realized that I had ridden horses all my life but didn't know a thing about it. With John's almost Zen-like help, I watched my horsemanship skills slide downhill rapidly. John's wife, Susie, gave me a bumper sticker for the back of my pickup that read "A Woman's Place Is on a Horse." She also made me a *mecate*, and we traded hate-to-wash-dishes stories. Sometimes my dishes stacked up for a week, but the guilt was gone. On a colt, astride my third hand-made saddle, wearing very worn leggins and nursing a pulled groin muscle from my last buck-off, I trotted through the rain. Riding beside me, the men told stories about how much they liked women who stayed at the kitchen sink where they belonged.

An old cowboy friend once lamented that he'd spent his life flanking calves. When he was young, he said, it was always, "Let them old men rope so they can stay on their horses." When he got old, it was, "Let them young boys rope so they can learn." He said he was always the wrong age and never did get to rope. For me, when I was young, it was, "Let them young girls wash the dishes so they can practice." When I was old, it was, "Don't let them young girls wash dishes, it will wreck their lives." When I was young and wanted to ride tough horses, the men wanted pretty ladies who could cook and sew. When I got old and could really cook and sew, the men wanted pretty ladies who could ride tough horses.

To make a long story short, I quit the horses and the men and became a college professor. I enjoyed tricking my young student cowpersons into enjoying freshman comp. I got to read their horse stories, and I could afford a dishwasher. Life seemed tolerable again.

Once upon a time, the job of riding colts was given to young boys or green hands. The best hands wanted to work with the Ph.D. candidates, the reining horses, the cutters. Nobody wanted to fool with the freshmen. John helped me realize that teaching freshmen, like riding colts, can be the most challenging and rewarding job on a college campus. I don't ride horses much anymore, but I still go visit the horse professors when I get a chance. I once asked John if anyone else decided to get a Ph.D. because they failed his horse classes. He laughed.

I failed John's roping classes too. He tried to teach me to rope and braid rawhide, but I never did my homework. John is an excellent big-loop riata roper. He is quite particular about his rawhide ropes and always makes his own. Rawhiding and rawhiders were once the brunt of jokes. They smelled bad, they were all ex-felons, and just how smart does a feller need to be to slice up cowhides? But John and a few friends and apprentices changed all that. Today rawhide braiders hang their work in art museums. John says he spends considerable time working on a hide, getting it ready for braiding, scraping it clear enough to see through, making sure each string has no flaws. He says he never learned to tie many fancy knots, just worked real hard on the strings. I apply what he says to writing. Instead of concentrating on a fancy style, I work real hard getting my stories straight and clear. A fancy rawhide riata with flaws in the strings can only be hung on the wall. Real art should catch something.

Not long ago, John cooked me a pot of beans. I've eaten lots of beans in my life, but his were the best. I tried to wash the dishes, but John elbowed me out of the way. In his eighties now, he seldom gets horseback anymore, but he washes lots of dishes. At first I thought, poor John, this is beneath his dignity, and tried again to insist that he let me wash. "I can get this chore done in a second," I said with cheerful resignation.

John had never before been cranky with me, but as he stood between me and the sink, he looked like a country dog guarding his supper dish. His back was bowed, he had his four feet planted solidly on each side of the sink, and he was looking at me over his shoulder and out of the far corner of his eye. If I've learned nothing else from John, I've learned that sometimes I need to shut up and stay out of the way. So I did. I felt pretty worthless and confused, standing there with my hands in my pockets.

After John established his territory, he joked. He's a storyteller and a good one. He said the doctor who put in his pacemaker told him he could do anything he wanted to do, so he promptly told his wife, Susie, that he didn't think he wanted to wash the dishes anymore. But Susie said that wasn't what the doctor meant. John jokes when he works horses too. But his jokes are only funny until you think about them for a few years.

John was just as intense washing those dishes as he is working with horses. He looked for those cloudy gray areas on the bottom of glasses and into those ugly dark crevices around pot handles. Watching him, I thought about my pots and pans at home: my grandmother's old blackened pie tin, the saucepan with the once-copper bottom, the wineglasses with twenty years of hard-water deposits. As John scrubbed, I was suddenly struck with déjà vu. I had washed dishes all my life and didn't know one thing about it.

For me, that is John's magic. It isn't the horses. Some of John's horse students say they learned the most from him while digging a hole or hammering a nail. I learned my best lesson while watching him wash dishes.

So, on what have I decided to stake my rural reputation? I failed all John's cowboy classes, but maybe I can still be a great dishwasher. I started young enough and have plenty of experience: in hunting camps, sheep camps, cow camps, farmhouses, and cook shacks from Montana to Mexico, Iowa to California. I think I have probably washed dishes until my hands bled in more buckets, tin pans, galvanized tubs, and dry sinks—using water from more rivers, creeks, stock tanks, windmills, springs, *tinajas*, wells, cisterns, and rain barrels—in more hail, sleet, snow, and blowing dust than any other living human.

I never quite admitted it until just here lately, but I felt pretty smug that long-ago night of my roommate's broken heart. Through the years I've told that story over and over again. Most people laugh, but it isn't funny.

Who washed the dishes? I did.

Introduction

Another Troublesome Dichotomy

*A cultural parallax, then, might be considered to be the difference
in views between those who are actively participating in the dynamics
of the habitats within their home range and those who view those
habitats as "landscapes" from the outside.*
Gary Paul Nabhan (91)

While teaching a new class called "Environmental Literature" at small, rural Sul Ross State University in Alpine, Texas, I was about to assign Henry David Thoreau's 1862 classic essay "Walking." One of the textbooks for the class, *American Environmentalism: Readings in Conservation History* (third edition, 1990), edited by Roderick Frazier Nash, contains a shortened version of the essay which Nash had renamed "The Value of Wildness." At first glance Nash's version seemed okay. But there were many innocent-looking little ellipsis dots where passages had been removed. Curious about what was missing, I compared Nash's edited version with Thoreau's original.

I was shocked! Nash, a highly respected history scholar at the University of California, had carefully deleted most of Thoreau's references to horses, cows, farming, and pastures. Missing are Thoreau's statements that he loves to see "domestic animals reassert their native rights—any evidence that they have not wholly lost their original wild habits and vigor"; that watching cows swimming the river is like watching the buffalo crossing the Mississippi; and that the "seeds of instinct are preserved under the thick hides of cattle and horses, like seeds in the bowels of the earth, an indefinite period" (*Portable Thoreau* 618). Nash's deletions, and his decision to take out one key paragraph and replace it with another, change the essay's focus from how wildness as a saving grace lurks beneath the surface of all things domestic to wilderness preservation propaganda. But the problem isn't new.

The wild/domestic dichotomy in American literature began with *Mayflower* Pilgrim William Bradford (1589/90–1657). His published journal, *Of Plimoth Plantation*, written between 1630 and 1647, is an account of early Plymouth history. Modern anthologies, biographies, and journal articles dutifully quote Bradford's fearful description of the Pilgrims' first sight of the New England coast as "a hideous and desolate wilderness, full of wild beasts and wild men"

1

(61–62). With no friends to greet them and the wide Atlantic behind them, the Pilgrim Separatists had indeed finally separated themselves from the corruptive influences of society. Although granting that "Bradford was no romantic," critic David Laurence finds in Bradford's words "the queer music and peculiar visionary irony of the American sublime." Laurence observes that Bradford accomplished here "in a sudden and singular leap what American writing in general must wait to achieve after a long period of provincialism." Laurence argues further that if we "search the record of American writing between Bradford and Emerson for the like of Bradford's 'American-ness,' we search in vain" (64, 56).

The sublime emotion contained in Bradford's famous passage does not come from his literal description of the Pilgrims' vulnerable position, but because we read it today from the perspective of knowing, as Paul Harvey would say, the rest of the story. We know how the story ended. We know that half of the Pilgrims died that first winter. What many scholars have failed to note seriously enough, however, is that Bradford also knew how the story ended when he wrote those lines. The passage was written not at the moment the Pilgrims sighted land, but ten years later. Contrast the *Plimoth* quotation with the following lines, written on the *Mayflower* during the actual sighting: "After many difficulties in boisterous storms, at length, by God's providence . . . we espied land. . . . And the appearance of it much comforted us, especially seeing so goodly a land, and wooded to the brink of the sea" (*Mourt's Relation* 15). This quotation has a hopeful, almost childlike faith in the new land and God's benevolence. At the time, trees represented life-saving firewood and material for homes, not wilderness.[1] But after only ten years on Massachusetts's soil, Bradford had already adopted the strangely American phenomenon of "remembering" a howling wilderness which never in fact existed. A great deal of the coastal plain from the Saco River to Narragansett Bay had been cleared for agriculture before the Pilgrims ever arrived. The forest had been continually burned, leaving it "for the most part open and without underwood, fit either to go or ride in" (*Mourt's Relation* 18–19). According to Bradford's own journal, the Pilgrims settled on cleared Indian farmlands that had been vacated by an epidemic in 1616 (Laurence 63). The first "savage" they had contact with walked into their camp speaking broken English (Holzer 32) and taught the newcomers to use fish to fertilize their corn. New England was not a wilderness when the Pilgrims landed, and the Wampanoags were not wild hunter-gatherers. They were domestic farmers and pastoralists.

Gary Paul Nabhan, in his excellent essay "Cultural Parallax in Viewing North American Habitats," recounts the many ways "four to twelve million" Native American people "speaking two hundred languages variously burned, pruned, hunted, hacked, cleared, irrigated, and planted in an astonishing diversity of habitats for centuries." He also notes that when these "newly arrived 'colonists' came down from the Bering Strait into ice-free country, they played a role in Pleistocene extinctions which amounted to a loss of 73 percent of the North American animals weighing 100 pounds or more" (92, 97). Yet our literature and history have led us to believe that Native Americans lived in perfect harmony with the "natural" landscape. Rebecca Solnit finds "the gap between our view of landscape and of history" to be "full of lost stories, ravaged cultures, obliterated names" (*Savage* 222). This gap is also full of a lost domestic. Although he is a staunch advocate of wilderness preservation, even Gary Snyder realizes that the "wilderness" was actually a "home" full of people and trails (7).[2]

In *Wilderness and the American Mind*, Nash makes another interesting observation: the "central turning point in the human relationship to the natural world [coincided with] the advent of herding and agriculture some 15,000 years ago. Prior to that time human beings hunted and gathered" (xiii). Somehow, although even the most ancient oral history culture would never claim to know or remember, historians *know* that hunting and gathering linearly preceded herding and agriculture—especially in America. Even though nature has its own agriculturists—ants, for instance, keep herds of milking aphids and raise crops of fungi—somehow hunting and gathering is imagined as more "primitive." So, although *Mayflower* Pilgrims settled on cleared Indian farmlands, although Native Americans had constantly burned both grasslands and forests in order to improve pasture for and direct the migration of grazing animals (Pyne), and although Mormon irrigators followed miles and miles of ancient Hohokam irrigation ditches[3]—we hold fast to the idea that before Europeans arrived to farm the land, America flowed with milk and honey, and sinless people hunted and gathered them without effort or harm. Ignoring the heritage of indigenous farmers and pastoralists, Americans still prefer to imagine their ancestors as simply reborn into a preagricultural land that had been created especially for them.

Because the fledgling nation wrongly (or possibly racially) imagined itself without a heritage, ruins, or long traditions like those that stimulated European authors, the transcendentalists of the nineteenth century searched for something inherently American from which to gain inspiration. If intuition and a metaphysical sense of God or higher laws were inspired through observing wild nature, as European romantics believed, then the spectacular mountains and forests of the New World should have an exhilarating influence on the writing produced by American transcendentalists. Thus, scenic landscape was the logical choice for sublime and superior inspiration with which to compete with European authors. The wilder the landscape, the more romantically superior the writing would be.

Beginning with William Bradford, American authors were continually at work imagining the American continent as empty, wild, and pristine, newly delivered from the creating hand of God to his chosen people. Recognizing this tendency and disapproving of the racial bias that erased the existence of the continent's former inhabitants and land managers, Henry David Thoreau was trying to imagine a more realistic definition for a wild American heritage when he wrote his 1862 essay "Walking." In it, Thoreau argues that wildness is not unique to any nation, government, or race, and is something that cannot be lost, something that should be both valued and feared. He makes clear that civilization can hide it, oppression can stifle it, education and religion can subdue it, but scratch the surface deep enough to draw blood, and wildness springs eternal. He explains that wildness can be found in the forests and in what we call wilderness, but he also finds it in domestic animals, in "tawny" grammar, in both "civilized" and "uncivilized" cultures, in libraries, in architecture, underneath calluses, in the migratory instincts of birds, in the simplest and obscurest of men, in soil, in the smell on a trapper's coat, in both bogs and spades, in the sound of a bugle on a summer night, and in the humble act of walking. "Wildness," he says, is imported by the cities, and men plow and sail for it, but all that searching isn't necessary. Wildness can be found everywhere, Thoreau says: in the library, in skin color, even in cows.

It is in "Walking" that Thoreau's famous line, "In Wildness is the preservation of the world," appears. He does not say that wildness needs our condescending protection, but rather that wildness will protect us.[4] The line is often misquoted as: "In *wilderness* is the preservation of the world." Nash adds to this mistaken interpretation in the introduction to his version of Thoreau's essay when he writes,

> Thoreau spoke a half-century before most Americans were prepared to listen sympathetically to his message. Nevertheless, his philosophy survived to become the intellectual foundation of the wilderness preservation movement and of aesthetic conservation. (*Readings* 36)

Although Thoreau definitely valued wild places, wildness and wilderness were not interchangeable signifiers in his mind, nor is wildness based on imagining the environment created by native people as an exotic otherness. One vivid example of the way Nash changed Thoreau's meaning occurs in the following paired passages. Thoreau's version champions a "wildness" he finds in skin color. He is attempting to use the American love of all things wild to blur the boundaries between races—one of Thoreau's favorite subjects—and expose the subtle racism sometimes exhibited even by our finest scientists and scholars:

A tanned skin is something more than respectable, and perhaps olive is a fitter color than white for a man—a denizen of the woods. "The pale white man!" I do not wonder that the African pitied him. Darwin the naturalist says, "A white man bathing by the side of a Tahitian was like a plant bleached by the gardener's art, compared with a fine, dark green one, growing vigorously in the open fields."

Ben Johnson exclaims, "How near to good is what is fair?"

So I would say,

"How near to good is what is wild!" (*Portable Thoreau* 611)

Nash, however, deletes Thoreau's original paragraph and inserts a sentence that actually appears several pages later in the essay. Through this manipulation Nash gives his own version a preservationist, antiagricultural, and racially whitewashed flavor that totally changes Thoreau's original meaning. Nash's version:

I would not have every man nor every part of a man cultivated, any more than I would have every acre of earth cultivated: part will be tillage, but the greater part will be meadow and forest, not only serving an immediate use, but preparing a mold against a distant future, by the annual decay of the vegetation which it supports.

Ben Johnson exclaims, "How near to good is what is fair!"

So I would say, "How near to good is what is wild!" (*Readings* 39)

The inserted paragraph appears in Thoreau's original essay right after the sentence, "Not even does the moon shine every night, but gives place to darkness" (*Portable Thoreau* 622). Thoreau follows this paragraph with the idea that even grammar rules should sometimes be broken in order to allow for freedom of expression. Through his metaphoric comparisons between forests and cultivated fields, moonlight and darkness, proper grammar and lingo, Thoreau explains how he believes the world needs, should value, and already contains some sort of balance between the "wildness" he is attempting to define and the constraints placed on it by society, education, government, and religion. He is defining the spirit that rises when power structures become oppressive enough to inspire an unknown scholar at a small rural school to take up a pen and challenge the giants of academia.

Through metaphor, Thoreau is emphasizing the importance of maintaining an equal balance when making judgments between the desirable and undesirable; he is not demonizing agriculture, nor is he advocating the preservation of wilderness. As Lawrence Buell points out, however, Thoreau is often appropriated by those with an agenda. He has been acclaimed as the first hippie by a nudist magazine, recommended as a model for disturbed teenagers, cited by the Viet Cong in broadcasts urging American GI's to desert, celebrated by environmental activists as "one of our first preservationists" and embraced by a contributor to the John Birch Society magazine as "our greatest reactionary."

On the subject of wildness/wilderness, Buell says that although Thoreau "celebrated wildness, his was the wildness not of the moose but of the imported, cultivated escapee from the orchard that he celebrated in his late essay 'Wild Apples'" (*Environmental* 314, 116).

Thoreau attempts to redefine the word *wildness* and to show how important it is to the sanity and happiness not only of humans but also of animals. In "Walking" Thoreau reminds us that the cow was not born domestic, but is in fact descended, like all people, from the savage. Also missing from Nash's version is Thoreau's observation that

> [a]ny sportiveness in cattle is unexpected. I saw one day a herd of a dozen bullocks and cows running about and frisking in unwieldy sport . . . and perceived by their horns as well as by their activity, their relation to the deer tribe. (*Portable Thoreau* 618–19)

Thoreau is rejoicing in the fact that the cow has not lost its wildness. Looking to nature for ways to understand human problems, he observes that each generation of "horses and steers [has] to be broken before they can be made the slaves of men."[5] Although Thoreau's comment could be interpreted as meaning that eventually horses and steers are mentally "broken," I would say he is using an older meaning, more familiar to people who depended on horses for transportation. In this context a broken animal is one that has lost its fear of humans and has become cooperative. If the situation becomes stressful enough, even the most well-"broken" horse or steer will fight back or run away and display its hidden "wildness." Thoreau argues that "[t]he seeds of instinct are preserved under the thick hides of cattle and horses, like seeds in the bowels of the earth, an indefinite period." And he loves "to see the domestic animals reassert their native rights—any evidence that they have not wholly lost their original wild habits and vigor."[6] But all of these statements about the wildness in domestic animals have been edited out of Nash's new version of "Walking."

Thoreau does not define the domestic and the wild as polar opposites in this essay, nor does he try to devalue or erase the domestic from our history. Through metaphor and a celebration of nature's willingness to bestow wild beauty on all, regardless of race and class, Thoreau is arguing that his neighbors should do likewise. Challenging class, he says, "When the trapper's coat emits the odor of musquash even; it is a sweeter scent to me than that which commonly exhales from the merchant's or the scholar's garments." Challenging race, he says the white pine produces blossoms "over the heads of Nature's red children as of her white ones" and that the cock crowing in the morning reminds him that where the birds live "no fugitive slave laws are passed" (*Portable Thoreau* 611, 628). Throughout the essay he pulls support for his thoughts from a diverse mix of world religions and cultures: Spain, Dahomey, the Hottentots, Chaldeans, Arabs, Poles, Russians, and Hindu. He quotes Confucius as saying, "The skins of the tiger and the leopard, when they are tanned are the skins of the dog and the sheep tanned" (*Portable Thoreau* 619). In short, the "wildness" Thoreau struggles to define cannot be bred out, beaten out, preached out, educated out, or domesticated out of any animal, including the human slave: an idea that also inspired Lev Tolstoy, Martin Luther King Jr., and Mahatma Gandhi. Thoreau was thinking about much bigger ideas than simply advocating the preservation of pleasuring grounds for the leisure class. Nash does American literature a sad disservice by narrowing Thoreau's complicated wild ideas down to support of preservation politics.

Numerous humanities scholars have been investigating this typically American dichotomy between the places where people live and a pristine, wild nature from which humans have been excluded. Donald Meinig's essay "The Beholder's Eye," written in 1979, may have begun the current discussion by describing the various ways humans imagine landscape: as nature, habitat, artifact, system, problem, wealth, ideology, history, place, and aesthetic. Meinig explains that each view has its own biases, advantages, and disadvantages. A few years later, Annette Kolodny published her landmark book which summarizes how relationships to land are often expressed using female-gendered metaphors (mother earth, virgin land) and verbs of sexual conquest (penetration, rape). She claims that "at the deepest psychological level, the move to America was experienced as the daily reality of what has become its single dominating metaphor: regression from the cares of adult life and a return to the primal warmth of womb or breast in a feminine [preferably virginal] landscape" (*Lay* 6).

Just as women are often valued primarily as "visual spectacle," wilderness as imagined by preservationists has a highly visual bias as well. Art critic Solnit explains that when the landscape is defined as a "visual spectacle," tourism becomes the only "normal and proper" human relationship with it ("Reclaiming" 31). Nature reduced to visual spectacle rather than unpredictable, powerful, and cyclic system promotes the idea of a safe, nurturing, and passive place—maybe even a helpless place. This is almost opposite to Thoreau's view of sublime nature.

Yet Lawrence Buell applies the idea of nature as constructed by the imagination to Thoreau's work when he argues that nature pilgrims desiring a retreat into Thoreau's "wilderness" have become an "American cult." They flock to

Walden Pond, trying to follow Thoreau's example and thinking they have "left the profane metropolis to find solace in the sacred grove," in spite of the fact that in reality the "grove" is part of the greater Boston area. This cult, as he calls it, has become almost a form of religion complete with disciples, evangelists, and saint ("Pilgrimage" 183, 188–89).

In the early 1990s, numerous humanities scholars began agreeing, at some level, that the dichotomy between wildness and home is not only imaginary but harmful.[7] William Cronon, in his controversial collection *Uncommon Ground: Toward Reinventing Nature* (1995), succinctly brought together the ideas that had been floating through the humanities for almost two decades. A professor of history, geography, and environmental studies, Cronon argues that wilderness has become a powerful but imagined human construct that is preventing a realistic evaluation of ecosystems and providing an unstable foundation for the environmental movement.[8] In an essay in Cronon's collection, Richard White argues that nature as wilderness has become a sacred place where humans not only cannot live but also cannot work: "Most environmentalists disdain and distrust those who obviously work in nature, and . . . have come to associate work—particularly heavy bodily labor, blue collar work—with environmental degradation" (172). Seemingly in answer to or anticipating White's challenge (although both books were published the same year), Buell admits that although Thoreau did not embrace the wilderness of the moose, he bears some responsibility for "abetting the memorialization of what he stood for as a leisure time activity. At least ostensibly," says Buell, "precious little work gets done at *Walden* once he builds the cabin" (*Imagination* 389).

Although scholars are now reevaluating the wild/domestic dichotomy as it applies to geographical places, the movement to remove domestic animals from "wilderness" has gone unchallenged as an imagination-based problem, but the arguments are parallel. Articles appearing in today's popular press are quite similar to articles that John Muir published at the turn of the century, although the language has changed a little. Today's rhetoric juxtaposes wild "natives" against domestic "invaders" instead of domestic "hoofed locusts" against wild "dainty nibblers." An article in *National Parks* claims that grazing by "non-native" animals, disturbing topsoil with their hooves, is threatening sixteen endangered native plant species ("Channel Islands" 1995). The hooves of "native" animals evidently do no harm in national parks? An ecologist at the University of Minnesota says in an article published in *New Scientist* that "the introduction of sheep and cattle grazing has resulted in widespread soil erosion" (Hecht). An article in the *Atlantic* states: "Overgrazing the West has allowed cheatgrass to overwhelm native plants, resulting in devastating problems with wildfires" (Devine).

I would venture to guess that many of the writers who publish in these popular magazines as well as urban environmentalists still gain more of their information about grazing from Muir's antisheep campaign than from modern science.[9] Continuously in print, Muir's books are still read and enjoyed by modern nature lovers and quoted faithfully by Sierra Club members and publishers of books and magazines designed to evoke emotion and sway public opinion.

On the other hand, a review of modern scientific research on wild animal "overgrazing" exposes wild versus domestic grazing as a false dichotomy. Wild animals are just as likely to "overgraze" as domestic ones. A 1996 study comparing grazing habits of rodents, insects, and snails found that rodents reduced plant mass by as much as 50 percent and "substantially" increased plant mortality, although plants that suffered both high mortality and poor growth as a result of grazing were rare (Hulme). A study at the Chihuahuan-Sonoran Desert Ecotone in Arizona supports this and asserts that wild rats may be the primary cause of desert brush invasion rather than the domestic animals usually blamed. They found that without kangaroo rats, "a shrub steppe quickly changed to grassland" (Brown and Husk 1990, qtd. in West 10). Ecologists Luc Belanger and Jan Bedard (1994) found that wild goose grazing reduced vegetation by 45 percent. And in an especially emotional plea, Canadian zoologist C. Davison Ankney warns that goose grazing on Arctic nesting areas is fast reaching a vegetation reduction of 100 percent!

In an invited paper that appeared in the *Journal of Wildlife Management* in 1996, Ankney expresses panic and outrage over the current environmental crisis resulting from a goose population explosion. Ankney's paper is accompanied by an alarming photograph taken in a brood-rearing area in Manitoba. Scientists built two exclosures in order to exclude all grazers from small blocks of salt marsh vegetation. The vegetation growing inside the exclosures looks in the photograph like a green shag carpet thrown down on totally bare mud that is pocked with water-filled goose tracks. This "embarrassment of riches" occurs in a place where all native predators are still in place except one—subsistence hunters. However, Ankney says that the problem has already grown beyond the bounds that hunting could rectify. Giant Canada geese, "once thought extinct," have reached such tremendous numbers, he says, that waterfowl biologists and hunters alike call them "sky carp." Snow geese are referred to as "tundra maggots."[10] The effect their "consequent habitat damage" will have on other wildlife is "unclear" ("Embarrassment" 217, 218, 219, 220).

Although he stops short of placing the blame for the crisis south of the Canadian border, the desperate zoologist recommends that the practice of feeding geese in U.S. wildlife reserves be stopped immediately. He explains that lesser snow geese once wintered only in coastal marshes of Texas and Louisiana, but they have recently expanded their range into safe and food-rich rice prairies in Texas, Louisiana, and Arkansas and grain fields in Iowa, Kansas, Nebraska, Oklahoma, and Missouri. This has led to increased fall and winter survival and enhanced female fertility. While many environmentalist magazines call for preservation of wetlands, more protection for waterfowl, and more hunting regulations, Ankney recommends immediate relaxation of all hunting regulations, even beginning what some would consider the "abhorrent" practice of commercial goose hunting. Managers must make these unpopular decisions, he urges, and begin the ominous task of reeducating the public about waterfowl management.

Because scientists are often at the mercy of funding priorities, and because funding tends to pour into the projects that receive the most public attention, scientists, like U.S. voters, have become slaves to the media. Apocalyptic prophecy traditionally draws the most attention and research dollars. Ankney laments that the goose population boom has received little media attention, and finds the absence of serious discussion in leading wildlife publications "remarkable." "Surely," he supposes, "if the reverse were true, i.e., declining goose populations, the resulting discussion would be deafening."[11] In answer to the question of whether wild or domestic life-forms are the most prone to overgraze, Aldo Leopold might say deer are worse than cattle, Alston Chase might say elk are worse than sheep, and Canadian waterfowl zoologists might say grazing geese are worse than all of them put together. The wild/domestic dichotomy that influences and has been influenced by American literature has clouded public opinion and is currently shaping the direction of modern scientific research through funding, publication, political, and publicity pressures.

The United States, through its powerful research and tourist dollars, has also exported this imaginary wild/domestic dichotomy around the world with devastating results to rural people. In Africa, ending a three-thousand-year-old culture, indigenous pastoral nomads have been forbidden to graze their cattle in newly created national parks in Tanzania and Kenya and yet cannot prevent wild animals that leave parks from grazing their reduced pastures. The motives behind the formation of these parks are sometimes hidden. Wildlife conservation, as Dan L. Flores observes, is often based on racial and class biases because it usually represents the interests of "the aristocratic sportsman who hunted only for trophies and for manly immersion in sport." *Pothunter,* meaning someone who hunts for food rather than for sport, has become a derogatory term. Flores says that urban elites who demand wildlife laws have

> convinced themselves that while it was "sporting" to use animals as live targets and symbols of wilderness prowess, ethnic immigrants, rural rednecks, and southern blacks who hunted wildlife and fished for food were a threat and should be regulated. (29–30)

In Africa, he says, the problem boils down to the title of a book a friend of his is writing: "White Hunters, Black Poachers" (35).

In South and Central America, "parks, debt-for-nature swaps, and preserves sometimes provide an excuse to displace indigenous and adaptive inhabitants, whose absence opens up the land for new exploitation" (Solnit *Savage* 299–300). Again the wild/domestic dichotomy seems to be at the root of the issue. A book called *Our Magnificent Wildlife* even features, almost on the same page, information about extinct, threatened, and endangered wild cow ancestors and a drawing claiming that one acre of African grassland can support forty-two tons of "wild" grazers but only seven tons of "domestic" grazers (169). The idea that domestic animals need more resources than wild ones also supports the rationalization that "more primitive" Third World populations can adequately exist on a fraction of the resources needed to support those living in a more "advanced" country like the United States. This economic dichotomy, again based on the wild/domestic dichotomy, divides urban and rural people worldwide.

One of the most controversial new theories regarding grazing was born in Africa. Allan Savory's Holistic Resource Management (HRM) theory, which is actually a complex, goal-based philosophical approach to decision making, includes the idea that the West has not been overgrazed but undergrazed, and that desertification is caused by long-term selective grazing—even by a single animal. A former tracker, Savory watched the seemingly destructive yet self-sustaining impact of wild grazers on African deserts. In order to restore western U.S. grasslands, Savory sometimes recommends more livestock (either wild or domestic or both) for shorter, more intense grazing periods, mirroring on a small scale the way wild grazers move across African savannas and once moved across the U.S. prairies. His theories rely on heavy manuring for fertilizer and on hoof action to "plant" seeds and to break up soil crust, allowing rainwater to soak in instead of run off. Savory believes heavy manuring increases soil health and productivity. Amish farmers concur with these ideas, claiming that it takes only about five years of their animal-based farming practices to restore "ruined," "worn-out," or even strip-mined lands (Ruth).

Although HRM often seems to mirror the rhetoric of agribusiness lawyers, Savory's ideas have not been readily adopted by skeptical U.S. stock growers, who are reluctant to add more livestock to their ranges, object to building more fences, and dread the intense—almost obsessive—management reputedly required by HRM. Extensive fencing is often recommended as a way to concentrate livestock numbers. However, I have personal friends who are currently experimenting with ways to concentrate grazing without fences: burning, loose herding, controlling water access, and utilizing weather patterns and elevation.

Dan Dagget, honored in 1992 as a top grassroots activist by the Sierra Club, visited HRM-inspired ranches across the West to write his Pulitzer Prize-nominated book, *Beyond the Rangeland Conflict: Toward a West That Works* (1995). The book describes numerous places that claim phenomenal results after adopting some version of HRM-inspired grazing management. On the Tipton Ranch in southern Nevada, for instance, Dagget found a "steep, barren pile of clay, which formed a dam that held back a settling pond for a gold mine." The site, "a scar visible for miles," was tackled in order to convert skeptics—which it did. Dagget tells the story eloquently, but suffice it to say that after cattle were forced to eat hay on the scar, trample scattered grass seeds into the clay, and defecate on the steep bank for only four days, the site had produced "thigh-high grass" by the end of the first summer (92–93).

David E. Brown, in a 1994 *Wilderness* magazine article, compares HRM-inspired results obtained on Rukin Jelks's Diamond C Ranch near Elgin, Arizona, with a neighboring research ranch managed by the National Audubon Society that practices "no-use" management (meaning no domestic animals). Brown found it remarkable that Jelks's range conditions were "frequently described as superior" to the neighboring Audubon property,[12] which hadn't "been grazed since 1968" (32), so he went to look for himself. His conclusion:

> Jelks' range is certainly well managed, and Savory's HRM workshops have obviously worked for him. Cattle numbers have increased from 220 to 650 with no apparent damage to the range. Nonetheless, claims that the Diamond C possesses greater land health than the Research Ranch are misleading. It is a matter of perspective. True, more nutritious green grass can be seen on the Diamond C than on the Research Ranch, but the tall stands of residual grass that Savory and other stockmen like to call "decadent growth" are a major objective of the Research Ranch's manager, Bill Branan. The Audubon property not only has taller and browner grass, it appears to have more forbs. Pronghorn antelope require both, and studies show that ground-nesting birds and riparian plants have benefitted from Audubon's "no use" management program. Jelks' ranch is, after all, managed for cattle; the Audubon Ranch's goal is not grass—it is biodiversity. (32)

This is an especially interesting position since taller grass and forbs are not necessarily ideal for birds. The cover that can conceal nests can also conceal predators and make taking flight more difficult. Wildlife managers recommend a "bare landing area at least 30 to 50 feet wide at the water's edge" for mourning doves, observing that they "prefer" sites free of ground-level vegetation which "could conceal predators" (George 15, 18). In addition, masked bobwhite quail numbers have declined with the expansion of tall shrubs into former desert grasslands (Alcock); some rare bird species, like the mountain plover, nest only in heavily grazed areas (Graul 1973, 1975; Ryder 1980; Leachman and Osmondson 1990; all summarized in West); and a 1997 study found that birds nesting in brush cover suffered higher nest predation than those nesting in open grass on rested pastures (Ammon and Stacey).[13] The Audubon stance also seems to privilege ground-nesting birds over their predators. In addition, while range scientists are still engaged in a hot debate over whether or not livestock grazing has caused the "invasion" of shrubs, "noxious" forbs, and succulents, Audubon managers have simply redefined brush and forb "invasion" as "biodiversity." Thus, with a slight shift in rhetoric, yesterday's range "degradation" becomes today's goal, and the "ideal" ecosystem, once again, changes. Just to confuse the issue further, another recent study found "slightly more" wildflowers and forbs in grazed areas than in ungrazed areas (Stelljes).

Yet another study found that domestic sheep grazing increased emergence of thistle seedlings by reducing litter and thinning the canopy of mature plants (Bullock et al.). And another found that sheep that were held off of feed and fasted for a certain length of time tended to be less choosy about what they ate when allowed into the pastures (Newman et al.). So, if domestic sheep were subjected to periodic fasting like wild grazers, couldn't their grazing patterns be manipulated, causing desirable plants to respond in the same manner that thistles do? Modern range managers currently claim to be able to do just that. The problem seems to center on *who* determines which plants and animals are considered "desirable."

The results of a study published in the *Journal of Animal Science* in 1995 indicate that reducing steer numbers in a riparian mountain meadow actually increased grazing and loafing along stream banks (Huber et al.). With fewer animals grazing, they obviously stay longer before reduction of plant mass forces their departure. I would ask the scientists whether or not increasing animal numbers might eventually cause natural rotation and migration (as Savory claims) similar to historic bison movement caused and directed by Indian fires (Pyne 108) and bison movement out of Yellowstone National Park during periods of starvation (Chase "Bison"). R. W. Ruess and S. W. Seagle found that "where grazing intensity is greatest, soils have the highest levels of soil microbial biomass." Other researchers found that removing domestic grazing animals reduced soil loss and stream sedimentation (Owens et al.). I would ask if these combined studies simply point to the fact that grazing animals deposit large concentrations of loose biomass along banks, which is then easily washed into the stream. I would ask whether streams carrying sediment from grazing animals are healthier or less healthy than streams without sediment, and healthier for whom: plants? insects? snails? fish? I would ask whether or not this loose biomass makes a significant contribution to riparian soil health. Our golf course mentality toward nature seems to equate "clean" with health. "Clean" is also sometimes sterile, and those who equate habitat with prosperity seem to forget the necessity of food chains. In any event, I would especially ask the scientists whether or not the same results would be obtained with "wild" grazers who would also deposit large concentrations of loose biomass along streams and cause sedimentation.

Data obtained in an extensive study of grazing and soils in a "global range" of environments, published in *Ecological Monographs* in 1993, support the "controversial hypothesis" that grazing can increase vegetation. The authors also found "no relationship" between grazing and damaged root systems, despite the "commonly held view that grazing negatively impacts root systems." The paper concludes vaguely that "all three below ground variables [root mass, soil organic matter, and soil nitrogen] displayed both positive and negative values in response to grazing," and warns that "current management of much of the world's grazing lands based on species composition criteria may lead to erroneous conclusions concerning the long-term ability of a system to sustain productivity" (Milchunas and Lauenroth). While it is almost impossible to control or measure all ecological variables (water, climate, soil microbes, air quality, time, insects, etc.) in order to accurately measure and evaluate results, scientists are trying.

On a more theoretical level, arguments about wild versus domestic animal grazing often take on the appearance of simple rhetoric. Some argue that the North American continent was a complete and balanced ecosystem immediately preceding European invasion, an idea that ignores native management practices and which Frederick Turner calls "'scientific' creationism" (40). The common apocalyptic view argues that modern ecosystems are evolving toward self-destruction rather than "higher" life-forms. In order to preserve the genetic "purity" of one endangered species, habitat borders must be rigorously patrolled; yet in order to preserve a viable genetic "pool" for another species, habitat boundaries need to be enlarged and corridors established. Some want western rangelands returned to "native" species; others theorize that the earth is in a constant state of plate tectonic recycling. Each time new land rears its sterile head from under the sea or through volcanic eruption, immigration begins. Charles Darwin once raised eighty-two separate plants, belonging to five distinct species, from a ball of mud taken from a bird's plumage (Carson 91). Yet the popular media and even agriculturists blame every "noxious" plant that has "invaded" the North American continent on domestic animals. Ignoring the fact that domestic grazers arrived in the desert Southwest during the mid-sixteenth century with the Spanish, biologist David M. Graber observes that due to mid-nineteenth-century cattle and sheep grazing "Eurasian annual grasses and some dicots have virtually replaced the native herbaceous species." Yet he fails to see his own contradiction when he ends the same paragraph with the sentence: "Nor is there good information on what the native herbaceous layer consisted of, should an opportunity arise to restore it" (128–29). If no one knows what species are "really" native to a place, how can anyone be sure the "natives" have been replaced? If plate tectonics is true, then there can be no "native" species, including humans. Perhaps a more accurate conclusion would be that minority and majority populations have recently cycled to favor one over another in a process that is in constant flux.

In an excellent synthesis paper published in the *Journal of Range Management* in 1993, Utah State University professor Neil West summarizes the issue:

> Unfortunately, policy makers have quickly turned what were academic working concepts about biodiversity into packaging buzzwords to fund politically popular programs. The evolving understanding of biodiversity being built by researchers was thus prematurely uncoupled from strong science. . . . We have land managers trying to implement actions based on fuzzy definitions, loosely worded objectives and inadequate methods of measurement and monitoring because a concerned and impatient public is breathing down their necks. (11)

Even conservation biologists admit that "[u]nexamined technical questions are legion" (Brussard et al. 920), yet still suggest that "[i]n the face of uncertainty, let the burden of proof be on those who would continue grazing to show how it benefits the native ecosystem" (Noss 616)—a policy that embraces a "guilty until proven innocent" philosophy and relies again on scientific creationism. Martin Lewis, in *Green Delusions: An Environmental Critique of Radical Environmentalism* (1992), concludes that no matter what the labels, ecoradical policies will produce ecological disasters.

For many years scientists enjoyed almost unchallenged acceptance of their research as fact, but humanities scholars are now arguing that "objective" science, like "objective" history, has feet of clay. When scientists begin their research under the assumption that the "original" North American ecosystem was a pristine wilderness rather than heavily managed farm and pasture land, or that some species are "native" and others are not, their data are based on an imaginary foundation. I believe that critical study of our myths, perpetuated and possibly invented by our own literature, can and should play a role equally as important as science when investigating environmental issues.

While scientists, humanities scholars, and rural land managers struggle with complex ecological and ideological relationships, many an armchair environmental journalist and radical has black-and-white answers. Pro–domestic animal magazines are also guilty of this: demonizing predators, the government, the universities, public education in general, and "environmentalists," a vague term applied to anyone who disagrees with them. It is no wonder that stressed

and desperate rural people are frustrated with the shadow boxing going on between journalists, academics, and federal policy makers, who are in turn being
pressured by a sometimes naive and easily manipulated voting public. Behind
the scenes, mega-corporations that have mastered the art of using the media
and pushing the public's hot buttons play one group against the other.

Especially frustrated are those who have lived on, observed, and managed
the lands in question for several generations and yet are seldom asked for their
observations or advice. Although scientists admit that short-term studies do not
always parallel long-term problems or dynamics (Leigh and Johnston), "[e]x-
perimental evidence is given almost exclusive credibility over personal experiences to a degree that seems almost religious rather than logical" (Masson and
McCarthy 3). Barry Lopez explains that a

> belief in the authority of statistics and the dismissal of Eskimo narratives
> as only "anecdotal" is a dichotomy one encounters frequently in arctic en-
> vironmental assessment reports. Statistics, of course, can be manipulated—
> a whale biologist once said to me, "If you punish the data enough, it will
> tell you anything." . . . The Eskimos' stories are politely dismissed not be-
> cause Eskimos are not good observers or because they lie, but because the
> narrative cannot be reduced to a form that is easy to handle or lends itself
> to summary. Their words are too hard to turn into numbers ("Country"
> 300).

In short, Lopez maintains that "anything a native says about animals . . . counts
for nothing with [scientists]. Useless anecdotes" ("Country" 300).

Observations by modern rural people whose families have lived on the land
for four and five generations are also usually considered useless anecdotes.
College-educated people who have managed farms and ranches for forty years
are frequently required to submit to the judgments and ideas of young, newly
graduated federal employees whose field experience can be totaled in hours,
and who may never even have seen the particular range they are sent to man-
age! As John Berger asserts, "The marginalization of animals is today being
followed by the marginalization and disposal of the only class who, throughout
history, has remained familiar with animals and maintained the wisdom which
accompanies that familiarity: the middle and small peasant" (27–28). Kent Ryden (*Mapping*) argues that a sense of place is an unconscious accumulative process. Over time, the place influences the jobs, foods, and living habits of its inhabitants.[14] Wendell Berry says that land "that passes rapidly from one owner
or user to another will not be adequately studied or learned and so will almost
predictably be abused." He concludes that "[g]ood farmers, like good musicians,
must be raised to the trade" (*Another Turn* 58, 4). Nabhan argues that it "may
take time for any culture to become truly 'native,' if that term is to imply any

sensitivity to the ecological constraints of its home ground" (93). This tedious accumulation of place-based wisdom, emerging "only after several generations in one general terrain" (Abram 269), is also rapidly forgotten once people's ties to the land are broken.

Edward Said's theories as explained in his book *Orientalism* (1979) have had a tremendous influence on my thinking. Although he is talking about the Far East when he describes the way the colonizer imagined the Orient as mysterious, primitive, exotic, ruled by passions, dying, and in need of the watchful "civilized" eye, his ideas can easily be applied to the relationships between the American West and tourists, rural and urban people, and wild and domestic animals. Said argues that the Oriental was spoken for and about by the colonist, and that the colonist's judgment held such power that the culture was actually influenced by those "expert" opinions, blocking a more authentic understanding. As Lopez observes, the fight for wilderness "hurts us in two ways. It preserves a misleading and artificial distinction between 'holy' and 'profane' lands, and it continues to serve the industries that most seriously threaten wilderness" ("Unbounded" 2).

The grazing dispute often appears to be more a struggle for power than a genuine desire to help science, agriculture, or the environment.[15] Environmentalists who sincerely think they are helping the small family farmer or rancher play into the hands of agribusinessmen and land developers when their demands for more regulations force the smaller operators out of business. Many of the most insidious myths about rural people and domestic animals were created not within the vernacular regional cultures but by urban writers who "Orientalized" the place and the people and animals who live there. Since the language of travel/postcolonial theory is unfamiliar to most readers, however, I will use words such as *stereotype* and *mythologize* to describe what Said would, more descriptively, call "Orientalizing."

Following the ancient cyclic pattern of conqueror and newcomer, many of today's agricultural problems are actually caused by "new" management practices that are often forced on stock growers by federal agencies before even newer goals and rhetoric, often demanded by the media, change funding priorities, which in turn change research objectives, which in turn change the goals a "progressive" agriculturist should be pursuing. Yesterday's uncleared land is today's old growth forest. Yesterday's bog, which only a lazy, uneducated manager did not drain, is today's priceless wetland. Yesterday's range improvements, like the productive varieties that replaced thin native meadow grasses, are today's introduced and demonized nonnatives. In 1965, Sally Carrighar said, "At this stage science is proclaiming many 'final' conclusions which are then revised in a few years; and the rest of us are convinced too easily by the self-confidence of the men of facts" (37). Her statement would have been true one hundred years ago, and it still often holds true today. Those who actually live and work the land for their living have often been the most reluctant to adopt unproven new ideas and have thus been called backward, stubborn, or ignorant.

In summary, a comparison of current research reported in professional journals with articles appearing in popular magazines indicates that the popular presses promote apocalyptic and unsubstantiated antiagriculture theories while scientists and rural people struggle inconclusively to find concrete differences between wild and domestic grazing and to determine whether grazing is harmful or beneficial. In fact, although the word *overgrazing* may be greatly overused, scientists, range management experts, and land managers have never been able to agree on its definition. It is time to tug on the word *overgrazing* and unravel the thread. Berry summarizes the issue impatiently: "The governmental and educational institutions from which by right rural people should have received help have not helped." Angrily, he concludes that he does not expect agricultural problems to be solved in the universities, which "have never addressed, much less solved, the problem of health in agriculture." And he doesn't expect the problems "to be solved by the government," either (*Another Turn* 12, 99).

* * *

Unlike Berry, I have not lost faith in academia or democracy. I have not joined the militia, the sagebrush rebels, or the wise use movement, although I have joined the Sierra Club. Sometimes seemingly unsolvable problems between people involve perception, the domain of the humanities. This environmental stalemate on grazing seems to boil down to a melodrama in which cows and sheep have been cast as villains, and elk and elands as heroic and noble savages—a very ancient story, as I have discovered while reading literary history. This imagined dichotomy between the wild and domestic began, at least on the European side of our literary genealogy, as early as Virgil's *Eclogues,* and so is buried deep in our collective psyche. Since our myths have placed it there, perhaps only exposure and reevaluation of these myths can open the deadlock and begin our progress toward more peaceful discussion, if not actual solutions.

Following Thoreau, one of the earliest North American authors to rethink, theorize, and rewrite the dichotomy between wilderness and the domestic home was Mary Austin. Although the concepts are never fully articulated by Austin scholars, many have noticed that her "nature writing" works against the grain of traditional American wilderness worship. In 1923, Carl Van Doren observed that she combined the warring moods of romanticism and naturalism. Henry Smith (1931), seemingly unaware of his own irony, found Austin "a little un-American, perhaps, in her humility." Attempting to place her on perhaps a more "American" pedestal, he argues that she has "done something of transcendent meaning, definitive if not yet definable"; she has enlarged the "American Naturists" tradition, and has "taken the unisonal melody of a Muir and scored it for full orchestra." Although Smith does not object to having Austin placed within the "nature literature" tradition of Thoreau, Muir, and Burroughs "if such classification bolstered her admirers' estimate of her," he does want to make one important difference very clear. Her interest in the environment, he says, was real, ethical, and political. She was not seeking a "retreat" from men, cities, and society, but a real avenue of approach to them; she was attempting to create new American myths (25–26).

Perhaps because of her strong personal and literary ties to Native Americans,[16] Austin never imagined the North American continent as an empty wilderness or without culture. With "un-American humility," she knew that indigenous populations had peopled, worked, and adapted their lives to the continent for centuries. Equally important, she also realized that the continent had adapted to native management practices as well. The vast prairies, the willow-lined creeks, the open parklike forests, even the giant redwoods were products of native management, not "nature."

A strong advocate of regional loyalty and literature, Austin believed that landscape would indeed inspire writers ("Regional Culture" and "Regionalism"). Instead of basing her writing on a mythic wilderness that existed only in imagination and could be aesthetically ranked into good, better, and best, however, Austin related to the landscape as home ("Holiday"; Wynn "Mary Austin") and believed its influence on the psyche was grounded in reality. She was opposed to any hierarchical ranking of one landscape over another (Norwood "Heroines"), and was so fiercely loyal to place that she believed any desire to return to a former homeland, through a mythic longing either for a lost Eden, for lost tribal lands, or for lost childhood places, was a sentimental, nostalgic journey that devalued the current home. After she left the Owens Valley, however, she herself struggled with these same nostalgic feelings of loss for the rest of her life. Although she was forced by circumstances to move often, she never advocated the constant relocation that has become an American tradition. Dudley Wynn finds that "[c]riticism of American rootlessness is implied in almost everything Mary Austin wrote" ("Mary Austin" 16).

Several Austin critics have compared her work with that of Thoreau, Muir, Audubon, and Burroughs.[17] Critics have also noted her environmental advocacy concerning water issues (Starr "Mystic"; Norwood "Photographer," *Made*; Blend "Mary"). Although Norwood says that Austin believed the desert to be "safe from the development which was sweeping the country" ("Photographer" 39), Benay Blend states more accurately that Austin thought the desert was in grave danger from development in Los Angeles and Southern California.

According to Blend's excellent in-depth summary of the Owens Valley water issue, Austin championed the underdog in the battle, defended the "rural way of life," and recommended a focus on cultural rather than economic conservation ("Mary" 18). In fact, Austin was in favor of irrigation development. She simply wanted to see the water used in the Owens Valley, where the water originated, not shipped to Los Angeles. Her objection was aimed not at irrigation development in general, as her novel *The Ford* (1917) further illustrates, but at the colonization of rural people and the appropriation of local resources to support urban development and wealth. Further, irrigation was not a "new" development in the area. Owens Valley Indian tribes had long depended on irrigated crops (Hoyer "Prophecy" 239; Lawton et al.). As this book progresses, I will explain how Austin's political activism concerning the Yosemite grazing issue also championed the underdog (in this case, shepherds), defended the rural way of life, and recommended a cultural rather than economic conservation focus.

Today, tensions between rural and urban interests have once again reached the volatile levels Austin experienced. Wendell Berry claims that while North American populations of most wild animals have been consistently on the increase since the turn of the century, human populations in rural areas, due to mechanization and "displacement of nearly the entire farming population," have reached apocalyptically low levels. The U.S. Census Bureau announced in 1993 that farmers, whose population dropped from 32 million during the 1910s and 1920s to only 4.6 million in 1991, will no longer be counted as a separate category (Berry *Another* 8–9)! This population decline should be an important counterargument to Frederick Jackson Turner's declaration that the frontier closed in 1890. His vision was based on the rise in rural population, yet this drop represents a devastating turn of events for rural communities, and one that has received little media attention. Small rural towns, unless they are able to attract wealthy urbanites into the area for recreation or hideaway subdivision living, have closed businesses and schools like ghost towns.

Tourism is often suggested as the solution to the problem. However, in May 1997 the Center of the American West at the University of Colorado at Boulder sponsored a conference called "Seeing and Being Seen: Tourism in the American West." The conference flyer advertised the discussion of ideas such as using folk societies (Indian, Hispanic, Mormon, ranching, mining, logging) as "attractive 'foreign' alternatives," turning people's homes into "veritable theme parks," and teaching residents to play to the camera. Provocative questions appeared on the flyer: "[D]oes tourism prove to be yet another form of extraction and colonialism?" What are the "relations of power in tourism"? "Does it devalue people by forcing them into subservient, seasonal, low-paying jobs?" In short, the conference organizers took exception to the idea that "outdoor recreation is typically benign. Austin, as I will argue later, was also violently opposed to turning rural communities into tourist traps.

* * *

As a direct descendant of *Mayflower* Pilgrim William Bradford, I am a thirteenth-generation rural American. My early childhood was spent fishing the Mississippi River, hunting, and exploring my family's wild Iowa farm. Later, I spent thirty years living and working on ranches in Arizona and Texas. Because of my background, I have always been interested in "nature writing" and the importance of plants, animals, and land in American literature. In the introduction to *The Ecocriticism Reader: Landmarks in Literary Ecology* (1996), Cheryll Glotfelty defines ecocriticism as "the study of the relationship between literature and the physical environment," and goes on to say that "[a]s a critical stance, it has one foot in literature and the other on land; as a theoretical discourse, it negotiates between the human and the nonhuman" (xviii–xix). As an ecocritic, I have one foot in literature and the other on rural grazing land, and I am continually trying to negotiate between cows and my fellow environmentalists. I believe serious research and publication should be important to the world outside academia, and I further believe that the most important current problem involving rural people is the grazing issue—the one point, and often the only point, on which I disagree hotly with environmental politics. The idea that domestic animals are somehow more destructive, less intelligent, and less valuable than wild grazers seems to be rooted in the wild/domestic dichotomy I find rampant in the popular press, science, and American literature.

Ecocriticism is a new form of literary interpretation that attempts to gain deeper insight into literature through an interdisciplinary investigation of the role played by the natural world. As Michael Branch points out, "ecocritics must wrestle with a simple paradox, which might be stated this way: 'nature' is both a cultural construct and a grounding in reality" (50). So, in order to maintain a balance between imagined construct and reality, I will blend perspectives from the humanities, the sciences, agriculture, and personal experience to expose the imaginary dichotomy between wild and domestic grazers. This dichotomy was flourishing during Mary Austin's day, was something she recognized as dangerous to rural American communities, and was something she attempted to combat. I think it is crucial to reevaluate her theories in light of modern concerns over grazing by domestic animals.

One gaping hole in both American literary criticism and Austin criticism, and one I believe holds tremendous potential for illuminating the grazing issue, is an investigation of animal representation. Although Austin's early writing contains numerous references to both wild and domestic animals, what little critical attention the subject has received appears almost as asides in a few scattered sentences. James C. Work observes that with self-forgetting sympathy, empathy, "rat-level inspection, offal-watching, and sky scanning," Austin looks at desert life struggles through the point of view of local residents, animals, and plants and neither condemns nor condones. He reminds readers that because Austin was writing at the turn of the century, "when each coyote and wolf had a price on its head and when anything with wings was considered only a challenging target, she extends a humanitarian fair mindedness to even the most repulsive of them" (41–44).

Reviewing *The Flock*, one critic notes that in the chapter "The Sun in Aries," about "lambing and the ways of lambs and ewes," the reader will find "more pure authentic science of behavior . . . than you will find in many pages of heavier reading" (Tracy "Mary" 24). Another says that "all the occupational and environmental factors of sheep-raising combine [in *The Flock*] into the potency of symbol" (Young 31). Yet another observes that Austin "stops for queer speculations on the development of the animal mind" and does not sentimentalize animals, yet this same critic finds only a simple pastoral theme that inspires a desire in the reader to "lie under the sky with dogs and flocks, lulled to sleep by the 'blether' of ewes and the bark of distant coyotes" ("A Review" 17–18).

This book will investigate the ways Austin questions and reinvisions the dichotomy between the wild and domestic through animal stories. Chapter 1 details Austin's theories about animal intelligence as she explains that by watching "wild" animals, humans actually learned "domesticity": homemaking, territory claiming, food storage, raising young, education, society, and religion. Austin learned to read animal sign and understand animal language, discovering in the process that animals understand people as well. She argues that white male pathfinders, frontiersmen, mountain men, and mountaineers were actually following ancient well-worn trails first laid down by animals, deepened by native people, and further deepened by rural people while bathing, doing the wash, getting water for soup, visiting neighbors to gossip, or shopping. Only an awestruck stranger could imagine the busy, settled, and heavily managed West as a pristine wilderness or a false utopia where social struggle did not or should not happen.

In chapter 2 I argue that the wild/domestic dichotomy is also a gender issue. Although the female grizzly is reputed to be the most dangerous of all North American wild animals, and although women have always lived and raised children in the "wilderness," the West in Austin's time was imagined as no place for a lady. I compare the subtle gendering in John Muir's and Jack London's animal stories with Austin's challenges to their stereotypes of women as naive, pampered nonfighters prone to madness, victimization, or sexual exploitation when exposed to "wilderness" conditions. I argue that because domestic animals are traditionally imagined as "females," they suffer from the same biases. I also argue that Austin's animal stories attempt to reverse these gender stereotypes, representing the western male as nurturing, the bachelor as lonely, and the wildest men as the most domestic.

In chapter 3 I summarize my own experiences with the domestic side of the wild through a personal essay. I grew up fishing, hunting, farming, and ranching in direct daily contact with animals. Just as Austin did, I adopted numerous baby animals and studied their ways. In my family, hunting did not fit the gendered and virile stereotypes that American literature and history have generated. Like Austin, I found hunting more sedentary than agriculture as I learned to be as still as a baby quail. Instead of the modern interpretation of traditional hunting as a masculinity contest in which males tried to obtain a trophy or gain status within the tribe, hunting in my family was simply a tedious method of obtaining cheap food. Like Austin, I also found so-called wild animals, when they were given the opportunity, to be curiously more friendly and domestic than the so-called domestic animals.

Next, I begin my argument that domestic animals are wilder than their reputation implies by comparing John Muir's sheep with Austin's sheep. In her book *The Flock* (1906), Austin defends both sheep and shepherds, almost point by point, from Muir's earlier published accusations. Austin found sheep intelligent, wild, and quite capable of taking care of themselves when the need arose. Privately, Muir also found sheep wilder than he could control, yet publicly he said they were stupid, helpless, and destructive, allegorically much like the common human masses. I argue that through the wild/domestic sheep dichotomy Muir supported a wilderness-is-better hierarchy, valuing all things wild over all things domestic, in order to help develop tourism. His views represent an elitist and constructed hierarchy of western land value and use. Through sheep, Austin, as a true leveler, struggles to understand the complexities of ecological interdependence and equality. Muir's book *My First Summer in the Sierra* (1911) may have been written in response to Austin's eloquent defense of sheep in *The Flock*.

In chapter 5 I use Austin as a theorist in order to illuminate Edward Abbey's domestic cow as a symbol. On the surface, Abbey cussed the fact that he found cows, and not deer, in the West's most remote and wildest canyons. In contrast, the bighorn sheep he found in national parks were so tame that they were reluctant to get up to let him pass on a trail. I will argue that Abbey was influenced by one of Austin's haunting sentences about cows in her book *The Land of Little Rain*. Abbey consistently presents the cow as an indigenous wild desert animal that has lived in the West for more than five hundred years, long enough not only to adapt to the harsh environment but also to become an important cog in desert ecology. Although Abbey is sometimes read as an environ-

mental journalist, through Austin I am able to offer a more complex reading of
his work as literature. With Austin as his inspiration, he used animal stories to
question hierarchies: gender, food, government, and religion.

In support of the wildness that can be found in domestic animals, I turn
again to personal essay in chapter 6 in order to relate my own experiences: my
personal close calls with dangerous domestic animals, domestic animals' weather
sense, and their fear of humans. I describe the cow's wild habits, territory claiming, friendly cohabitation with antelope, and fighting spirit. I argue that the
more one really knows domestic animals, the less domestic they seem. I would
speculate that horned mama cows have killed and crippled many more men in
the West than mama grizzlies. In my world cows are sacred—as they have
been throughout the ages.

Because both of us have lived in the rural West and know its animals intimately, Mary Austin and I believe that the dichotomy between wild and domestic animals is a construct of the imagination that influences the way Americans, both in Austin's day and today, view environmental and conservation
issues. Reevaluating this dichotomy through Austin's writing enables me in
the final chapter to combine the tenets of deep ecology with a vision of a truly
democratic, multicultural, human society based on the earth as home and an
inclusive ecosystem that deserves our greatest respect, but not our condescending protection.

Chapter One

Walking Ancient Domestic Trails

*To project a feeling of power and speed, automobile manufacturers name
their products Jaguar, Mustang, and Falcon, even though the clientele they
wish to attract has no personal knowledge of these animals. Somehow
jaguars and mustangs still project an image of power in a man-made world
full of engines and machines that ought to convey energy in their own right,
without borrowed feathers and claws from nature.*
Yi-Fu Tuan (*Dominance 72*)

In the chapter "Kachinas in the Orchard" in *Land of Journeys' Ending* (1924),
Mary Austin argues that instead of being domesticated or developed, the peach
"came to us in almost its present perfection" from the Persian Gulf and "went
wild again and made itself at home in the fields of the Hopitu-shinumu, between first and second mesas" in northern Arizona. She remembers reading a
pamphlet that attempted to prove that it was a peach, not an apple, that "the
Serpent plucked for Eve." So she asks,

> Where else would [the peach] naturally come, if actually out of Eden, but
> to the only place left in the world where the great Snake is still a deity and
> has dances performed in his honor? . . . Was it, then, homesick, all these
> centuries of trim orchard rows, for a dark-skinned desert tribe, mud huts,
> and the call of the five-notched flute?

According to Austin, the wild and the domestic were equal parts of a never-
ending cyclical process rather than a permanent linear change. Wild peaches
became domestic, then went wild again, becoming indigenous to the Southwest
("Kachinas" 269–83). The North American fossil record shows that both horses
and camels were once indigenous to the continent, died out, and were reintro-
duced, although only the horse survives in the "wild." The bison, on the other
hand, was not indigenous but arrived in North America along with humans after the Ice Age. In one story about an outcast dog, Austin asks if perhaps wolves
became wild when they learned to fear humans for some reason:

> There used to be in the Little Antelope a she dog, stray or outcast, that had
> a litter in some forsaken lair, and ranged and foraged for them, slinking

savage and afraid, remembering and mistrusting human-kind, wistful, lean, and sufficient for her young. (*Land* 62)

Animals, including humans, who are not petted, who are treated badly or hunted, can become wild. If the reverse is true, they become domestic. Austin also posits the interesting argument that since all animals can become tame when they are not hunted, perhaps hunting developed not before but after domestication as a way to entertain the youth. In an unpublished manuscript about how society organizes itself, Austin suggests that young males have always tended to "draw away into bachelor gangs," and that through woodcraft leagues and Boy Scout organizations we try to "put it to the best of use" (AU 760, box 490). Hunting may have actually developed as a way to encourage animals to fear humans and thereby help humans avoid starvation and animals avoid extinction.[1] When a human or predator population begins to outgrow its food supply, the supply is more likely to be depleted if prey animals are too tame and easy to kill.

In her poem "Thanksgiving," Austin lists numerous "domestic" foods that Native Americans introduced to European immigrants: turkey, cranberries, celery, pumpkin, maple syrup, potatoes, tomatoes, lima beans, succotash, peanuts, clams, popcorn, and corn (*Children* 146–48). She depicts domestic Aztec women working the cornfields in Mexico, Indian girls tending flocks of "wild" turkeys, and Indian boys stealing "wild" melons from tribal fields (*Western* 147–60; *Trail* 106, 132). Contemporary ethnobotanist Gary Paul Nabhan describes a growing list of plants that Europeans have traditionally labeled as "wild" but were actually cultivated and domesticated, heavily used, and constantly transplanted to new locations by native people. Donald Worster notes that many supposedly "natural" plants like cottonwoods, burro bushes, and willows growing along streambeds were placed there by Indians to slow water currents or trap silt (33). Even "wild" rocks and boulders, Austin says, were placed in streambeds by Indian and early Hispanic irrigators to make the water run smoother and sound happier (*Land of Journeys' Ending* 93).

While domestic plants, animals, and rocks may initially have been appropriated from the wild for their usefulness, they were also appropriated as pets and curiosities. From early times, most world cultures have exhibited the rare and exotic in menageries and zoos as a way to represent wealth and power. Harriet Ritvo states that collecting exotics, as well as their exotic keepers, promoted in the British imagination an "increasing inclination to view the wild as a source of entertainment and relaxation."[2] Ritvo also reasons that when wildness was "easily circumscribed and controlled," walled in or walled out, it was not only "no longer much of a threat," it might actually have seemed "threatened or endangered" (368–75). Possibly in both historic and more modern times, as animals were appropriated from the wild, either because of their usefulness or as symbols of wealth or power, the most highly collected became the most threatened. Today's desire to reintroduce "native animals," "native plants," and their "native keepers" throughout the West may simply be new forms of appropriation, possession, control, entertainment, display of sovereignty, or attempts to recapture a romantic past.[3]

According to Juliet Clutton-Brock, "People have been moving animals and plants about, by accident or by design, for at least the past 10,000 years, and the effects have caused such changes in the world's floras and faunas that it is often difficult to know whether a particular species is indigenous or exotic" (12). When our most endangered flowering cacti have disappeared from the desert, we will rediscover them someday in Japan, England, or in Tucson and Phoenix subdivisions where they have been shipped for gardens. Even rocks have become so popular for various human projects from landscaping to lining stream banks under bridges that they are threatened. One rock-selling entrepreneur in Arizona is currently under fire from tourists, the Hualapai tribe, and the Arizona Department of Transportation, to name just a few (Gripman). I might also add that animals, birds, weather, and geologic forces have been moving things around as well.

The most common reason for members of native cultures to appropriate animals from the wild may have been as a way to learn the animals' ways and gain wisdom for the tribe. Austin's stories frequently include Native Americans who have adopted baby animals. Sometimes children simply adopt young birds and animals as pets, like the Zuni lads who hatch a condor's egg under a turkey hen or raise an elk calf (*Trail* 245, 132). Sometimes the reason for their appropriation is similar to the colonizer's reasons, as when an Indian boy takes a mountain lion from his lair as a "nine days cub." Taking the cub, Austin explains, was one of "the first fruits" of the boy's courage. The boy taught the lion to jump over sticks, snarl when he smelled a Navajo,[4] and curl his tail under his legs and slink on his belly when he passed a man who didn't like the boy and his strange pet. The lion, as narrator of the story, tells the reader that the boy "had to beat me over the head with a firebrand to teach me that trick." After the lion was grown and had killed three humans, he decided to give up the domestic life and return to the wild (*Trail* 96–123).

The word *domestic* is itself problematic in that "[e]very scholar has his own definition" for it (Bahn 141), ranging from "tame" to "controllable" to "genetically altered." Since species evolve naturally in the wild, since domestication does not always change the nature of an appropriated species, and since a species can be simultaneously cultivated and wild, historian Ritvo asks thoughtfully, "At what point did a species cease to be wild?" (367). According to Christopher Manes, native people had no words to differentiate between wild and domestic (18). Even modern Native American writers like Louise Erdrich blur the boundaries between wild and domestic animals. In "Skunk Dreams" Erdrich finds that elk fed grain at feeding stations are not wild animals—"how could they be?" But they are not domestic either—they are something in between. She also tells about a turn-of-the-century journalist who broke a pair of buffalo calves to the yoke, exhibited them at county fairs, and even "knit mittens out of buffalo wool" (91, 92). The plants her ancestors used for food were not classified either as "wild" or "domestic," and the animals who shared their world were often not even classified as "animals" but as other tribes.

Austin was obviously very interested in defining or blurring those boundaries too. Among her papers preserved in the Huntington Library are many articles she clipped and saved which show her interest in the domestic side of the wild: "How Mountain Plants Behave When They Go to the Seaside," "The Meaning of Animal Sounds," "Insect Musicians," "Making a Bear Living," "Air-Carrying Spider," "Social Institutions in the Animal Kingdom," "The Morals of Beans," "Can the Lower Animals Hear?" "The Wolf That Wooed a Collie," "Nature's Reasons for Monogamy," "A Remarkable Partnership" (between Spanish bayonet and moth), and "How Plants Endure Heat and Cold" (AU box 131, folders 1 and 2). Austin thought the imaginary dichotomy between wild and domestic was similar to the one she had discovered between savage and civilized people—mostly a matter of unfamiliarity: the more one studied plants and animals, or lived next door to them, the more one realized how domestic their lives actually were.

While many of Austin's contemporaries imagined the North American continent, especially the West, as a preagricultural Edenic wilderness where nobody worked and where the wealthy visitor simply dressed in wild or working costumes (as in traditional pastoral) and pretended to be wild or workers, Austin argued for a more domestic reality. In the real West, she says, everybody works: Native Americans are not home during the day because these are "working hours." Bird-folk have to "get their living." Wildlife is "busy" doing chores, gathering, hunting, butchering, storing. Plants know "their business," clouds do their "work," rain and glaciers do their "ploughing," and the wind does its job of trying the pines for "their work upon the sea" (*Land* 57, 75, 7, 69, 95). Even symbolic water is "busy" breeding food for trout, and "the high note of babble and laughter falls off to the steadier mellow tone" of mountain water that knows "the proper destiny of every considerable stream in the West [is] to become an irrigating ditch" (*Land* 78, 83, 79, 86). All humans, nonhumans, and even inanimate rocks and plants obey the stern dictation from the "lord" of the mountain streets, who declares, "Come now . . . I have need of a great work and no more playing" (*Land* 75).

According to Austin, even coyotes and wolves work. In the story "How

Howkawanda and Friend-at-the-Back Found the Trail to the Buffalo Country Told by the Coyote," Austin's coyote narrator asks the mastodon if the "tame wolves" that were following the Indians were wolves or—. Before he can finish his question, the mastodon responds, "Very like you, Wolfling, now that I think of it . . . and they were not tame exactly; they ran at the heels of the hunters for what they could pick up, and sometimes they drove up game for him." Austin calls Coyote "The First Father of all the Dogs" and claims he showed the Indians where to find game. After the Indians made the kill, she says, they would throw the First Father of all the Dogs pieces of liver. A Blackfoot Indian further interrupts the story to add, "Why should a coyote, who is the least of all wolves, hunt for himself when he can find a man to follow? . . . Man is the wolf's Medicine. In him he hears the voice of the Great Mystery, and becomes a dog, which is a great gain to him" (*Trail* 51–52). Clearly Austin is blurring the distinctions here between wolf, coyote, and dog, going beyond the common pioneer tendency to call all wild canines wolves. She is also blurring the distinction between domesticator and domesticated.

During times of severe hunger, her coyote narrator explains, people began to starve because of drouth and because they couldn't go into other tribes' territories for food. When the human hunters became too weak to hunt, the wolf/coyote/dogs took over hunting duties for the tribe and brought food back to the camp—as is their nature—until the rains came again and the human hunters were able to regain their strength. Further into the story, the man builds a fire to keep from freezing. While the fire warms his front side, the wolf/coyote/dog sits against his back—thus the name of the story: "How Howkawanda and Friend-at-the-Back Found the Trail to the Buffalo Country Told by the Coyote." The two partners eventually find a trail across the Sierra, with help from geese and bighorn, and return to the tribe with a map (*Trail* 50–69).

Austin's story describes a working relationship between human and animal that is mutually beneficial. John Berger asserts that this attitude toward animals has changed, calling modern zoos "an epitaph to a relationship which was as old as man" (21). In rural areas, however, where people's lives and animal's lives are still intertwined, human-animal relationships are still often reciprocal partnerships.

Although turn-of-the-century easterners imagined the indigenous people and "wild" animals of the West as living lives of idyllic leisure, Austin's stories blur all distinctions between human and nonhuman work, between hunting and herding, gathering and farming, domestic and wild. Her wild mountain streams domestically "graze" in perennial snow "pastures" and blur into very domestic Indian irrigation ditches, distributing "chiefly the sorts of [plants] that are useful to man" (*Land* 88). One "stately, whispering reed," she observes, is useful for both war and peace: its light, strong shafts for arrows, its sweet sap and pith for sugar (88). She argues pointedly that "you get the same rainbow in the cloud drift over Waban [mountains] and the spray of your garden hose" (99). Consequently, Austin wrote about wild animals as though they were neighbors who lived next door. She thought only an animal who did not drink water would be difficult to get to know (32).

Austin's writing is full of the domestic side of "wild" animals: where and how they build their homes, how they adapt to the climate, how they raise their young, where they gather their food and find water. She argues, in fact, that "wild" animals actually taught humans much of what we call "civilization." In 1918, while her contemporaries were writing about a "pathless wilderness," Austin explained in *The Trail Book*[5] that ancient animal trails showed even the Native American where to find water, food, salt, river crossings, and mountain passes.[6] Throughout the book she uses animal narrators, choosing the animals who probably made the trails to tell the stories. In the desert, for example, looking for roads, she uses a roadrunner as narrator. Following Spanish explorers across the ocean and telling stories about things that happened on the beaches is a pelican narrator. In still another story, a mountain lion remembers a salt trail that is "older than the oldest father's father of them could remember" (11). In "What the Buffalo Chief Told," an old bison has heard "that when the Pale Faces came into the country they found no better roads anywhere than the buffalo traces." An unpublished Austin manuscript claims that the American bison had such a feeling for topography that "our best national trails and many of our accepted railroad gradings still follow the buffalo traces" (AU 760, box 49). According to Austin, even old Indian trade trails, like the ancient one to Chihuahua, Mexico, simply follow animal migration trails. When the buffalo decided to move, the Pawnees moved with them. "They follow the herds," explains the old bull in *The Trail Book*, "for the herds are their food and their clothes and their housing" (9–11).

Humorously, Austin reminds the reader that keeping track of who first made the trails is not always easy. When the coyote is about to tell a story about how *he* helped a human find a trail across "the backbone of the world," a bighorn jumps down off a crag and states, "That should be my story, for my people made that trail, and it was long before any other trod in it." We learn that the "railroad that passes through the Rockies, near Pikes Peak, follows the old trail of the Bighorn" (*Trail* 290). But during the telling of the story, we find out that a wild goose trapped by wind currents also played an important role in helping to find the pass. When an Indian tries to credit the moose and wapiti for making a trail, a mastodon interrupts: "Then you must have forgotten what I had to do with it" (13). Then, when the mastodon actually tells the story about how *he* showed a boy the trail to the sea, we find out it is not really the old bull who deserves credit but mastodon cows who knew the trail across the marsh. The cows were led by an old female, as is almost always the case in the animal world—the bucks, bulls, rams, and stallions trail behind.

Austin believed that humans even learned patterns for society from animals. In an unpublished outline and manuscript for a book on animal social patterns, she indicates that every kind of human society is found among animals: mating, family, school, pack, herd, flock, hive, and the cooperative colony. She finds animal societies very matriarchal and domestic, centered on home, food, and raising young. Although scientists usually explain these similarities as projections of our own social patterns onto animals, we may as easily have copied our social patterns from those we observed in animals (Douglas 33). Austin, of course, believed that is exactly what happened. Sarcastically, she writes, "Along about the middle of the last century, when Western civilization began to take an intelligent interest in its own predicament, there was a pleasant notion abroad that man himself had invented Society" (AU 760, box 49).

Although today we imagine native people as living without any form of land ownership, Austin says that native people learned to claim and defend territories by watching animals. While neighborly sharing is a highly cultivated trait among both animals and Indians, and both wolves and "Indians never refuse food [to a visitor], if they have it, even to their enemies" (*Trail* 211), Austin maintains that "[i]n thickly populated districts, hunting packs will fight for control of the ground, or well organized packs will migrate to new grounds where they will deliberately drive out earlier occupants" (AU 760, box 49). Modern writer Mary Douglas naively believes that "[e]quals, that is friends or enemies, recognize no territorial or property constraints," and she tries to equate land ownership with oppression by saying, "Patron-client relations have a strong territorial aspect" (34). In the animal world, however, only equals— those animals who prefer the same habitat or rely on the same prey—claim and defend territories from one another. Almost every modern scientific animal study begins by determining "home range," which means the area claimed and occupied by the animal(s) being studied. Even the so-called gentle animals claim territories: "Mule deer never come down into the river bottoms where the white-tail are found but keep to the broken hills" (AU 267). Austin also explains that the territories of unrelated species sometimes overlap, and that the meekest rabbits are capable of eating elk, wolf, and Indian out of house and home ("Na'yang-Wit'e, the First Rabbit Drive" *Basket*).

If humans and animals fail to defend their territories, Austin explains, they, like the mound builders, will discover that the Lenni-Lenape have "fished *our* rivers and swept up the game like fire in the forest" (*Trail* 145; emphasis added). What tougher form of land ownership laws ever existed than those Austin describes in *The Land of Little Rain*: "the boundary of the Paiute country was a dead-line to Shoshones" (34)? Instead of paying for the land with money, native people and animals often paid with their lives, through either war or starvation: "The people began to starve because of drouth and because they couldn't go into the other tribes' territories for food" ("The Ford"; *Flock* 217; *Trail* 53–59).

Animals also taught people that the prey base determines the size of a territory, and that the largest meat-eating predators travel the greatest distances, which Austin says explains both the great awe in which Indians held the Spanish conquistadors and why the Indians "never did get it out of their minds that they might be eaten" by the horses (*Land* 13; *Trail* 201). In "How the Iron Shirts Came Looking for the Seven Cities of Cibola: Told by the Roadrunner," she explains that after a Pawnee watched horses sicken, die or grow well again, and have colts, he came to "the conclusion that they were simply animals like elk or deer, only more useful" (*Trail* 236).

Austin believed that by watching animals, humans were able to adapt more quickly to an unfamiliar place. Animals showed them what sort of houses to build: dark houses of earth in order to "keep their brains underground" in the desert, or snow tents in the mountains (*Land* 25, 27). In *Children Sing in the Far West* (1928), she describes prairie dog home-building techniques:

Old Peter Prairie-Dog
Builds him a house . . .
With a door that goes down
And down and down,
And a hall that goes under
And under and under, . . .
With a ceiling that is arched
And a wall that is round . . .
And the hall and the cellar
Are dark as dark. (57)

If one is a fisherman, one needs to live near places where fish congregate, so Austin predicts we will find a heron's feather beside the irrigation weirs and "mallards squattering in the crescent pools below the drops" (*Flock* 20). If people are not to be trapped by their enemies, their houses should have "back doors" like those of the "furry people." She observes that by "knowing the type of house used, you can tell more about the kind of life lived by that tribe than any other one thing" (*Land* 56).

By watching animals, Austin argues, we also learn that certain places are not safe for home building. On a mountain slope, after a rockslide, she hears the "houseless cry of a cougar whose lair, and perhaps his family, had been buried under a slide of broken boulders on the slope of Kersarge" (*Land* 96). On another occasion, Austin learns that it is not wise to build a home in a pretty canyon where she finds even "trout floating . . . belly up, stunned by the shock of sudden flood" (*Land* 135–36). But what taxes her most "in the wreck of one of [her] favorite canons by cloud-burst" is "to see a bobcat mother mouthing her drowned kittens in the ruined lair." In the end, however, Austin always accepts nature on nature's terms: "After a time you get the point of view of gods about these things to save you from being too pitiful" (*Land* 96).

Austin believed that wisdom and education came from many sources, ranging from miners, who like animals preferred hunch and instinct over science, to *curanderos,* who like animals used local plants to cure illness (*Land* 44–45, 88). Writing that the Indians know that animal fat is an antidote for wild hyacinth poisoning, Austin muses innocently,

> The Indian never concerns himself, as the botanist and the poet, with the plant's appearances and relations, but with what it can do for him. It can do much, but how do you suppose he finds it out; what instincts or accidents guide him? . . . One might suppose that in a time of famine the Paiutes digged wild parsnip in meadow corners and died from eating it, and so learned to produce death swiftly and at will. But how did they learn, repenting in the last agony, that animal fat is the best antidote for its virulence; and who taught them that the essence of joint pine (*Ephedra nevadensis*), which looks to have no juice in it of any sort, is efficacious in [treating stomach] disorders. But they so understand and so use. (*Land* 88)

She knew that, like most things, Indians probably learned these cures from animals. In *The Flock,* she relates how Arabian shepherds learned about coffee by watching their goats eat the berries (126). Humans teach animals useless "tricks," which are usually never *new* to the animal but something the animal is already capable of doing: fetch, roll over, lay down, bark. Animals, on the other hand, teach humans survival skills: trails, patterns for society, and medicinal uses for plants.

In addition to recognizing the wisdom gained by watching and learning from animals, Austin also recognized the metaphoric and symbolic power in animal stories themselves. Animals as archetypal partners, helpers, teachers, gods, and half-humans appear throughout world myths. Always looking for ways to level hierarchies, Austin claimed that even some of our arts came from animals. In "The Father of Song-Making," she says the coyote taught the Indian to sing (*One Smoke* 35). The Greeks learned to dance, she says, by watching shorebirds and wild goats; the Indians by watching cranes and elk "prancing before the does on the high ridges; old, old dances" (*Trail* 202, 297).[7] Austin believed that common sense, local legend, and homey skills passed from generation to generation, influenced by land, local plants, and animals, were perhaps even more difficult to acquire than an elitist homogenized education. "Particular artists and thinkers have their superiority proved by the degree to which the common people fail to understand them," she says (AU 625).

Animals were the first art subjects; animal blood was probably the first artist's paint; and, John Berger notes, "it is not unreasonable to suppose that the first metaphor was animal." They were once, says Berger, a central part of our world. We depended on them for food, work, transportation, and clothing, and yet, he says, "to suppose that animals first entered the human imagination as meat or leather or horn is to project 19th century attitudes backwards across the Millennia. Animals first entered the imagination as messengers and promises" (7, 3–4).[8]

Even our knowledge of religion has traditionally come from animals, but as Austin humorously relates in a story about the making of a shaman, animals can't help those who are not humble enough to listen to animal voices. In one of her stories a future shaman goes on a vision quest. Although rabbits ran into his hands, he swam with deer, trout rose "in bubbly rings" under his arms, and squirrels ran over him, he laments that "the Holder of the Heavens would not speak to me" (*Trail* 170). Not satisfied with a constant bombardment from a whirlwind of animal voices, a shaman, Austin hints, waits for the booming human voice that will drown out thunder. Yet, although the "persistence of these marvelous creatures in literature and imagination tells us how important they are to the health of our souls," as Gary Snyder points out (74), animal stories have usually been relegated to the children's story level and are seldom studied by serious scholars.

Interestingly, even the most ancient stories seldom divide animals into "domestic" and "wild" categories. According to the Greeks, the Muses' well, from which all poetic inspiration flows, sprang from the hoofprint of Pegasus, a mythological flying horse that existed somewhere between not only the domestic and the wild, but between the animal and the bird. Mythic dragon slayers rode both tigers and horses. Wild forest-dwelling male centaurs and satyrs combined human form with that of horses and goats, and women became trees, cows, or canyon echoes. Native American stories are full of humans who suddenly change into birds, coyotes, or buffalo, and back again. Even biblical cherubim (I Kings 88:6–7) and seraphim (Isa. 6:2) combine human and animal traits. As a student of world religions and myth, Austin realized that animal stories operate at a subconscious, archetypal level, and she used them as symbols and metaphors in order to produce literature which she hoped would dissolve boundaries between wild and domestic, human and animal, friend and enemy, good and bad, sacred and profane, and spiritual and material, thus reimagining religion, language, racial stereotypes, and power structures. Yet even when she was writing myths, Austin attempted to stay as close to the reality of her animal characters as possible. Racial and cultural prejudices, for instance, seem foolish when one looks closely and realistically at the animal world. Although some feathered creatures choose to take their baths in water, observes Austin, roadrunners maintain sparkling clean feathers with dust baths (*Land* 15). Bathing in water, dust, or sweat is cultural, she decided, not godly.

Austin believed that many of society's problems stemmed from the human need to judge, rank, and exclude. One of her most interesting animal characters is the half-god/half-devil, half-real/half-myth, half-animal/half-human "lazy dog" called Coyote, who thoroughly mixes boundaries and hierarchies. In 1829, Edward Bennett admitted that it seemed "impossible" to offer a physical description of the domestic dog that would distinguish it from the wolf and other wild canines. He was not concluding, however, that wolves and dogs should be considered a single species. Instead, he argued that "the moral and intellectual qualities of the dog" distinguished it from the wolf (qtd. in Ritvo 366). Since stealing is a sin, especially within cultures that prize material possessions, only canines with high morals who do not steal should be classified as dogs.[9]

Coyote, whether real or in one of his many mythic disguises, is a natural thief among those who do not share willingly. Austin relates that while the shepherd gladly butchers sheep to feed his "moral" dogs, he fights continually against the "thieving" varmints (*Flock* 250). Austin finds this double standard humorously intriguing:

> It is a trick man has played upon the dog to constitute him the guardian of his natural prey, . . . [and i]t is notable that the best sheep dogs are most like wolves in habit . . . as if it were on the particular aptness for knowing the ways of flocking beasts developed by successful wolves that the effective collie is molded. (*Flock* 136–37)

She argues that the partnership between wolf, sheep, and shepherd benefits all three: the wolf (as morally converted dog) protects the sheep from its own kind, the sheep furnish food for both, but since "dogs can't discriminate between pastures" (*Flock* 143), humans do their part by claiming and defending territories for grazing. As long as all three partners do their jobs, nobody starves—except, of course, the wolf or coyote that hasn't learned, forgets, or simply chooses not to beg for his or her food. Austin cleverly mocks this ethical dualism between predators and dogs in "Lost Dog" (1909) as she describes two women who adopt and feed "every halt and blind and hungry and hurt dog" who comes along. The women are very poor and constantly struggle to keep "the wolf away from the door," yet they always have at least one lazy dog living in their house, sitting in their laps, and eating their food.[10] Austin acknowledges the fact that the wolf deserves some of his/her ancient reputation for gluttony and blood, but like Shakespeare, Austin seems to respect "bandit airs" (*Land* 19) and wonders if the British-inspired groveling courtier system of class, patronization, and preferment is actually superior to Old Man Coyote's system.

Throughout her writing Austin carefully balances her animal stories so that right and wrong, good and bad remain obscure. Coyote is friend, counselor, and fire-bringer to one boy but tries to lead another boy into the desert to die of thirst and become a meal for himself and his friends the buzzards. The buzzards help Coyote by mesmerizing the boy with their endless circling ("The Fire Bringer" and "The Merry-Go-Round" *Basket*). In one story a pocket hunter is saved during a snowstorm by a band of wild sheep (*Land* 28); in another a hermit miner saves a wild sheep trapped in the snow ("The Golden Fortune" *Basket*); and in yet another a trapped wild sheep is killed by a starving coyote and a man because, explains the coyote, "when one *must* kill, killing is allowed." And besides, responds the coyote, "It was pure kindness, for he would have died slowly otherwise of starvation" (*Trail* 50–69). In one story cougars gluttonously kill sixty sheep in one night (*Flock* 183), but a heroic cougar kills thieving humans in another story (*Trail* 123). Rabbits are "foolish people" good only to furnish meals for meat eaters (*Land* 12), smart and skillful enough to catch the sun in a snare (*Basket* 24), or punished because they were so clever and selfish that they never let the Indian people win at gambling ("Na'yang-Wit'e, the First Rabbit Drive" *Basket*). All animals, including the human animal, should remember to share and should not try to prove themselves too wise. In summary, her stories question all dualisms. What looks like destruction can be neatness or rejuvenation. Rain or fire can be both heaven-sent and apocalyptic. Religion or witchcraft, cleanliness or filth, beautiful or ugly, useful or worthless, weed or flower, food or garbage can change with perspective.

Austin does not rank killers, scavengers, and prey into hierarchies or dichotomize them into good/evil, helpless/self-sufficient, or stupid/intelligent; she simply points out the ecological interdependence of all. She observes that "[t]he hawk follows the badger, the coyote the carrion crow, and from their aerial stations the buzzards watch each other" (*Land* 20). Whether the coyote depends more heavily on the crow to find them both a rabbit, whether the crow depends more heavily on the coyote to make the kill, or whether both depend on the miraculous dirt to decompose the sick, dead, putrid, and waste in order to provide food for the grass that feeds the rabbit is hard to say.[11] Our modern obsession with cleanliness, with burying our dead and our garbage, has done much to destroy this interdependence.

Austin also quarrels with the hierarchies and rankings imposed on the animal world by modern science. Although Darwin actually developed his ideas by observing unique species that had developed through inbreeding on each of the isolated Galápagos Islands, evolution is more generally conceived as a linear development from single-celled organisms *up* to more complex organisms.

This provides a "scientific" basis for the idea that humans are a "higher" form of life because they evolved later and thus have a more sophisticated form of intelligence. Manes observes that although "Darwin invited our culture to face the fact that in the observation of nature there exists not one scrap of evidence that humans are superior or even more interesting than, say, lichen, . . . [a]l-most all of us, including biologists, refer to 'lower' and 'higher' animals"—with humans at the "apex." He concedes that the human thus becomes the "apparent *zenith* of evolution by virtue of this brain size, self-consciousness, or some other privileged quality" (22–23; emphasis added).[12]

Although supposedly replacing creationism with facts in the public mind, the theory of evolution retained the hierarchical ranking inherited from the Great Chain of Being. "Lower" life-forms evolved into "higher" life-forms, with humans as the last, and ultimate, creation—with only angels and God above them. As all stockmen know, however, evolution can easily both improve and degrade. Although size, weight, bone diameter, and colors can be selectively changed, modern breeders are not able to make cows out of pigs or vice versa. Breeding domestic animals is a matter of crossing animals belonging to either a single species or two closely related ones. All modern cattle breeds still closely resemble their ancient, extinct wild ancestors. New species have not been created. Cattle and bison are subspecies of a single species, and they can readily interbreed to produce "cattalo" or "beefalo." They are susceptible to the same diseases and compete for the same habitat. Europe's wild white cattle look very much like white bison—small curved horns, hump, curly hair over upper face and shoulders (Hartung 213). Cross-breeding can create offspring with different colors, sizes and other slight "improvements" that line breeding can solidify, but inbreeding of closely related individuals eventually causes retardation (blindness, mental deterioration, smaller size, albinism, etc.).[13] Thus, some "endangered species" found only in isolated, genetically impoverished colonies are blind, tiny, and colorless.

In fact, scientists have never created or observed the creation of a new species. Some biologists even argue that all North American wolves and coyotes are really a single species. The red wolf, for instance, according to some, is a cross between a wolf and a coyote. Although most people would guess that the red wolf's chief enemy is the rancher, efforts to "protect" it are actually meant to isolate it so the "species" does not become extinct because of further interbreeding with coyotes. Today some scientists favor very fine classification divisions based on unique color or size, and what were once considered a subspecies are given full species status (see Brown *Wolf,* for example). This is similar to classifying humans into different species on the basis of hair, eye, or skin color, or on weight and height. We have lost many subspecies to extinction, but our losses of species are few.

Austin challenged the hierarchy implied by misinterpretation of evolutionary theory, offering instead the Native American view that different species are simply different tribes or nations interdependent on one another and of equal worth and equal intelligence. Cassandra Lee Kircher points out that it is "animal instinct, not endurance or skill or luck," that helps the Pocket Hunter "find safety" during a blizzard. She cautions that Austin does not imagine animal instinct in the same way naturalistic writers in the late nineteenth century imagined it. Austin's characters do not "fall prey to their desires," nor do their instincts "lead to barbarism"—the suppression of instinct does (26–28).

Among Austin's collected papers is an article she clipped and saved entitled "Was Darwin Wrong?" (AU folder 1, box 131). Probably inspired by it, she argues in an unpublished book manuscript that "Dawn Man" was a lowly scavenger, not a romantic hunter. Before "Dawn Man" was accepted by the dog as a hunting partner, he may have followed the predators and taken the leavings of their kills:

> If the original wolf pack killed as unreckoningly as the wolf of today when he makes a successful raid on a domestic flock, killing far in excess of his immediate needs, there would have been good eating and cheap for the Dawn Man who followed the wild pack. (AU 760, box 49)

She also writes that "Cape Bushmen of today are found on the trail of the African lion . . . a notable huntsman who frequently leaves a generous portion of his kill, and being full fed, is himself harmless." Animals and humans once lived (and some still do) in close contact with one another as partners and competitors.

Archaeologists today are beginning to agree with her. British archaeologist Paul Bahn, for example, acknowledges that he is "fully aware of the impact which *Man the hunter* has made on archaeological thinking," but says that recent scholarship has reexamined the man-resource relationship in prehistory. Instead of "trying to pinpoint the origins of domestication, many scholars would now argue that such cradles of invention are illusory." He also points out that domestication of animals "was not irreversible, e.g., the gazelle in the Near East, or the Barbary sheep in North Africa" (142; emphasis in original). Austin further argues that weapons were not crucial to food choices or survival. During her day, among the Bushmen of South Africa and the Papagoes of southwestern Arizona, a young man's ability to run down an antelope or deer and take it with his bare hands was still the customary test of his ability to support a family (AU 760, box 49).

Austin was writing her animal stories, however, at a time when everyday contact with animals was becoming rare. With the coming of the machine, animals gradually disappeared into a "wilderness that existed only in the imagination" (John Berger 17). Once food came from the grocery store and transporta-tion from machines, animals were still studied and watched, yet it became more and more difficult for those whose lives did not depend on them and who did not live with them on a close daily basis to separate fact from fancy. As our knowledge of animals became more speculative than real, the shape-shifting half animal–half humans common in myth and folklore began to cause a psy-chological tension (John Berger 11). Discussing Shakespeare's animal allusions in *Othello,* Jeanne Addison Roberts observes:

> Some tension and uneasiness about the true nature of man-animal rela-tionships may help to trigger the comic explosion in an audience at the ap-pearance of Bottom as an ass and Falstaff as a deer, but the laughter de-pends finally on a secure confidence in the superiority of man and the absurdity of the conjunction. When an audience's values become confused or the barriers between species are suddenly eroded, the loss of human form is no longer funny—witness the terror in Kafka's *Metamorphosis.* (80)

Austin is continually eroding those barriers when she writes about animals as "furry people." William J. Scheick finds this tendency in Austin's writing an-thropomorphic, a "form of colonization," and calls her descriptions a "failure" (42–43).

As an example of Austin's "frowned upon" anthropomorphic writing, Scott Slovic and Terrell Dixon include her story "Scavengers" in their environmen-tal reader *Being in the World: An Environmental Reader for Writers* (1993). They suggest asking students to imitate Austin for an undergraduate writing assignment, implying that her anthropomorphic style is perhaps unacceptable today, but a good way for "beginning" writers to exercise their imagination (43–48). I think Austin would boil up out of her grave like a big black thunder-head and hurl lightning bolts at them if she could. James C. Work also faults Austin for employing personification, pathetic fallacy,[14] and anthropomorphism, although he finally calls it "empathy" and stresses that empathy is "the exact word we want" (303).

Empathy was easier to conjure when animals and people led more similar lives. Austin observes that Indians once had "the faculty of quail for making themselves scarce in the underbrush at the approach of strangers," for example, and that "[y]oung Shoshones are like young quail . . . learning what civilized children never learn, to be still and keep being still." Shoshones wintered "flock wise," going up "each with his mate and young brood, like birds to old nesting places"; a campoodie at noon resembled "a collection of prodigious wasps' nests" (*Land* 56–58). Austin also notes that both Shoshone and coyotes ate desert tortoise. She describes an occasion when an old rancher sixty miles from a Bible made up a ceremony in order to bury an old mountaineer, and "[t]he tall, hard-riding Texans and Tennesseans, [as] clanking in their spurs, [came] down to be pall-bearers, lean as wolves" (*Flock* 222).

John Berger summarizes the plight of modern people who no longer live the same kind of lives animals live or work with animals on a daily basis when he says, "today we live without animals [and] in this solitude . . . anthropomorphism makes us uneasy" (11). Contemporary humans who feel any sort of empathy with animals usually anthropomorphize the animals' desires, imagining that they want to be loved and cared for with no responsibilities. Yi-Fu Tuan also sees this highly sentimentalized view of pets as caused by our distance from animals in the modern world:

> Wild animals and even farm animals were becoming less and less the common experience of men and women in an increasingly urbanized and industrialized society. It was easy to entertain warm feelings toward animals that seemed to have no other function than as play-things. Moreover, humans needed an outlet for their gestures of affection and this was becoming more difficult to find in modern society as it began to segment and isolate people into their private spheres, to discourage casual physical contact, and to frown upon the enormously satisfying stances of patronage, such as laying one's hand on another's shoulder. (*Dominance* 112)

Humans, therefore, shower animals with "love" and patronage rather than respect, and project onto them a childish personality. Thus we have adult poodles with bows on their ears and matching nail polish on their toes instead of hunting partners and teachers.

In order to be taken seriously by an increasingly urban population, science attempted to purge all traces of emotion, empathy, and anthropomorphism from animal research. Recent scholarship, however, has begun to reevaluate this purging. In *When Elephants Weep: The Emotional Lives of Animals* (1995), J. Moussaieff Masson and Susan McCarthy build a strong case that by insisting on "objective" research, science has actually hindered our knowledge of animals, just as "objective" history hindered our understanding of the past. In addition, this distancing of humans from animals has resulted in the idea that animals are simply an "otherness subservient to human needs" (Oerlemans 1).[15] Peter Fritzell, in *Nature Writing and America* (1990), argues that our insistence to dehumanize animals is actually an anthropocentric defense mechanism that keeps us feeling "special" and further promotes the dualism that separates humans from nature (98–99). But these antianthropomorphic biases seem to be changing. A recent article in the *Chronicle of Higher Education* states that modern scientists feel that "critical application of anthropomorphism" could help research in animal behavior (McDonald A8).

Granted, Austin does sometimes drift too far into anthropomorphism. She equates pines with "tall priests" who "pray for rain" (*Land* 105), her mountains sometimes weep out mountain streams like "tears" (*Land* 113), and coyote fathers sometimes tell their "cubs" bedtime stories (*Children* 75). In her children's books, trees, water, and glaciers talk (*Children* 15–16, 184). Even in her adult books, birds and animals express emotions and communicate to some degree, even with humans. I don't like pine-tree cathedrals, wolves dressed in granny gowns, talking horses, or mice who wear shoes, but I like Austin's hawks who "come trooping like small boys to a street fight," clouds that "dance to some pied piper of an unfelt wind," and desert dust spirals that rise like a genie out of a bottle (*Land* 37, 134, 138).

Austin's world is actually more animistic than anthropomorphic. Plants have brains. Desert winds run "loose" and herd sheeplike clouds around sky pastures. Water "lolls," "leaps," and "runs away"; the Sierra is "white fanged." Animism, according to Manes, is a belief that "the phenomenal world is alive in the sense of being inspirited"—this includes cultural artifacts and natural entities, both biological and "inert"—and that the nonhuman world is "filled with articulate subjects, able to communicate with humans" (18).

Austin says that humans who refuse to listen to animals and try to rely only on their own intelligence sometimes pay with their lives. Predators "on the plains where water-holes are far between," for example, ". . . will not follow after the flocks, for meat-eaters must drink directly they have eaten." Shepherds who tried to take their flocks where the predators refused to go were sometimes found dead or crazed for lack of water (*Flock* 182). This kind of listening and watching is not the animal watching we see today in zoos, scientific studies, and tourist attractions. Today animals are watched as subjects, exotics, beautiful objects, symbols, or curiosities, but never as teachers.

Through stories about animal intelligence, Austin challenges the science-based dualism between human intelligence and animal instinct, which in turn challenges the entire system of animal hierarchies. She continually preaches that humans and animals are equally intelligent (*Work* 43), and animals perhaps even more so in most circumstances. Modern man uses an animal's "lack of common language, its silence" to guarantee "its distance, its distinctness, its exclusion, from and of man" (John Berger 6). But Austin explains how animals speak and how to understand their language. She explains how antelope communicate by flashing their white rump patches (*Flock* 228), and she tells us that coyote hunting packs are able to execute intricate relay races in order to bring down game that a human hunting pack "would need a great deal of palaver" in order to accomplish (AU 760). In support of animal intelligence she writes, "Last-evening coming down from Fort Tejon at the top of the hill, looking down the *canada* I saw a whole family of coons playing tag. I watched them a long time and I think there were rules to the game" (AU 267 p. 19). Just as Europeans once considered Indians to be animals because they had no language, denying animals language relegates them to a "lower" level of development and existence.

In a highly touted book, *The Spell of the Sensuous* (1996), David Abram presents a sophisticated academic argument supporting the importance and influence of animistic communication with the nonhuman world. He treats with great respect the kind of knowledge that people who live in direct daily contact with animals and the natural world accumulate through their senses: "In indigenous, oral cultures, nature itself is articulate; it *speaks*" (116; emphasis in original). He also compares trackers' ability to "read sign" on the land to our modern ability to "read sign" on the page:

> As nonhuman animals, plants, and even "inanimate" rivers once spoke to our tribal ancestors, so the "inert" letters on the page now speak to us! *This is a form of animism that we take for granted, but it is animism nonetheless—as mysterious as a talking stone.* (131; emphasis in original)

Abram relates that while he was abroad living with indigenous people, his own senses jumped to alertness. Once he returned to the United States, however, he gradually began to lose this heightened awareness. The more "books and articles and discussions" about animals that he read or held, the more the feeling of communication faded: "Indeed, the more I spoke *about* other animals, the less possible it became to speak *to* them (25; emphasis in original).

One hundred years ago, Mary Austin was already questioning the wisdom behind privileging human language, especially scholastic English, over all other forms, when animals with their more highly developed senses of smell, hearing, and touch could read signs their educated human counterparts did not even realize existed. She asked whether humans' ability to read, interpret, and communicate across species through birdcalls, animal muscle tension, hackles, scent, and tracks might be more difficult and therefore a more advanced form of communication than understanding academic discourse. These ancient languages are lost to the average "civilized" person, but they are spoken fluently and passed from generation to generation through stories in cultures where animal-human contact is still prevalent.[16] As John Berger notes, it was once thought that normal humans lacked the capacity to speak to animals, although exceptional human beings could (6). Manes explains that "in an attempt to re-animate nature, we must have the courage to learn that new [I would say very ancient!] language, even if it puts at risk the privileged discourse of reason—and without a doubt, it does" (24).[17]

Abram says that indigenous hunters are so familiar with the calls and cries of animals that they are able to "generate and mimic such sounds," and thus "to enter most directly into the society of other animals" (141). Austin explains the same phenomenon as "mind conscious mind reacting on mind shaping the world. Mind in trees and birds and flowers. That is how they come to resemble one another" (AU 363). The ability to read animal signs and learn again to communicate with animals could be a first step toward reintroducing modern humans back into the natural world from which they think they have been expelled.

Amazingly, Austin is still ahead of her time. She takes communication with animals one step further than the most progressive modern thinkers have yet attempted. Not only does she claim that some people are quite capable of understanding animal language to some degree, she also claims that animals are capable of understanding human language. She argues that sheep not only understand ancient salt calls and come to the shepherd, but sometimes associate the call with any prominent rock on which a shepherd might stand in order to make the call. When they are hungry for salt, they will congregate around a rock, communicating their need to the shepherd through silent "words" understood by both (*Flock* 130). In "The Folk Story in America" (1934), Austin relates how hunting dogs "could listen with pride or chagrin to their own stories as told by their owners." Because the communication between sheepdogs and shepherds went on every day, all day, "sheep dogs not only recognized familiar tales of their own adventures, but could, when the adventure was a lively one, relive it joyfully, and even get the drift of an unfamiliar tale told about some other sheepherder's dog" (11). She observes that shepherds can say to a dog what the dog cannot say to another dog, and says that she has known "some collies that only know Basque and a *patois* that is not the French of the books," or only speak Paiute (*Flock* 146; *Basket* 104). These claims sound like anthropomorphism at its worst, but those who work daily with animals would agree with Austin, at least to some degree; and some of us also believe that animals are often capable of understanding humans better than other humans can.[18] Sounding mysterious and mystical while simply telling a natural truth about sheepdogs, Austin claims her proof that dogs could understand shepherds' stories by following shepherd-dog signs and signals that could not possibly pertain to their present surroundings was "probably the most important contribution to the story-teller's art that Mary will ever make" (*Earth* 265).

Chapter Two

Gendering the Wild and Domestic

*Thus, in the Western myth, where nature is constrained to bear the
otherness of men, the landscape becomes not only transcendental but also
feminized, a yoking together explainable only by nature and women's
common function as factors in male otherness. The need to define the
masculine as not-feminine seems so powerful as to mandate the
construction of the animal as female too.*
Suzanne Kehde (135)

In "The Bitterness of Women" (1909), Austin reminds her readers that the
most feared and dangerous wild killer in the American West is a female, not a
male. The story tells how a female grizzly bear changed the life of Chabot, a
handsome womanizing shepherd, who had scorned the love of a faithful but
plain Mexican woman until,

> [s]omewhere up in the blown lava-holes of Black Mountain there was a
> bear with two cubs, who had said to them, bear fashion: "Come down to
> the flock with me tonight, and I will show you how killing is done. There
> will be dogs there and men; but do not be afraid, I will see to it that they
> do not hurt you."
>
> Along about the time Orion's sword sloped down the west, Chabot heard
> their gruntled noises and the scurry of the flock. Chabot was not a coward;
> perhaps because he knew that in general bears are; he got up and laid
> about him with his staff. This he never would have done if he had known
> about the cubs; he trod on the foot of one in the dark, and the bear mother
> heard it. She came lumbering up in the soft blackness and took Chabot in
> her arms. (*Western* 79)

Chabot does not die, but his face is scarred beyond repugnance, and in desperation he marries the faithful Mexican woman who still loves him in spite of his
new ugliness. In this story, Austin very intentionally connects the female gender to wildness and strength.

A serious student of psychology, Austin knew that in order to make a difference in the American consciousness her stories would need to plumb a deeper,
more mythic level than stories about humans provided. Dudley Wynn claims

that Austin's ideas about "racial memory" predate Carl Jung's theories (*A Critical* 16). A good example, perhaps, is Austin's recognition of a gendered anima/animus within the human psyche.[1] Her emphasis on the importance of gender in animal stories operates at a psychological level and reverberates far beyond the simple battle of the sexes. Through the anima/animus, Austin's animal stories challenge gender stereotypes and the myth of a womanless West, reminding the reader that women and men of various species have always lived in the "wilderness," together raising families, providing food, and setting up housekeeping. Just as the dichotomy between wild and domestic animals was constructed by people who did not know them, the mythic Wild, Wild West—which was no place for a lady and idealized the lone male in the wilderness—was constructed by eastern writers, not by rural westerners. Knowing that animal stories operate on psychological, subconscious connections, Austin became a stickler for exposing, deconstructing, and rewriting gender misrepresentations in animal stories; she especially seemed to target John Muir and Jack London.

In his famous essay "The Water-Ouzel" (1894) Muir, an Austin contemporary, eloquently simulates his own fitness for wilderness living and his ability to write about it. Identifying with the ouzel, Muir describes the bird as a "singularly joyous and lovable little fellow" who flits about the most isolated and beautiful of the Yosemite canyons, "ever vigorous and enthusiastic, yet self-contained, and neither seeking nor shunning your company" (*Mountains* 410). Muir allegorically compares the "sweet and tender" music that flows "from *his* round breast" with the lyric writing that flows from Muir's own pen "like water over the smooth lip of a pool, then breaking farther on into a sparkling foam of melodious notes" (212; emphasis added). Curiously, Muir always refers to the ouzel as a male and states that he is "found singly; rarely in pairs, excepting during the breeding season." Muir insists that even during nesting the solitary bird is a male, referring to the nest building with language associated with architecture and carpentry rather than the more female "nesting":

> The ouzel's nest is one of the most extraordinary pieces of bird *architecture* I ever saw, odd and novel in *design,* perfectly fresh and beautiful, and in every way worthy of the genius of the little *builder.* . . . [T]he little *architect* always tak[es] advantage of slight crevices and protuberances that may chance to offer, to render *his structure stable* by means of a kind of *gripping* and *dovetailing.* (415; emphasis added)

Only once during the entire essay does Muir faintly admit to the possibility of a female presence when he describes the "young just out of the nest making their odd gestures, and seeming in every way as much at home as their experienced *parents*" (416–17; emphasis added). However, even this sentence seems to imply that the female bird frequents the canyons only when the male is with her; the single ouzels living alone in their cozy little mossy nests along the rushing streams and booming waterfalls are males—according to Muir. Nest building is for a wilderness hideway, not hatching eggs.

From the beginning, so the story goes, the American wilderness was never imagined by women in the same way that it was imagined by men. John O'Grady points out that neither the Pilgrim women nor Mary Austin were pilgrims to the wild by choice (*Pilgrims* 123). When William Bradford's young wife, Dorothy May, first saw the November-shrouded New England coast, she either fell or jumped overboard and drowned, never setting foot on the new continent. Suicide? No one, including Bradford, ever quite says (Grabo 275). However, these widely accepted Pilgrim (his)tories often leave out the fact that Bradford's second wife, the widow Alice Carpenter Southworth, sailed into the "wilderness" alone and of her own free will. In spite of the fact that not one scrap of a diary, journal, or letter from Pilgrim women survives, our (his)torians unquestioningly assume that the Pilgrim wives, unlike our own great-aunts, grandmothers, and modern selves, never helped make the decision to move, never badgered their husbands into the move, or, with rolling pin in one hand and fist on hip, never simply said, "Pack, Dear, we're moving."

When Austin began writing, the terms *domestic* and *wild* had been heavily influenced by both European and American romanticism. Through romanticism wildness became a strange paradox joining the sacred with the forbidden that was often expressed through a sexual or gendered metaphor—thus a "virgin" wilderness was also "no place for a lady." Annette Kolodny argues that the North American continent was commonly represented as a female presence: virginity, motherhood, rape, ravishment, fertility, gratification, receptivity, nurturance, abundance, satisfaction, breast, womb, despoliation, betrayal, birthplace (*Lay*). When the wilderness was given not only a female but a virginal image, virile males became the only rightful inhabitants. Kolodny finds that "implicit in the call to immigrate then, was the tantalizing proximity to happiness" (*Lay* 7).

Early in his career, even Wallace Stegner found the pioneer West no place for a lady. "From John Colter on," he says, "*man* with *wild* blood had found the Rockies a place of *savage* freedom, but the mountains apparently offered nothing to the homesteader." Stegner describes the West as a place where "*girls* screech[ed] at the rattlesnakes" and where conflicts arose between the "freedom loving *man* and the civilizing *woman* . . . *wildness* versus *civilization* and danger versus the safe and tamed (*Sound* 26, 65, 195; emphasis added). As Cheryll Glotfelty summarizes, "[T]he American wilderness has historically been constructed as a man's world" ("Femininity" 450).

Austin feared this evolving tendency to imagine the West as composed of wild, virginal places and the idea that only males belonged there. With almost parallel description, but with allusion to a woman's happy adaptation to wild places and her ability to write about them, in "The Cheerful Glacier" (1904) Austin specifically rewrote Muir's ouzel story, changing the bird's gender and deleting Muir's description of male feathers: a "tinge of chocolate on the head and shoulders" (*Mountains* 410). Austin recognized the tendency to leave women out of (his)tory and literature, and set out, through animal stories, to describe the West as the home for both genders it had always been.

Austin's ouzel, a little mountain soprano, is very specifically female: "*She* came whirling up the course of the stream like a thrown pebble, plump and slaty blue, scattering a spray of sound as clear and round as the trickle of ice water that went over the falls." She flitted far up into an ice cave until "the sound of *her* singing came out wild and sweet, mixed with the water and the tinkle of the ice" (*Basket* 65–66; emphasis added). With lyric onomatopoeia Austin challenges Muir to a duel of pens and also corrects his claim that ouzels spend the winter along frozen streams. Muir's version describes all Yosemite's birds except the ouzel as being restricted to the sunny north side of the valley, stoically and cheerlessly enduring the winter. But the "ouzel never calls forth a single touch of pity," Muir claims; "not because he is strong to endure, but rather because he seems to live a charmed life beyond the reach of every influence that makes endurance necessary" (*Mountains* 411). Austin's version is more concrete and seems to mock not only Muir's version of the ouzel's existence but also his own reputation for carrying only a crust of bread on his hikes:

> The ouzel always went downstream at the beginning of winter, when the running waters were shut under snow bridges and the pools were puddles of gray sludge, down and down to the foothill borders, and at the turn of the year followed up again the wake of the thaw. . . . For though she did not mind the storms and cold weather, one cannot really exist without eating. (*Basket* 67)

The female animal, plant, or human in the wilderness appeared in Austin's writing time and again as she tried to combat the accumulating subconscious stereotypes.

In 1903, although they had not yet met, Austin and Jack London both published books featuring female dog characters living in the "wilderness." In *The Call of the Wild* (1903) London creates the quintessential virile wilderness male. The book also implies, through several female dog characters, that the manly wilderness is no place for a lady, not even a female dog. London's male dog, Buck, and a female dog, Curly, sail into the "savage" north on the same ship. On landing, Curly and Buck immediately must fight "wolfish creatures" as a test for survival of the fittest in the wilderness. The male dog adapts quickly to the wolf manner of fighting, but the female becomes an easy "victim" after "she, in her friendly way, made advances to a husky" (15). The resulting dog-fight is brief, brutal, and has undertones of gang rape—an obvious end result that any friendly, naive female who ventures into the all-male wilderness should expect:

> There was no warning, only a leap in like a flash, a metallic clip of teeth, a leap out equally swift, and Curly's face was ripped open from eye to jaw.
> It was the wolf manner of fighting, to strike and leap away; but there was more to it than this. Thirty or forty huskies ran to the spot and surrounded the combatants in an intent and silent circle. Buck did not comprehend that silent intentness, or the eager way with which they were licking their chops. Curly rushed her antagonist, who struck again and leaped aside. He met her next rush with his chest, in a peculiar fashion that tumbled her off her feet. She never regained them. This was what the on looking huskies had waited for. They closed in upon her, snarling and yelping, and she was buried, screaming with agony, beneath the bristling mass of bodies. (*Call* 15)

In *The Land of Little Rain*, published the same year as *The Call of the Wild*, Austin creates a female dog character who challenges both the idea of a savage wilderness and the idea that women are unfit to live there. Austin was very aware of and very opposed to American literature's stance that the wilderness was no place for a lady. Women had been cast as persecuted maidens in Puritan sermons, as fainting virgins who must be protected in the works of Cooper, and as mothers who did not "light out for the territories" in Twain (Fiedler); or they had simply not been imagined at all, as in Emerson, Thoreau, Whitman, and Muir. In contrast, Austin describes the desert wilderness as a home and presents as inhabitants both an Indian woman and a female dog who are quite capable of fending for themselves:

> There used to be in the Little Antelope a she dog, stray or outcast, that had a litter in some forsaken lair, and ranged and foraged for them, slinking savage and afraid, remembering and mistrusting human-kind, wistful, lean, and sufficient for her young. I have often thought Seyavi might have had days like that. (*Land* 62)

Both women and female animals, Austin argues here, not only survived but were well able to raise their children in the wilderness. It was so-called civilization, not wildness, that changed their homes into dangerous places.

Sometime between 1904 and 1906, Austin became a personal friend of London's and part of a group of writers headquartered at Carmel. One by one, almost matching animal character for animal character, she challenged the stereotypes London used to exclude women from wild places: their inability to fight, their physical and mental weaknesses, their inability or unwillingness to handle hard work, and London's strange double standards concerning sexuality.

Challenging London's implication that women were more prone than men to madness in the wilderness, Austin took exception to another female dog in *The Call of the Wild*. After London's fictional dog team is attacked by a wild band of starving Indian dogs, only Dolly, "the last husky added to the team," who "had never been conspicuous for anything, went suddenly mad." London's description of her sudden onset of "madness" sounds like a mixture between rabies and the insanity of a female pursuing a male:

> She announced her condition by a long, heartbreaking wolf howl that sent every dog bristling with fear, then sprang straight for Buck. He had never seen a dog go mad, nor did he have any reason to fear madness; yet he knew that here was horror, and fled away from it in a panic. Straight away he raced, with Dolly, panting and frothing, one leap behind; nor could she gain on him, so great was his terror, nor could he leave her, so great was her madness. (29)

The male dog is saved when the sled-dog driver brings an axe down "upon mad Dolly's head"(29).

Although Austin resisted creating a comparable "mad" animal character, she was able to come fairly close the next year (1904) with a half-coyote/half-human male who seems to be struggling with madness in "The Coyote-Spirit and the Weaving Woman."[2] A Coyote-Spirit, explains Austin, wants to be with humans, but because of his wolfish nature, he immediately thinks of devouring them.[3] So, as soon as the Coyote-Spirit meets the Weaving Woman, he wants to "eat her up, or to work her some evil." However, instead of running away from madness in horror, like London's male dog, the Weaving Woman cures the Coyote-Spirit of his madness, and he is able to become a fully human man again, happily marrying a girl who tends goats (*Basket* 43–58).

Another "mad" Austin character created after *The Call of the Wild* was published is an Indian woman who is obviously "pursuing" a male, but for good reason. In the story "A Case of Conscience" (1909), a very British male "mates" with an Indian woman and they produce a child. When he decides to return to civilization, he takes the child with him. The Indian woman pursues him until he decides to give back the baby, and Austin's narrator comments, "I believe he thought he had come to that conclusion by himself." Mother and child then return to their wilderness home (*Western* 45–50).

At the end of *The Call of the Wild*, Buck's transformation from soft, domestic dog to wild, virile beast is complete when he mates with native females, and the resulting wolf cubs inherit some of his markings (87). "Mating" with native females was, again, an idea Austin disagreed with violently, referring to it as "mahala chasing" and comparing native women to another form of "game":

> You can guess, however, that all this warring of rifles and bow strings, this influx of over lording whites, had made game wilder and hunters fearful of being hunted. You can surmise also, for it was a crude time and the land was raw, that the women became in turn the game of the conquerors. (*Land* 62).

Imaging the wilderness as a man's world promoted the treatment of native women as sexual "fair game" with no resulting responsibility attached. As Kolodny explains, Indian women became an "emblem" representing a place where Europeans expected to be entertained ("Unearthing" 172). Both animals and native women survived just fine in the wilderness, Austin argues, again allegorically, until "civilized" men arrived.

The Austin-London battle of the dogs also takes on complex political overtones when one of Austin's human characters is compared to yet another female dog character in London's *White Fang* (1906), interestingly created after London and Austin had become friends. London's female dog's fur is ominously, mysteriously, and perhaps racially and politically tinged with

> a faint reddish hue—a hue that was baffling, that appeared and disappeared, that was more like an illusion of the vision, now gray, distinctly gray, and again giving hints and glints of a vague redness of color not classifiable in terms of ordinary experience. (108)

Like London's none-too-subtle color symbolism in the "red sweater" worn by his dog-beating villain in *The Call of the Wild* (10–13), this red fur obviously brands the female dog as a Satan character. London's she-devil dog had rejected domesticity and "run away with the wolves." Like a frontier whore (who also often dressed symbolically in red), the fallen dog is able to survive in the wilderness by using her sex for the benefit of her adopted wild pack. Seeming to "smile" at the domestic sled dogs in an "ingratiating rather than a menacing way," she lures even the most sensible dog away from his human protectors. Following the female "decoy," the sled dogs become easy prey and simple meat when "the rest [of the wolf pack] pitches in an' eats 'm up" (*White* 110, 104). Patiently the she-devil dog helps her wild pack pick off and devour the domestic dogs one by one; eventually she lures one of the two male humans to a similar death. As the wolves are about to devour the second man, the she-devil's spell is broken with the timely arrival of human male reinforcements (119).

In response, Austin invents a comparable devil character in human form, but a male. *The Flock* (1906), published the same year London published *White*

Fang and while Austin and London obviously were discussing and comparing each other's work, features a red-tinged, social-Darwinistic, female-stealing shepherd. The devil-shepherd believes that his manhood is proven by his ability to compete with and beat his fellow shepherds to the grass:

> "Tell me," I said to Narcisse, who because of the tawny red of his hair, the fiery red of his face, the russet red of his beard, and the red spark of his eye, was called Narcisse the Red, "tell me what is the worst of shepherding?"
>
> "The worst, madame, is the feed, because there is not enough of it."
>
> "And what, in your thinking, is the best?"
>
> "The feed, madame, for there is not enough of it."
>
> "But how could that be, both best and worst?"
>
> Narcisse laughed full and throatily, throwing up his chin from the burned red chest all open to the sun. It was that laugh of Narcisse's that betrayed him the night he carried away Suzon Moynier from her father's house.
>
> "It is the worst," said he, "because it is a great distress to see the flock go hungry, also it is a loss to the owner. It is the best, because every man must set his wits against every other. When he comes out of the hills with a fat flock and good fleeces it is that he has proved himself the better man."
> (*Flock* 157–58)

An important distinction between the two authors as they portray their respective "devil" characters is that Austin is less judgmental than London. Austin did not shy away from accepting both the good and the bad in human nature for both the male and female genders, but she did refrain from imposing the worst of human characteristics on animals. Her ideas are also more complex than simple social-Darwinistic survival of the fittest. Her female characters are often old, blind, thin, and timid—yet still able to survive quite well in the wilderness (*Land* 61–67).

Austin obviously objected to the flawed and stereotypic roles in which London cast his female dogs: naive victims like Curly; mentally weak females susceptible to madness like Dolly; the wily, red-tinged fallen whore of the wild frontier; or pampered house dogs like "Toots, the Japanese pug, or Ysabel, the Mexican hairless—strange creatures that rarely put nose out of doors or set foot to ground" (*Call* 6). In contrast to London, Austin's female animals are not helpless, pampered pets; nor are they unfaithful to their domestic duties; nor are they mentally weak.

Austin also found, and countered, a dangerous gender bias in the work hierarchies in London's dog stories. *The Flock* features a hard-working female sheep-herding dog as a comparable character to London's hard-working male sled dogs. No pampered pet, Austin's female dog is so torn between her herding duties and her duties as the mother of a new litter of puppies that she travels miles on bleeding feet trying to do both jobs:

> At Los Alisos there was a bitch of such excellent temper that she was thought of more value for raising pups than herding; she was, therefore, when her litter came, taken from the flock and given quarters at the ranch house. But in the morning Flora went out to the sheep. She sought them in the pastures where they had been, and kept the accustomed round, returning wearied to her young at noon; she followed after them at evening and covered with panting sides the distance they had put between them and her litter. At the end of the second day when she came to her bed, half dead with running, she was tied, but gnawed the rope, and in twenty-four hours was out on the cold trail of the flock. One of the vaqueros found her twenty miles from home, working faint and frenzied over its vanishing scent. It was only after this fruitless sally that she was reconciled to her new estate. (*Flock* 141–42)

Austin repeatedly challenges gendered work hierarchies through her animal stories, asking what higher calling either males or females could aspire to than raising children, providing nourishment, or producing art for use in their own homes. Ursula K. Le Guin jokes derisively that "it is hard to tell a really gripping tale of how I wrestled a wild-oat seed from its husk, and then another, and then another, and then another, and then another. . . . No, it does not compare" with hunting stories (149). But that is exactly what Austin was trying to accomplish. She didn't want to privilege hunting as "wild" work; she wanted to find a way to write about making baskets, cooking, wrestling with wild oats, and gossiping that touched the universal and God.

Annette Kolodny sees the "domestic professionalism" of child training, nursing, handicrafts, home management, and cooking as a scheme to keep women oppressed (*Land Before Her* 165), but Austin thought true art was the ability to make everyday skills strange and beautiful. Although perhaps only part of her public book-selling myth, Austin's "Indian name" was supposedly *See-goochee*, meaning "the woman who gives good things to eat" (Hoyer "Prophecy" 245). She took greens from her garden to trade for meat in shepherd camps (*Earth* 248) and was famous for her pies; and when she died, friends found 135 jars of homemade jams and jellies in her house at Santa Fe (Church 3). Instead of valuing their work, Austin declares, women give it away to hirelings. According to Benay Blend, Austin did not believe that domestic chores "confined" women to the home, but rather that "the domestic sphere should be expanded to encompass the world" (Blend "Building" 78). In Austin's mind the domestic represented freedom and wildness.

Austin uses animals to add mystery, beauty, and the universal to women's stories. In one story, she argues that wolves, if given a choice, would freely choose domesticity. Austin's female Native American narrator in "Wolf People" (1934), Antelope-over-the-Hill, tells that the Wolf became a dog "of its own free willing," not by force or by being caught as a cub and raised to be tame. Antelope-over-the-Hill says respectfully that Wolves are a people, with their own leaders and chiefs, and friendly toward Indians. The Wolves and Indians helped each other during the hunt by signaling to one another. When Wolves heard Indians singing a hunting song, they would arise and drive the game toward the Indian hunters because "men are more skillful at the kill, and Wolves on the trail" (*One Smoke*). Through this Indian-wolf partnership more food was available for both (*Trail* 51).[4] Supposing that one gender can or would need to force domestication on another and thinking that because humans are smarter we are able to force domestication on animals are examples of condescending anthropocentric thinking. At the end of *White Fang*, obviously influenced by Austin, London's domesticated wolf mates with a collie sheepdog, siring a litter of puppies. Through his male dog characters, Buck and White Fang, London also wrestles with the boundaries between wildness and domesticity.[5] In fact, a comparison of Austin's and London's dog characters regarding subtle differences in psychology, politics, and sexuality, which characters appear first, and who influenced whom would make an interesting study.

* * *

If most Americans, either during Austin's day or today, were told to close their eyes and imagine an elk, a bighorn, or a moose, a virulent horned male, probably silhouetted against the sky, would pop into view. But if they were asked to imagine domestic cattle or sheep, the representative animal pictured would be a docile, stupid, unhorned female. In *The Land before Her: Fantasy and Experience of the American Frontiers, 1630–1860* (1984), Kolodny explains that the female gender, when associated with the land, is usually either virginal (wilderness) or motherly (civilization). Thus the archetypal gendered pairing is wild male animals and humans with the virginal wilderness playground, and motherly, nurturing types with domestic places.[6] According to Christian mythology, agriculture began as a curse. When Adam and Eve fell from grace and were thrown out of the Garden of Eden, their punishment was to sweat and "till the ground" (Gen. 3:18–23). Thus, observes Kolodny, the biblical "fall" was reenacted on this continent over and over again as the frontier moved west and innocent, free, wild men who belonged in the wilderness were tempted to "settle down" and till the ground in order to support the domestic daughters of Eve. I argue that the animals associated with agriculture were saddled with the same subconscious baggage connected to the female gender and that some of today's prejudices against domestic animals and agriculture stem from this identification with the female.[7]

Domestic animals have a long history of imagined villainy. During the sixteenth and seventeenth centuries both the Catholic Church and Protestant sects burned animals at the stake as witches, just as they did women. Most of these animal "witches" were domestic animals: horses, cows, pigs, and dogs.[8] With a few interesting exceptions, the domestic animals in American literature are usually either "fallen" working animals (Steinbeck's work teams, Hurston's mules), a form of transportation (horses in Leopold, McCarthy, and Abbey), a Gothic food source (Sinclair's meat), a sacrifice (Dillard's unblemished red heifer), or a symbol of the destructive masses (Muir's sheep). In contrast, the great wild animal characters in American literature are lone males who live in the wilderness without women: Melville's great whale, Hemingway's marlin, Faulkner's bear.

Wild males are imagined as big, strong leaders with the skills to live off the land, their lives free, violent, and unencumbered by such boring domestic responsibilities as tending children or practicing sexual restraint. Wild males are free to collect harems and serve any female who comes into heat. Even today, writers perhaps unintentionally imagine wild and domestic animals with a strange sexual double standard. When Gretel Ehrlich, who is touted by Annie Dillard as Wyoming's Whitman, describes life on a Wyoming sheep ranch in *The Solace of Open Spaces* (1985), the book is so full of sex even corncobs have erections (130). Yet, although Ehrlich writes about "fifteen hundred sheep," "fifteen thousand sheep," "two thousand sheep," "two hundred ewes," lambs, branded lambs, orphaned lambs, even "a lamb with two heads," not a single domestic ram appears (*Solace* 67, 19, 1, 20). In contrast, we breathlessly watch, with Ehrlich, a wild "Big Horn ram in rut chase a ewe around a tree for an hour. When he caught and mounted her, his horns hit a low branch and he fell off. She ran away with a younger ram in pursuit" (*Solace* 68).[9] Although domestic sheep have lambs, they apparently do not, at least publicly, have sex.

(His)tory, politics, religion, and literature, somehow connected to the idea of "virgin land," have always imagined wild bachelorhood as an ideal existence. Thus, frontiersmen, mountain men, and cowboys are represented as romantic, handsome, aggressive, self-reliant, and, of course, happily single.[10] As long as the cowboy is trailing steers (males) north on his gelding (male), he retains his stature as knight; but once he becomes identified with bawling female cows, he loses much of his appeal. Taking a band of silly female sheep into the wilderness is nothing short of sacrilege! But these stories, again, did not originate in the rural West.

Austin challenges the happy lone male in the wilderness myth most effectively in "The Last Antelope" (1909), in which a lonely bachelor shepherd makes friends with a lone antelope and a lone juniper tree. Having heard the story from rural men, Austin explains that it is an animal story "such as men seldom think of telling to women, not because they are untellable, but because they seem perhaps to belong so exclusively to the male life, such tales as 'The Last Antelope' " (*Earth* 215). Melody Graulich notes that in this story Austin "sympathetically explores male experience in the West," and she speculates that Austin may have considered it her "best native folk story about the lone male in the wilderness" (*Western* 202). The missing female presence provides the story's subtle tension.[11] The shepherd, juniper, and antelope are frozen in a moment that can only end tragically because they have no mates. Even junipers need both male and female trees in order to reproduce. The moment cannot last, and because the life span of the antelope is the shortest, he ages fastest. The poignancy of their lonely situation is intensified when they make friends with one another and blur the boundaries between wild and domestic. When the antelope freely joins the shepherd's flock for protection from the coyotes, we realize that the story could have had a happier ending. If the antelope had only had a mate, he could have raised a family within the protective circle of the flock.[12]

Western males in Austin's work are not so virile and indestructible as Muir, London, and the dime novels portray them. She rightly took exception to Muir's claims that leadership in nature naturally belongs to the male. Deer, for example, Muir writes, are "led by old experienced bucks whose knowledge of the topography is wonderful" (*Our National* 535). Elsewhere, Muir observes a band of wild sheep perform miraculous feats of mountaineering:

> The main band, headed by an experienced *chief,* now began to cross the wild rapids between the two divisions of the cascade. . . . After crossing the river, the dauntless climbers, led by their *chief,* at once began to scale the canyon wall, . . . [and] the *ewes follow* wherever the rams may lead. (*Mountains* 425; emphasis added)

Instead of being led by fearless, majestic males, Austin's bighorn sheep and mastodons are led, as hunters know is true, by old females (*Land* 96; *Trail* 29). When traveling with females, the bucks and rams either embed themselves safely within flocks and herds or follow behind them. Yet, it is not her intent to denigrate men. Humorously, although she finds shepherds only possibly as intelligent as their dogs and "certainly" not as handsome, she still finds them appealing.[13]

Austin's gender switching is more complex than simple competition between the sexes. Although English-born critic Vernon Young (1950) thinks that Austin had an "obsessive repugnance toward the male animal" (29), a closer look, especially at her earlier work, reveals affection for desert-dwelling men in every line. Austin's male characters are cooking pocket hunters, gentle shepherds, shy vaqueros, prospectors who rescue babies, or Mexican miners who quit their jobs so they will not eat better than their families. If the males are bachelors, they are humble nurturers, not knights-errant. Wild Indian husbands like Winnenap are somewhat henpecked, and romantic storytelling stage drivers occasionally fall sick like mere mortals.

When Austin began writing, male western characters, like rural women, had been sadly misrepresented in literature written by eastern, urban, and European authors. Zane Grey was a New York dentist. Frederic Remington's studio was in New York, and Owen Wister was an easterner who went west for his health in the summers. Yet Grey, Remington, and Wister were considered quintessential representatives of the western male in Austin's day just as they are today. And the pattern continues. Although a native westerner, Walter Van Tilburg Clark was a second-generation urban academic; Jack Shaefer had never been west of Ohio when he wrote *Shane* (1949); Louis L'Amour lived in Los Angeles; and even Gretel Ehrlich was a California–New York urbanite before she became, as Edward Abbey says, an "instant redneck" (*One Life* 3). Western myths, "formulaic western narrative," hierarchies, masculinity, and violence in western films and literature are credited to westerners (Tompkins) when they should be credited to their eastern or urban creators. Much serious critical work needs to be done to sort out authentic western literature, art, film, and photography from works with a western setting peopled with characters who wear cowboy clothes, ride horses, and use bad grammar, and who were invented by artists and authors who came from outside the rural western culture.[14]

Austin also reverses gender in her animal stories in order to create new myths about the western male, again elevating domestic duties to their proper status as wild work. When Austin says in *The Flock* that cougars often "go in companies," or that one can throw a hundred-pound wether "across *his* shoulder" and carry it "miles to *his* young in the lair, with hardly a dragging foot to mark *his* trail"; or when on a mountain slope, after a rockslide, Austin hears the "houseless cry of a cougar whose lair, and perhaps *his* family, had been buried under a slide of broken boulders," the actual animal in each case is obviously female, but Austin switches gender in order to give the male animal nurturing characteristics like compassion and family ties (*Flock* 183; *Land* 96; emphasis added).[15]

Austin's male characters, both animal and human, often enjoy and perform domestic homemaking skills. She writes of male sheep adopting lambs, male mastodons adopting human boys, Scottish shepherds knitting (*Trail* 22; *Flock* 24, 63), Indian males and bears catching fish with their hands[16] or digging roots like Indian women (*Basket* 112; *Land* 27; *One Smoke* 35), shepherds cooking savory meat on a fire (*Land* 58), and a pocket hunter describing his nonsticky "kitchen" (*Land* 23). Women's work and domestic chores are actually closer to the kind of work that "savage" people, bachelors, and "wild" animals perform daily in the wilderness than the leisure "freedom" imagined by outsiders. As Kolodny notes, mealtimes recur in the "real woods with distressing iteration" (*Land before Her* 137–38). Much of the legendary self-reliance attributed to male pioneers was simply their ability to cook and sew for themselves and set up housekeeping on their own without a woman's help.[17]

Although the West has traditionally been imagined as a "man's world" where women were treated like property, the first place women gained the right to vote was not in the East but in Wyoming in 1869. The entire West had already granted women suffrage by the time it was forced on the East Coast in 1920. In the rural West, as Graulich notes, Austin already felt liberated, already felt equal, and already felt self-confident (*Earth* afterword 387; Taylor 122–23).[18] Austin realized not only that this imagined dichotomy between the wild and domestic was false, but also that it encouraged treating the West as a place of wild "otherness." Thus the West served as a place where easterners could test their manhood on local native women, animals, and land. This idea encouraged colonization of the West as a playground, encouraged extracting resources for the benefit of eastern and urban societies, attracted undesirables, and encouraged treating women as whores or "fair game." Austin's aim was to rewrite both male and female gender myths so the West could be imagined as a home.

Sometimes Austin even felt the need to rewrite gendered Native American stories. She ends "The Basket Maker" chapter in *The Land of Little Rain* with a sentence stating that Seyavi knew she would not be reborn a coyote. Most critics interpret this to mean that because she had lived a good life, Seyavi would not be reborn a thief. But Austin does not subscribe to a negative attitude toward coyotes, nor does she attempt to present her female characters as sinless angels. This line is not about animal villains, but about blurring false boundaries between genders. The coyote in Native American stories is a trickster-god figure, and as David Leeming notes, this trickster-god is "always male" (163). Transcendentally looking to nature in order to discover a higher truth, Austin does not find that all real coyotes are males. Her stories are full of female coyotes who go "gossiping" about the desert. She observes that coyotes are the worst at thieving "in the spring when young are in the lair," and she often listens at the lairs "when the sucking pups tumble about and nip and whine" (*Land* 56; *Flock* 177, 182). The gentle old Native American basket maker Seyavi may believe that because she is a woman she cannot be reborn as a thieving, ribald coyote-trickster-god, but Austin is not so sure.

Chapter Three

"My First Daughter Was an Antelope"

*According to the family tradition . . . the original founder of the family
had been one Pierre Daguerre, who accompanied the Marquis de Lafayette
from France. . . . There was also the traditional assurance that the
American Daguerres were collaterals of the distinguished French chemist,
Louis Jacques Mande-Daguerre, inventor of the daguerreotype. . . . They
were plain people, neither rich nor poor, devoid of airs, loving the soil,
. . . largely rural in their affiliations . . . fishing parties, wild-berryings,
and hazel-nutting . . . never bookish.*
Mary Austin (*Earth* 12–15, 21, 34)

My pets were usually wild: baby turtles, flying squirrels, fawns, coyote pups, or cottontails. I once raised a red fox that liked to sleep curled around a blaring TV speaker. I had a little red harness and a leash and would take "Freddie" walking when I went to town, just to watch people's reactions. Freddie was very well behaved on a leash and would trot out in front of me, his giveaway tail floating on the breeze. People would smile at me as they walked past us, stop in their tracks, spin, and say, "Hey! That's a fox!"

The trouble most people have when trying to raise young animals is failing to do their homework: studying animal ways and finding out what they eat. A baby vermilion flycatcher, for instance, will starve without flies, and no amount of birdseed or habitat will help. I always fed young mammals some combination of Carnation Evaporated Milk and white Karo syrup. Too much syrup produces diarrhea, too little produces constipation. Another problem most people have is in performing only half of an animal mother's duties. Nests and dens are kept clean because baby animals only defecate and urinate when stimulated by the mother's tongue. So after a feeding, the surrogate mother must "lick" her baby's butt with a damp cloth.

I've always been a sucker for beady black eyes. No bird or animal ever came to my door hungry and left the same way, although I'm careful not to make welfare cases out of them. After my divorce, I once even adopted a jumping spider who set up housekeeping in my air-conditioned apartment between the window and screen where flies couldn't go. I tried to talk him into either moving on into the house to catch flies for me or going back out into the wide world. But he was a very independent little spider and preferred his spot.

So occasionally, when he looked hungry, I'd open the window and chase a fly in his direction. He had no idea I was helping him. Technically, I suppose I wasn't, I just made it possible for him to hunt. He had to catch the fly all by himself, and he had an ingenious method worked out. Flies always seem to crawl up a window screen, and in a fairly straight line. So he would wait in a dark crevice at the top of the screen, creeping along until he was directly in line with the fly that was crawling up toward him. When the fly got close enough, he'd jump out and grab it, sort of like a bulldogger—so I named him Harley May after an old rodeo cowboy I know.

Sometimes Harley missed, but in just a few minutes the fly would be crawling up the screen again. I imagined the fly trying to count coup, like I've heard Indians used to do when it was considered more honorable to risk their own life to touch an enemy than to kill. Lots of times the spider came right out in plain sight and crawled toward the fly, who kept right on moving toward the spider. Sometimes the fly lost his nerve and flew, but after a few deep breaths, he would try to count coup again—or something.

What kind of person has flies and spiders for friends?

I'm choosy, too. I don't like spiders that have to build webs to catch flies— they are too messy to live with. And I don't like those fancy, shiny spiders with the long, skinny, pointed legs that might like to bite me. I don't like those female spiders who eat their men and build crazy Picasso-looking webs that feel like nylon. I don't like great big hairy, slow-moving spiders with deep voices either, or the kind that set up long, thin trip ropes across trails. Those ropes must be intended to blind or decapitate humans because they sure can't catch flies. I imagine that the ropes are made by glory-seeking spiders who want to hang a human. I've even been around some spiders who were after cowboys. Their trip ropes were just about a foot higher than a horse's head and stretched between trees. I always wondered just what those spiders intended to do with a cowboy if they caught one.

But back to my personal preferences. I don't even like all little black-and-white spiders. Harley was short and chunky and fuzzy and looked like a cross between a teddy bear and a spider, so he was easy to love, but some of his relatives liked to hide and jump out and scare me. When I opened a cupboard door, jumped, and screamed, I imagined that I could hear them giggle. So I didn't make friends with them. I don't like to be laughed at.

That's why I liked Harley so much. I always knew just where he was, and he never tried to scare me. If I wanted to feel very, very secure, I could shut the window so he couldn't come in my house even if he wanted to. If I was bored and needed some entertainment, I would open the window and chase a fly in his direction. Maybe he was the ideal friend for a selfish person: there when I needed him, tucked away when I didn't.

I also liked the fact that Harley jumped on his fly and grabbed it. That seemed a much more honorable way to catch flies than spinning a big nasty web, tying a line around a toe, and taking a nap until the float bobbed. And since flies go to bed at sundown, I felt sure Harley went to bed then too. That made him much easier to live with than the ones that prowl around in the dark while I am sleeping.

* * *

Socrates, the guy who started rhetoric, said a writer should be a gadfly. To Montaigne, the father of the essay, writing was undefinable. In French, his native language, the word *essai* means a test, an attempt, or a trial. Montaigne insisted that his essays were based on ignorance. Shakespeare seemed to agree and called his own writing "looking at truth askance." Hemingway said the secret was going to Paris; Langston Hughes recommended the rhythms of jazz; and Chekhov favored dung heaps as the source of inspiration. On the other hand, Samuel Johnson said a writer should strive to make the world better, and Kafka said writing was the reward for service to the devil. But all of those old men are dead.

I am a teacher. I study literature with my students and teach college freshmen how to write essays: five paragraphs, a thesis, topic sentences, support, audience awareness, and Standard English usage. Tell me what you're going to say, say it, and then tell me what you said. That's my job.

I usually begin the semester with a motivational lecture, explaining that writing an essay is like planting grass. First you make a plan, then you prepare the ground. You loosen the soil by digging, enrich it with fertilizer, and fill uneven spots. You buy seed for the kind of grass you want to grow. Each kind of grass, I explain, has advantages and drawbacks: some can handle more traffic, some needs more shade, some more water. Once the seeds are sown, keep the ground moist—watch it carefully and don't let it dry out. Keep the weeds pulled. Mow it.

"Do you have a yard, Miss?" asks a voice from the back of the room.

"Well, . . . no," I stammer.

I stare at the student for a moment. I always seem to have at least one of these in every class. The student who is never paying attention, who asks stupid questions in the middle of a good lecture, the student with the cowboy hat and sunglasses, desk tipped back against the wall, no pen.

No . . . I don't plant grass, don't mow anything, don't water anything, don't even pray for rain anymore. I like my grasses wild. Sometimes, when I'm walking, I might strip a seed stalk between my thumb and first two fingers and fling the tiny seeds into the wind, like shooting dice. Maybe that's planting, but I don't look back. I trust its fate to quail or packrats, or some cow to grind it into the rocks.

I like my grasses mixed. I want black grama on west-facing slopes, sacaton along creek bottoms, and tobosa in rotten flats to warn me to slow down. I want some bear grass, some bluestem, some sprangletop. I like it weedy with loco, catclaw, tasajilla, sacahuista, Mormon tea, and sotol. I want some whitebrush for the bees and some creosote to smell after a rain. I like it ragged, windblown, parched; tough, patient, and fast. I've seen West Texas gramas shoot up, bloom, and produce seed in two weeks after one last-minute October rain.

I just don't respect green grass. Mowed grass never moans or blooms. The tiny orchids in shades of lime green, white, orange, yellow, and blood red dangling from the seed heads of wild grasses are my favorite flowers. Mowed grass never spun a spur rowel. But if mowing must be done, then I prefer critters or wind and lightning—twenty sections at a time in thirty minutes—whoom!

I stop to catch my breath.

"Jeeze," says the student with the sunglasses, smiling now. "You coulda just said no."

* * *

Like most daughters, I keep a framed picture of my mom and me on the bookcase. However, unlike most, my bear-slayer mom and I are both dressed in cammo. I hold a Remington twelve-gauge automatic shotgun; Mom's scoped .243 Savage lever action hangs from a sling over her shoulder. Stretched between us is a dead bobcat. We each hold one hind leg and grin at the camera like Hemingway wannabes. Behind us stretches an endless expanse of southern Arizona desert, the only kind of playground I ever had. Until lately, I never realized how unconventional my boring old polyester-clad parents were.

My dad didn't hunt with "buddies" but with his wife and kids. He never drank whiskey or owned the latest hunting fashions or gimmicks. Hunting was not a virility thing in my family; it was a domestic chore. We were pothunters. Our rifles were sighted in on the money, but there was no fancy checkering on the stock or engraving on the barrel, and seldom any varnish or bluing left.

My dad was a moonlight teacher. At night, after his blue-collar day job, he taught gun safety courses to kids for the American Rifle Association for many years. Pointing a gun indiscriminately, climbing through a fence with one in hand, or shooting without knowing my target would have been grounds for even more severe child abuse than I was used to, but I don't remember ever not knowing those rules. I was whipped for lots of things—giggling in church, catching trout with my hands, playing with bait, making my little brother eat mudpies—but only once for the way I handled a gun: when I got my first BB gun, I shot all the windows out of the barn while shooting pigeons. Mostly, I thought what I got whipped for was worth the whipping. I'm quite proud of the fact that I once made a man who has addressed a joint session of Congress eat mudpies; and for reasons I've never analyzed, I've always been proud of shooting those windows out of the barn. I've told that story a thousand times.

Like Huck, I grew up barefoot. I fished the Mississippi River, built fires and picnicked on its islands, swam in it—but only under strict guidance. I don't remember ever being afraid, but I deeply respected that old river and knew that just under that smooth, quiet, milk chocolate surface beat a bloody heart. I once read a modern story written by a man who had recently taken a boat trip down my old Mississip. He complained about the flood control dikes, the locks and dams, the way the U.S. Army Corps of Engineers had tamed the river, making it conform to the needs of society. He said that we have stripped the river of its power and its will and its natural dignity. I smiled to myself. He didn't know my river.

Samuel Clemens did. He wrote some great essays about it and said that only the naive see the Mississippi as tame and harmless. To a riverboat captain, every sun glint, every dimple on the surface, reveals some hidden snag, reef, shoal, or undercurrent. Clemmons wrote, "That silver streak in the shadow of the forest is the 'break' from a new snag and he has located himself in the very best place he could have found to fish for steamboats." But that would also be the best place to fish for fish. Those same dimples and slanting lights that talked to riverboat captains, my grandfather read for food. Instead of backing off with warning bells ringing, our little boat would quietly slip its way in deep among the snags, and my grandpa couldn't swim.

The river was always changing: on the surface, along the banks, in the channel, and around the islands. Sandbars, snags, whirlpools, and undercurrents would be there today and gone tomorrow. Clemens said that once he had truly learned the river, all the "grace, the beauty, the poetry" went out of it for him. Yet no one else ever wrote about it with such grace, beauty, and poetry. I think Sam Clemens sometimes lied.

Probably because the DeGear side of the family was illiterate until my father's generation, and because my father refuses to consider alternative spellings for the family name (like Duger or Daguerre), we haven't been able to track his family back past Illinois pioneer and War of 1812 soldier Peter DeGear (1786–1835). All we know is that they were never far from a river. I've heard it said that no modern family actually needs to hunt for their food. But I think my family did.

Before plastic buttons were invented, my dad, uncles, and aunt hunted washboard, sand, and paper-shell clams in shallow water, feeling around on the muddy bottom with their bare feet. They slept in their boat at night, their backs so sunburned from bending over and pulling up clams that they had to sleep on their stomachs. If the water was too deep to wade, they rigged a trick to catch clams on bare hooks. Once the boat was loaded, they'd pull ashore and cook the clams in a big vat until the shells opened. Then they'd scrape the meat out, save it to ferment for fiddler net bait, and sell the shells to the button factory—by the ton. During the depression, my dad, uncles, and aunt did everything from hunt snapping turtles to spear carp to gather blackberries and sell what they couldn't eat door to door. They also can-fished, ran hundred-hook trotlines, seined for their own minnows and crawfish, hunted turtle eggs with a stick, sculled for ducks, and sawed down bee trees. In their spare time they cut fence posts and firewood. Their dad, my grandfather Bill, was a commercial fisherman who drove carp, sheepshead, and buffalo into nets like cattle. After a life on the river, he'd found enough freshwater pearls to give one to each of his three granddaughters. That freshwater pearl ring is one of the few pieces of jewelry I've ever owned.

During my own childhood, my dad's blue-collar wages stretched only so far. We made every tank of gas, every fishing license, every bullet count to produce meat, furs, or bounty. I don't remember ever coming home empty-handed. But we often rose at 3:00 A.M. to be the first fishing boat on a lake or to be hunched in a wet duck blind before daylight. At 10:00 P.M. we would still be at it, again struggling in the dark to clean fish or singe pinfeathers. If there was a heavy dew, we'd hunt night crawlers with a flashlight until well past midnight.

"Sleep? Goddamn it, you can sleep when you get old."

My skills were good one day and bad the next. I learned what kind of fish I had on the hook by the way one took my bait, how to play and land one that weighed ten times what my line could handle. Then I'd go for days without a nibble. To keep my spirits up, Mom would make a bet that I would catch the next fish. But if I caught the most, then Dad reminded me that he and Grandpa spent half their time filing my hooks or dipping my fish. Once, after I was grown, fishing ranch creeks while the experts fished a trophy lake, I beat all the old potbellied bass fishermen in a stringer-weight tournament. Yet, on another occasion, also after I was grown, just wanting to look, I let my dad's full stringer swim away to die a wasteful and agonizing death.

"Je-sus-Christ!"

I'm still surprised he didn't make me dive until I found it.

* * *

Up until I left home at about seventeen, I had eaten more wild meat than tame. Today, when I read that Native American hunter-gatherers led an idyllic life of leisure, I laugh. Those who think hunting is easier than herding, or that herd-

ing is more sedentary, have never done both for a living. We have a secret saying in my family that is often recalled when the moment requires heroic sto-
icism—"Let it drip." The saying evolved during childhood instruction periods
spent watching a snowy deer trail, waiting for some blundering town hunter—
who thought hunting was hiking—to start the deer moving. A whispered conversation between me and my father during a six-hour period on an agonizing
ten-degrees-below-zero morning might go something like this:

"Daddy, I have a cramp in my leg."

"Be still."

. . .

"My toes are frozen."

"Shut up and be still, Goddamn it."

. . .

"(sniff)"

"Let it drip."

One day, riding choppy waves on a Minnesota lake, my little brother, suffering from terrible seasickness, threw up regularly the whole day (Dad called it
chumming), but he was never allowed to stop fishing. I cut my feet pollywog-
ging Mississippi sandbars for freshwater clams and was kicked on my butt by
a single-shot twelve-gauge shooting my first squirrel. I'm sure I've walked
around the world a couple of times carrying guns and dead animals. I never had
a boyfriend in high school because weekends were spent calling coyotes, tramp-
ing after javelina, scouting elk bed grounds, or loading and unloading a boat.
Neither rain nor sleet nor human exhaustion were excuse enough to let a rod
tip droop or make noise sniffling up a runny nose.

"What, you have to go to the bathroom? Je-sus-Christ!"

The first house my newlywed parents owned was underground, buried in
the side of a slippery, steep bank on the Mississippi. Maybe that makes me part
muskrat. Actually, the "house" was the basement to a normal house we never
quite got around to finishing. My pregnant mother used to sit hunched over
her swollen belly there, holding a dead muskrat between her legs, her elbows
resting on her knees, while my father skinned off the pelt. Twice during the
same pregnancy, she broke out up and down the insides of her legs with poison
ivy rash contracted off the muskrats' hides. She'd catch poison oak trying to go
to the bathroom on some island where Dad would grudgingly finally let her
out of the boat. If she didn't go hunting with him, Dad would come home and
throw a dead goose in bed with her.

Mom, the *Mayflower* descendant in the family, eventually became a vice
president of the Arizona Bank, but she wasn't much of a storyteller. When
hunting stories were told, she just listened and laughed. "You lie, and I'll swear
to it," she'd tell Dad. The only way I ever heard about her successful bear hunt

was through a story I read in the newspaper: "his wife also shot a bear." Mom chattered like a dang squirrel, but she didn't tell stories.

"The hell you say."

I'm the female storyteller in the family. I like to tell stories about Dad calling in a mountain lion when he was trying to call in a bear. He prefers to tell stories about hunting with my brother. I like to tell that I killed six deer with six shells over a six-year span; my dad prefers to tell about the day I forgot to load my gun (we always carried them unloaded in a vehicle). I like to tell about Dad bagging all but the buffalo (which he thought was a stupid hunt) in the Arizona grand slam and being the second-highest-point (two points for a coyote, six for a bobcat, one hundred for a lion) varmint hunter in 1964, one of those predator hunters Edward Abbey cusses so eloquently. Dad likes to tell about the day I got "buck fever" and couldn't shoot a big deer in Blue River Canyon. He always forgets to say that after three days of skunked hunting, I found the spot, led him in there, and helped him drag the damn deer out. I've also corrected him a thousand times, explaining that I expected him to shoot and was just waiting. I didn't know he was waiting on me.

"Yes, dear."

One other time, too, I couldn't shoot. I was grown, married, and hunting alone. I had glassed a rocky side ridge and spotted a mule deer buck laid up under a big Spanish dagger near the rim. Checking the wind, I made a long sneak and came down on him from above. When I got within range (three hundred yards for my custom glass-bedded .270), and not wanting to be caught unprepared, I lay down behind a rock, got a good rest, held my breath, and whistled. Nothing happened.

I waited, then whistled again, then tossed a little rock. Still nothing.

So, I got up and crept closer, repeating my strategy of rock, rest, whistle, rock. Again nothing happened. The buck must be sound asleep, I thought. My sneak somehow turned into a game to see just how close I could get before the buck woke up. I got so close I could see him breathing and finally actually hit him with a rock. Then the dagger exploded with antlers. He just kept on getting up. He was the biggest deer I'd ever seen. He ran straight away from me down the side of the mountain, and I had him in my sights the whole time, my finger on the trigger.

But I couldn't shoot.

"What the hell was the matter with you, anyway?"

I told that story at a Terry Tempest Williams round-table discussion, and my fellow environmentalists nodded knowingly. They thought the moment had been an epiphany for me and that I had given up my sinful life of blood lust. Creeping close enough to see the deer breathing, they thought, made me realize that I was killing a living animal. I let them think they understood my story and never explained. But in truth, it was a difficult downhill running shot, and wasteful. My only vital choice would ruin the best meat. Besides, with all those antlers, he wasn't going to be very good to eat. It was a shot a pothunter's kid would be whipped for taking. I didn't shoot because I had been raised better.

"Well, I'll be damned!"

I do remember once, though, when I didn't shoot because I was just over-whelmed with the moment. I was hiking along the rim, trying to get a glimpse of some wild Barbary sheep that had been imported by a neighboring rancher and had eventually gone wild all over West Texas. The sheep ranged in the high, unfenced country, and I hoped to get a picture of one. My dog, "Perro" (a very creative name meaning "dog" in Spanish), was with me. An Australian shepherd, Perro was a frustrated working dog because I didn't allow him to work cattle. I didn't want the cattle trained to let a dog bluff them because I was afraid that then the cows would stop fighting predators off their calves. So, Perro's job was mostly to be my best friend. The ranch raised a little band of Spanish goats that he was allowed to play cow dog with. Whenever I came home from town, he'd gather his goats into a tight wad and make them greet me. I'm sure they hated him.

On this particular day, Perro trotted beside me. I spotted some of the wild sheep across a canyon about the time he did, and my normally well-behaved dog took off barking. I figured that was the end of my chance to see any wild sheep, so I concentrated instead on picking my way through the rocks, down toward a pour-off I liked to visit. Suddenly, I was face-to-face with a full-curled, panting Barbary ram. Perro had brought me one! I was so shocked that I com-pletely forgot the camera dangling from my neck until the sheep, realizing its close proximity to a human, had bailed off the side of the rimrock to what I ex-pected to be its certain death. Of course, to my amazement, it found tiny hoof holds on the side of the rim. I have the story, but I missed the picture. So, I guess my dad is right—I have suffered from buck fever.

*   *   *

For twenty years I lived in old ranch houses at the end of long dirt roads. As Annie Dillard noticed in the Galápagos, critters always seem to want to be close to humans. At the 7W Camp on the Nail Ranch, rattlesnakes denned under the house. There was seldom a moment during the summer when I couldn't find one somewhere in the yard if I looked. A warm day in winter would bring the thousands of yellow jackets that denned in the walls and attic down into the house in a sluggish stupor. I slept on a screened-in porch, and every night I would holler at the frogs to please go to sleep, but they never did.

They'd croak, "Sex? Sex? Anybody want sex?" all night long.

Lightning hit the tin roof regularly, and water from the Clear Fork of the

Brazos came out of the tap black. The 7W Camp doesn't exist anymore. The ranch bulldozed it off the face of the earth because no one but me ever liked living there.

My second home, on the Tippit Ranch, had been abandoned for twenty-five years before I moved in, and stands abandoned now. The house water was all spring fed, and somehow, a little frog had taken up residency in the toilet. I'd flush him away, but in a few seconds he'd pop right back up. It was always fun to listen to guests shriek when they went in the bathroom, "Hey, there's a frog in the pot!"

I'd holler back, "Yeah, I know. It's OK. He lives there."

I tried not to think about what he ate.

At the Willow Springs Camp on the 06 Ranch, skunks denned under the house, and we killed one rattlesnake in the living room, one in the bathroom, and two on the back porch. If I found rattlers in the pasture, I always let them live—I liked to joke that they helped keep away tourists—but if I found one inside the house, that was crossing the line. Snakes always return.

I learned that once trying to rescue some baby phoebes from a red racer. I had been sitting on the screened porch with a cup of coffee, trying to write. Before I could begin, some Say's phoebes who had built a nest out in the carport started crying and carrying on, so I went to investigate. A big red racer was lying along a pipe wall-brace and across their nest. He hadn't eaten any of the baby birds yet, but I knew that was his plan. About that time, the teenage cowboy who worked for us on the ranch walked by, and since boys always want to kill something, I asked him to kill the snake. But he talked me out of it and suggested we just scare it real bad and maybe it would go away. We did, and I went back to the porch and my notes.

In a few minutes, the phoebes were crying again. Sure enough, the racer was back. His hunger had outweighed our scare. This time I talked the teenager into making the kill and went back to my writing feeling proud of myself for saving those baby birds. But that feeling didn't last long. I got to thinking about the snake. Who did I think I was, deciding that a baby phoebe was worth more than a red racer? Did the racer have a nest of babies somewhere too? Would my house be overrun with mice this winter as just punishment?

Before I could soothe my conscience, the phoebes were crying again. The racer had damaged the sides of the nest, and one of the babies had fallen out. I picked it up, put it back, and once again went back to the porch.

I'd hardly sat down when the birds were calling me again. This time my cat, who had followed me out to the carport on my last trip, found the baby phoebe first. After a few "Here Kitty, Kitty, nice Kittys," I grabbed her and took the rescued baby bird back to the nest.

Well, now I really had troubles. My cat wasn't going to forget where she found a nice, juicy baby bird, and in a few minutes she had another one. This time she wasn't about to let me sweet-talk her out of it either. I couldn't bring myself to kill my cat, even though her motives weren't nearly as noble as the snake's. She had a bowl of cat food available at all times and a bowl of milk most mornings. She didn't need to hunt and kill for her survival. But she was my cat! She sat on my lap when I was lonesome.

So, I gave the phoebes a good lecture. I told them I was sorry, but that next time they needed to think about where they built their nest. Sure, the carport was out of the rain, but phoebes can raise a lot of baby birds between rainstorms around here. They were safe from raindrops that might never come, but the pipe where they built their nest could support the weight of a snake, and a cat walked through that carport a hundred times a day. I also told them about a little hawk I'd seen dive-bombing a badger and said that they needed to toughen up, peck the cat on the head or in the eye, fix their nest, and keep their babies from jumping out. They had some responsibility around here too. I was not going to keep coming to their rescue.

Well, of course, the cat got the rest of the babies one by one. The phoebes did try to chase her once, but they weren't very good at it. They cried pitifully when their nest was empty. I told them I was sorry and plugged my ears with my fingers, being real thankful that I don't have God's job.

* * *

School districts in rural areas are too poor to send buses long distances after one kid, so when my daughter started school, I had to take her. Serious rainstorms often left us stranded on one side or the other of the creek. I would park the ranch pickup on one side of the creek and my own on the other side. My daughter and I would hike back and forth in the dark, through the raging black water, in order to get her to school on time. Instead of feeling sorry for ourselves, we almost regretted dryer weather, because once the motor was turned off and we were out in the dark, cold air, the morning changed.

For the first few steps I would hear only silence. Then I would hear rubber boots swishing through water and déjà vu would sweep over me. The air was cold and smelled wet. It was that time of day just before gray dawn when no one is awake except birds, animals, and my family. A killdeer would screech at us for invading her domain. Somewhere in the dark ducks would mutter softly, whispering in duck talk. They probably said something like "Listen to that racket, will you. They just don't make hunters like they used to." My father could mutter just like that and talk ducks down out of the air. These ducks thought my daughter and I couldn't hear them. They just don't make ducks like they used to.

My daughter's school called one day to let me know that she qualified for free lunches under migrant labor relief. I guess I spent most of my life in abject poverty and never knew it. The houses where we lived were always old; the electricity went off at the first hint of a storm; the phone too. Nobody picked up the garbage. I fed scraps to the wild critters, burned what I could, and carefully washed cans and broke glass jars so animals wouldn't get their heads caught trying to reach food. I thought everyone did.

My first daughter was an antelope. She was a wedding gift, blind with pink-eye and so tiny that I could fold her matchstick legs and hold her in the palm of my hand. I named her sappily "Dolly." I got up every two hours a night for a month to warm a bottle and "lick" Dolly's butt. Like a new mother, I rushed her to the vet every time she sneezed. The first time, when the vet squirted a line of clear salve across her tender diseased eye, she groaned with pain. Me—a tough old hussy who had assisted with C-sections to deliver dead and rotten calves, baited catfish hooks with stink bait, and field-dressed deer—I fainted dead away.

The fainting spell reminded me of Ka-nook. During the 1960s I found myself one of the first female ag majors in my college and also the only female in most classes. A loud-mouthed, hard-drinking, cussing Canadian we affectionately nicknamed "Ka-nook" teased me unmercifully every time there was blood, shit, or slime. Once, during an especially nasty C-section on a sheep, the seven-foot, 250-pound obnoxious ape, to the surprise of the class, hit the floor in the feminine swoon he kept waiting for me to display. When he woke up, I smiled my most condescending Apache smile. But this time, empathizing with the pain of an animal I cared deeply about, I found myself on the floor too. Maybe I had misjudged Ka-nook.

Dolly was gentler than any dogie calf I'd ever raised. When feeding time came, I simply opened the screened door and she would tap-tap into the kitchen like a little girl in high heels. Although her bottle always stimulated a rattle of antelope "pellets" across the floor and a flood of urine, like any doting mother I found it easy to clean up. Her fluffy white rump was just too cute to cover with a diaper, and I hated to make her stay outside.

The night a pack of coyotes had her trapped in the yard fence, she let out one sharp little bleat that I had never heard before, but it woke me from a sound sleep. I was running before my feet hit the floor. The coyotes got her tail and a patch of skin off her ribs, but nothing more. From that night on, I left the yard gate open, knowing that her only defense was running, that confining her put her in more danger.

Although I kept the yard watered and green, she never took a bite but preferred instead the ugliest, most dried-up-looking weed stalks she could find—and dog food. When her pellets started looking like dog shit, the vet said maybe I should feed the dog behind closed doors to keep her out of it. I had a very small mongrel yeller dog, and Dolly would try to stomp him in order to get more dog food. They fought like brother and sister and yet took naps together.

We lived on a long eighteen-mile dirt road from town and could see visitors coming for several miles. The day I recognized the local game warden's truck, my heart caught in my throat. I gathered Dolly in my arms and raced toward the creek, folding her legs and bidding her to "stay," which sometimes she did. The game warden had just stopped by to swap stories, and of course he needed a glass of tea. We sat on the porch and rocked while he, for some reason, turned the talk to antelope.

"Yessiree, the last antelope I ever saw in this country was running on those hills right out there," he said, and pointed toward what locals called "the Antelope Hills."

As if on cue, Dolly stood up right under his pointing finger, her unmistakable white antelope rump shining in the sun. He choked on his tea and sputtered, "Is that an antelope?"

What could I say? No?

"She's a pet," I confessed, and threw myself on the mercy of the court. Luckily, he was an old game warden and merciful. He said he guessed there was no law against having her as long as she wasn't in captivity.

"Oh, no!" I said hurriedly. "She's free to come and go at any time." He finished his tea and drove back to town.

One day while I was watching Dolly graze, she suddenly began to run in circles. I tried to catch her and calm her, but she was wild! Her eyes showed white around the edges, and her tongue lolled. Round and round she ran, sides heaving. Frantically, I talked soothing talk and tried to stop her. Then, as quick as she had begun, she stopped on her own, puffed for a second, and returned to nibbling dry weeds. After that, her "fits" gradually increased in frequency, duration, and effort. I finally figured out that she was simply building her stamina for flight.

When Dolly turned two, I began to worry about her love life. Since I had moved her from the country she was born in, no males were available. I wondered if she was lonely. I worried that even if I took her back to the land of her birth and turned her out, the other antelope might not accept her, or she them. I had seen how antelope bucks treat their women, and I wasn't sure I wanted my Dolly to be subjected to harem life. Did I know anyone with a nice, fat, hand-raised buck who might prove monogamous?

I never had to solve the dilemma. Dolly disappeared one night during a fierce hailstorm when the creeks flooded and several jackrabbits were found stoned to death. I couldn't track her because of the heavy rains. Sometime later a neighbor told me that he'd heard some oilfield roughnecks say that when they finished that job, they were going to take the tame antelope with them. The roughies were gone, but I never knew if coyotes got her, if she drowned, was stoned, stolen, or what. And I never tried too hard to find out. It was easier somehow not to know.

My real daughter's first kid was a white-tailed deer fawn she called "Little Bit." She let him drink Cokes out of a glass until I spanked them both. I didn't spoil my second kid.

* * *

Although I've lived in mountain lion country all my life, the only live ones I've ever seen were asleep under a friend's living-room couch or held in the arms of a child. I have slept like a baby in grizzly country right after the first thaw, when bears emerge from their dens very hungry and very crabby. After a life around animals, I can remember being truly terrified only once—one midnight when I switched on a light in my own bathroom.

For some reason it had been a good year for miller moths, and they had invaded my old ranch house by the millions. That sounds like exaggeration, but anyone who came to see me during the moth crisis knows. For a month, I never turned on a light after dark—except once.

The moths hung in big dark bands, like bats, around my ceilings, behind picture frames, behind curtains. Chalky pink moth excrement painted my windows opaque. Furniture, walls, clothes, food, everything was covered with pink moth shit. I tried chasing them away, spraying them away, vacuuming them away, but nothing worked. I remember once, after battling them for several hours, just sitting in the middle of the floor and crying. I don't cry often.

Just at dusk, when the house became darker than the world outside, the moths would congregate on the windows. I would dash around, removing screens, in order to turn them loose. But they only crawled back inside through the many cracks after twilight. Turning on a light after dark stirred them into a frenzy of fluttering paper wings, each headed in a different direction.

The night I woke up sleepy, shuffled to the bathroom, and snapped on the light without thinking I thought they were going to smother me. Nothing in Edgar Allan Poe or Alfred Hitchcock has ever been so terrifying as being caught inside that whirling cloud of flying moths, feeling the wet drips of pink excrement hit my face and arms and hair. I was so disoriented by the sense of suffocation and panic that I couldn't find the light switch for several long minutes. I couldn't get enough air to scream.

I can snore in grizzly, lion, or rattlesnake country, but one moth inside my house will keep me awake. Nothing I've ever read about moths tells this side of them. I've often wondered if Annie Dillard or Virginia Woolf ever really knew moths.

* * *

I was kissed by a wolf once, too. It was part of the entertainment for partici-
pants in the 1993 Environmental Writing Institute at the Teller Wildlife Ref-
uge in Corvallis, Montana. "Koani" was a black female wolf. Her owners used
her to educate the public about wolves. Prior to her visit, we were primed with
a slide show explaining wolf behavior and taught how to "greet" a wolf. Then
Koani was brought out of her cage on a leash.

We all got down on our knees in a circle and the wolf went from person to
person, licking us in the face. When she came to me—possibly still smelling
faintly of cow—she licked and licked and licked until the handler finally pulled
her off and I could breathe again. My fellow environmental writers were de-
lighted. My face burned from something in her saliva. I was amazed to find a
full-blooded wolf more affectionate than most dogs. The handlers said they had
to build a special pen that allowed the wolf free access into their home because,
lacking her pack social life, she needed much affection and human contact.

As Koani dragged her thin vegetarian handler around the yard like an old
woman with a spoiled poodle, we were told about the wolf's amazing strength.
The handlers said Koani made a very bad dog because she would revert to her
wild predator attack nature when a child or another animal ran from her.

When I was four, a coon dog grabbed me by the back of the neck and tried to
shake me dead. Royal Grabel loved that hound as much as I loved Dolly. He
also knew that I had been raised never to tease or torment any dog, and he
knew his dog knew me well. All I had done to provoke the attack was wear a
fuzzy, gray, raccoon-looking coat and knock on their door to ask if the Grabel
kids could come out and play. Without a bark, the dog broke its collar chain and
grabbed me. It was a registered redbone hound, famous among local hunters
and worth three hundred dollars in 1951. Royal thought briefly about shooting
the dog while I was in the hospital. My dad and the rest of the county thought
he was nuts.

"Je-sus-H.-Christ, Grabel?"

I never thought the dog should have been shot either. Why? Well, after I was
grown, I was helping with a saddle-shop booth next door to an old East Texas
hog hunter at a folklore festival. A fancy lady, dripping with diamonds, stopped
to chat with the old man. I eavesdropped on their conversation when she asked
him for what kinds of hunting his dogs were good.

"They're hog dogs, Ma'am," he said politely, frowning at her incorrect pro-
noun use.

"Hogs? Don't they hunt anything else?" she asked incredulously.

"Jeeze, Lady," he answered, quite indignant and defending his dogs, "cain't
everbody make a welder!"

Even at four, I knew that not all dogs were coon dogs, and a good one was rare
indeed. Kids, on the other hand, seemed fairly common and easy to replace.

Some of the things I know and some of the things I don't know make me wonder about school. I have studied sonnets time after time after time during my twenty-one or so sporadic years of learning and teaching college literature, yet I still have to stop and look up the difference between Shakespearean, Spencerian, and Petrarchan. In contrast, I was nine years old the last night I stumbled after Herb and Eldon Hueneke's pack of hounds through invisible wet miles of corn stubble and briared timber, hunting coons. Yet, when I am ninety, if I am sitting on my porch some black, moonless night and faintly hear coon hounds baying in the distance, I'll know what they are saying. Of course, I won't know the dogs and won't be able to pick out their different voices, but I will know whether or not they are cold trailing. I will know the moment they start barking treed.

I will still know, at ninety, which direction to look and how long to wait for a bobcat to come in to a call or how to tell by a single drop of blood if a deer is lung or heart shot. I will always know how deep to fish for largemouth, sunfish, crappie, perch, walleyes, stripers, rainbows, browns, fiddlers, bullheads, flatheads, or channel cat; when to use spinners, shiners, flies, or salmon eggs, and when to use leaders, floating line, sinkers, or bobbers; when to release the drag or set it; how to file hooks, tie knots, or hold the line softly between my fingers, and when to set the hook. I will never, however, remember for more than an hour the difference between those three kinds of sonnets.

Chapter Four

Hoofed Locusts or Wild Eco-Sheep?

*How could they justify relocation of some of the nation's poorest people.
. . . How could they talk about a benevolent system concerned with the
renewal of the spirit for hundreds of urban dwellers while they destroyed
the spirit of hundreds of local people?*
Bruce J. Weaver (168)

Around the turn of the century, just before Mary Austin wrote *The Flock*
(1906), she watched as Los Angeles stole the water from her Owens Valley
neighbors.[1] She watched as John Muir led a push to expand Yosemite Valley's
boundaries, taking extensive private lands away from rural people in order to
"preserve" and "protect" those lands inside the new national park's boundary.
She watched as some of those newly "protected" lands quietly became railroad
right-of-way, laying the foundation for the most lucrative big business the West
ever produced: tourism.[2] Finally, she watched as the new national park closed
thousands of acres of high Sierra meadows to summer sheep grazing, putting
many of her Owens Valley neighbors out of business. Austin had probably also
just read Frank Norris's *The Octopus* (1901), a novel suggesting that California
and the nation were at the mercy of a huge, ruthless, manipulative railroad
monopoly.

As Norris's novel opens, a band of sheep has accidentally wandered onto a
railroad right-of-way into the path of a fast-moving train. He describes the
scene as

> a slaughter, a massacre of innocents. The iron monster had charged full
> into the midst, merciless, inexorable. To the right and left, all the width
> of the right of way, the little bodies had been flung; backs were snapped
> against the fence posts; brains knocked out. Caught in the barbs of the
> wire, wedged in, the bodies hung suspended. Underfoot . . . the black
> blood, winking in the starlight, seeped down into the clinkers. (Norris 42)

As Norris's images of sheep as innocent victims of the thundering machines of
big business suggest, much of the rhetoric and symbolism regarding private
and public land, rural and urban conflict, water rights and railroads, socialism,
capitalism, and democracy centered on sheep. During these high-stakes land

battles between businesses promoting tourism, cities seeking water rights, and local residents trying to preserve their communities and livelihoods, two authors in particular concentrated their politics into literary allegories using sheep: Mary Austin and John Muir.

According to William F. Kimes's excellent annotated summary of Muir's early published work, Muir began cursing sheep publicly in 1872 through numerous articles in the *San Francisco Examiner,* the *Oakland Daily Evening Tribune, Century* magazine, the *San Francisco Daily Evening Bulletin, Scribner's Monthly,* and the *Overland Monthly.*[3] Two books written by Muir before the century's end, *The Mountains of California* (1894) and *Our National Parks* (1901), also condemn sheep. These writings had been instrumental in gaining popular support for the banning of sheep grazing within Yosemite National Park's boundaries, and Austin was obviously aware of them. She briefly mentions Muir in her first book, *The Land of Little Rain* (1903), as a "devout man" (94), and they evidently met in 1904.[4] Although Frank Stewart claims that Austin was "thirsty to meet" Muir and was "swept away" by his stories (134), Austin pointedly notes in her autobiography that Muir had a "habit of talking much, . . . the habit of soliloquizing" (*Earth* 298). I read Austin's 1906 book, *The Flock,* as a series of direct challenges to Muir's published denigration of sheep and sheepherders.

In a paper published in 1982, Vera Norwood notes that Austin's book was "written at a time when John Muir was referring to sheep as 'hoofed locusts'" ("Photographer" 39–40).[5] Although Norwood argued later that Austin was "inspired in part by John Muir's call to preserve natural landscapes," a close reading comparing Austin's and Muir's views illuminates strongly opposing ecological perspectives. Muir favored preservation of "pristine wilderness" as a place for leisure and study, not work. He revered those parts of the West that most resembled Europe's mountains, waterfalls, and lush woodlands as inspirational to writers and artists. Austin, on the other hand, believed land should be valued as home and argued that ranking land into hierarchies according to its attractiveness and preserving the most beautiful places encouraged abuse of the unbeautiful. On literal and symbolic levels, Muir and Austin both desired to protect natural resources from ravaging hordes, but their perceptions regarding who those hordes might be differed considerably. Muir feared the common rural masses and their domestic animals. Austin feared the unquenchable urban thirst for water and recreation. Muir wanted to preserve beautiful places for escape and enjoyment. Austin wanted to preserve sustainable rural communities.

Using a complex collected-essay pattern that Carl Bredahl calls "divided narrative," Austin constructed *The Flock* as a boundary-blurring collection of sketches about sheepherding in the Sierra, merging nonfiction and myth into a multivoiced, dialogic narrative (49). This communal narrative genre, later of much interest to class and postcolonial theorists such as Mikhail Bakhtin and Trinh T. Minh-ha, enabled Austin to work within the nonhierarchical oral tradition and disclaim an (author)itative voice.[6] Carefully crediting her sources in the first chapter, Austin cites historic California sheepherders, from Hispanic landowners to the "Basco" shepherds:

> I suppose of all the people who are concerned with the making of a true book, the one who puts it to the pen has the least to do with it. This is the book of Jimmy Rosemeyre and Jose Jesus Lopez, of Little Pete, . . . of Noriega, of Sanger and the Manxman and Narcisse Duplin, and many others. (*Flock* 114)

With this introduction, Austin creates for herself a humble, journalistic persona and gives authority to the common working-class shepherds.

Following a detailed history of the sheep industry in California, Austin romanticizes shepherds' work in the Sierra with lyrical allegoric vignettes of sheep management, shearing, shepherd ways, grazing the Sierra, weather sense, flock mentality and habits, sheepdogs, wars with cattlemen, predators, the Tejon Ranch, and the coming of a national park. Through what she calls the "pale luminosity" of sheep dust rising along the Long Trail, Austin conjures "the social order struggling into shape" (57) and follows the ancient storyteller's tradition of using sheep to represent the human masses. Carefully presenting the wild habits of domestic sheep, Austin's allegory ranges from Thoreau to biblical authors who predicted that the meek would inherit the earth and were quite familiar with docile flocks that could quickly explode into an uncontrollable sea of running anarchists.

In the chapter titled "The Sheep and the Reserves," Austin blatantly argues against Muir's call to ban grazing within Yosemite National Park for the sake of developing tourism, declaring that even the rangers often sympathized with law-breaking shepherds and looked the other way while they sneaked back into their old summer haunts. The rangers, she claims, "despised . . . the work of warding sheep off the grass in order that silly tourists might wonder at the meadows full of bloom" (*Flock* 193).[7] Austin obviously wrote *The Flock* as a response to political activism promoting tourism and national parks, as well as the underlying economic and cultural class divisions such activism encouraged. Her final chapter, "The Shade of the Arrows," uses a Paiute saying that "no man should go far in the desert who cannot sleep in the shade of his arrows" to warn about visiting a "wild" place when one does not truly understand how to survive there. This saying seems to be the theme of the entire book: working shepherds belong in the Sierra and tourists do not.

Although Austin's story line in *The Flock* is obviously based on a political controversy raging in California at the turn of the twentieth century, these were also ancient conflicts. A glowing 1906 review in *The Nation* compares Austin to Virgil:

> Badly stated, [*The Flock*] is no more than a study of the sheep industry in California, with a slender thread of historic narrative, a picture of sheep herding, a word for irrigation. This summary of *The Flock*, however, bears about as much relation to the actual achievement as a statement that the first book of the Georgics is a treatise on agriculture. ("A Review" 17)

The struggle Austin illuminates in *The Flock* is also quite modern. "Are You an Environmentalist or Do You Work for a Living?" asks Richard White in the title of a provocative essay which proposes that modern environmentalists, while "celebrating the virtues of play and recreation in nature," often "take one of two equally problematic positions toward work." They either "equate productive work in nature with destruction" or "ignore the ways that work itself is a means of knowing nature" (171).[8] Austin allegorically attempted a similar literary argument almost one hundred years earlier; further, she saw grave political danger in imagining sheep, symbolic of common people, as ravaging hordes.

Muir scholars have traditionally interpreted Muir's sheep allegories as eco- rather than anthropocentric. Thomas Lyon, for example, observes that "Muir's conversion of the lamb . . . into a devilish, 'hoofed locust,' . . . is a fine example of his imaginative inversion of cultural values" (30). However, I argue that as an allegory, Muir's hierarchical reversal, which places a higher value on wild sheep than on domestic, is xenophobic and riddled with allusions to class divisions, and exhibits a chilling elitist aspect. Austin challenged Muir's tendency to privilege what Thorstein Veblen had just labeled "the leisure class" over work-based local communities and the desire to appropriate rural places in order to provide playgrounds. As regional, indigenous people of various races were pushed aside for the "greater public good," which almost always turned out to be oppressive, urban, and in some way promoting big business, Austin rose to defend her friends and neighbors. In *The Flock* she blends natural history, politics, and allegory into a genre-blurring narrative championing local shepherds in their losing battle against the quickly developing tourist business.

Realizing how powerfully Austin had structured her literary argument supporting working shepherds, Muir may have felt that both Yosemite National Park and tourism itself were threatened. Muir's book *My First Summer in the Sierra* (1911) may well have been written in reaction to *The Flock*. Although today we read *My First Summer* as a published journal, forty-two years passed between the actual experience and the writing and publication of the book. Muir supposedly spent the summer of 1869 working for Pat Delaney as a sheepherder in the Sierra, but he wrote *My First Summer* in 1910. According to editors of Muir's papers, the original journal from which Muir supposedly composed

the book is "missing." The collected papers do, however, contain another unpublished journal entitled "Twenty Hill Hollow," which Muir began on January 1, 1869, and kept while working in the fenced pastures of the San Joaquin
Valley for John Connel. The papers also contain Muir's working draft of *My
First Summer* (hereinafter "Draft"). Both documents reveal extensive contradictions and changes between Muir's private observations, publication drafts,
and early and later published work.[9] If Muir actually worked from an early
journal when he wrote *My First Summer*, the journal was probably heavily
rewritten. In an interesting analysis comparing the "young" Muir as sheepherder and journal keeper with the "old" Muir as author, Michael Cohen says
that *My First Summer* is "deceptively straightforward," and although "an
honest and truthful book, it is also narrated with all the skill that a novelist
might muster" (*Pathless* 350–51).

By the time Muir published *My First Summer*, Yosemite was embroiled in a
bitter struggle between those who lived and worked in the Sierra and those
who wanted to preserve it as a national park. Muir had also married into a very
wealthy California family by then, and his circle of friends now included the
nation's educated, wealthy, and political elites. Understandably, although wanting to claim sheepherding expertise through personal experience to give his
opinions more weight, he also wanted to avoid the stigma attached to the occu-
pation. His glacier theories had once been dismissed as the simple ideas of a
sheepherder (Teale 18), and he never quite recovered from the sting of that
insult.[10]

Muir tries to make it quite clear to the reader of *My First Summer* that he
had agreed to go along with the sheep only as a respectable scholar eager for
the opportunity to study the geology and biology of the high mountain meadows, and that he was merely supervising the real sheepherder to make sure he
did his job (5). Through this stance, Muir is able to emphasize the class division
between himself and the common shepherd, a tendency Leo Marx describes as
creating a "distinction between the countryman who actually does the work
and the gentleman (or poet) who enjoys rural ease" (99). Yi-Fu Tuan calls it a
"special kind of play," common in both Eastern and Western cultures, in which
"the high-born pretend to be simple farmers, thus imitating children who in
their games pretend to be engaged in serious work" (*Dominance* 31). White
argues that today, "environmentalists have edited [the labor of the body] out
[and] . . . replaced it with a story of first white men at strenuous play or in respectful observation." The reason, he says, that "environmentalists so often
seem self-righteous, privileged, and arrogant" is because they identify nature
with play and make it "a place where leisured humans come only to visit and
not to work, stay, or live" (177, 173). In truth, though, when John Muir first ar-

rived in California in 1868 he was a penniless thirty-year-old drifter in desperate need of a job, not a gentleman scholar on holiday.

On the subjects of sheep, shepherds, and sheepherding, Muir contradicts Austin's descriptions in *The Flock* almost line for line. Austin's sheepherder seldom carries a six-shooter; Muir's usually does (*Flock* 83; *My First* 129). Austin goes into raptures over the wonderful meals she has eaten at a shepherd's fire; Muir says the sheepherder's food is "far from delicate" (*Flock* 82–83; *My First* 81). Austin argues that "[t]he smell of sheep is to the herder as the smack and savor of any man's work"; Muir makes fun of the sheepherder's desire to sleep next to the sheep "as if determined to take ammoniacal snuff all night" (*Flock* 93; *My First* 129). Austin calls ridicule of shepherds simple prejudice and argues that the fact "[t]hat most sheepherders are foreigners accounts largely for the abomination in which they are held and the prejudice that attaches to the term" (*Flock* 55–56). Muir claims the sheepherder wears "everlasting clothing" consisting of pants waterproofed by drips of "clear fat and gravy juices" that have clustered into stalactites and become imbedded with bits of nature. These greasy clothes do make the sheepherder a collector of specimens, jokes Muir derisively, again keeping the class divisions clear, but he is "far from being a naturalist" (*My First* 130).

Austin persistently questions cultural, educational, political, and language hierarchies, while Muir just as persistently characterizes himself as superior to shepherds because they are, in his view, dirty, uneducated, and racially other. While being out in wild nature inspires Muir to a deep appreciation, the same exposure does not seem to work on his fellow shepherd, who, according to Muir, ignores the wild beauty that surrounds him (*My First* 41). Not so, insists Austin; the shepherd simply finds it difficult to put his appreciation into words. She maintains that "it really is not exigent to a sense of natural beauty to be able to talk about it" (*Flock* 258) and claims that silence is sometimes a sign of great love that cannot be expressed in words.[11]

Austin also suggests that because shepherds often spoke an(other) language, outsiders came to the "unfounded assumption" that most of them were "a little insane." She suggests further that their outdoor life "nourish[es] imagination and they have in full what we oftenest barely brush wings with" (*Flock* 61–63). Although Muir claims that mountain hardships produce strength and wisdom in discriminating gentlemen such as himself and his fellow mountaineers, he believes this same solitary outdoor life adversely affects the shepherd: "seeing nobody for weeks or months, he finally becomes semi-insane or wholly so" (*My First* 24). Austin states emphatically that "[w]ith all my seeking into desert places there are three things . . . I have not seen,—a man who has rediscovered a lost mine, the heirs of one who died of the sidewinder and a shepherd who is insane" (*Flock* 65). Muir just as emphatically states, "The California shepherd, as far as I've seen or heard, is never quite sane for any considerable time" (*My First* 24). Commenting on today's version of this argument, White asserts that modern environmentalists, "[h]aving demonized those whose very lives recognize the tangled complexity of a planet on which we kill, destroy and alter as a condition of living and working, . . . can claim an innocence that in the end is merely irresponsibility" (185). Modern versions of this debate often use much the same rhetoric, and domestic animals still allegorically represent these clashing cultures and class values.

Wherever she found it, Austin challenged the stereotype of rural people as ignorant and illiterate. She recognized art in humble places, granting sophistication to basket makers and pocket hunters, and remembering that she never found a better companion with whom to discuss French literature than a dark shepherd she called "Little Pete." She respected and recognized shepherds as creative: poets, wood-carvers, musicians, philosophers. Believing that the perception of ignorance often simply stemmed from language barriers, Austin writes defiantly that "these Bascos are a little proud of the foolish gaspings and gutterings by which they prevent an understanding" (*Flock* 60, 63). Austin's defense of sheepherders reflects her pattern of respectful representation of indigenous and regional cultures.[12] She often preferred the company of Shoshones, Paiutes, and settlers from Old Mexico to that of her white neighbors, whose creeds were "chiefly restrictions against other people's way of life" (*Land* 106). Comparing the attitudes of Muir and Austin toward the working shepherd exposes many of the stereotypes about the poor and racially other that the environmental justice movement has recently begun to scrutinize (Flores).

On the surface, it would seem that John Muir, having actually worked as a shepherd, had the best personal knowledge of sheep and is therefore the more reliable authority. Muir actually worked sheep at least four times. He sheared sheep during the late summer of 1868, and that fall and winter he herded for John Connel in the fenced pastures he would later call the "bee-pastures" of the San Joaquin Valley. A year later he again worked in fenced pastures, this time for Pat Delaney. In the summer of 1869 he went with another shepherd and a band of Delaney's sheep into the Sierra (Limbaugh and Lewis's chronology). In fact, however, the "Twenty Hill Hollow" journal, which was written while Muir worked for Connel, reveals his inexperience with herding. In the journal, Muir describes losing one hundred lambs and two hundred "old sheep" in one night, after which the boss asked Muir if he had ever lambed a band of ewes. Muir writes, "I answered that I had not, & that I had not the slightest idea of the duties."

The boss quickly relieved Muir of the ewe band and sent what would have been considered an easier-to-care-for band of wethers, castrated male sheep.

However, Muir also found the wethers wild and totally uncontrollable. His journal describes spending the first day trying to "train" them to behave, running them with the dogs. This training proved to be another error in judgment; the next day's entry notes that "a good many of my sheep are dying." All along, Muir blames his losses not on his own lack of shepherding skill but on the weather—San Joaquin Valley weather, not Mount Whitney's ("Twenty" 46–53). Muir was born in Scotland, a country where sheep had grazed steep green hills for thousands of years, but he was no shepherd.

In *The Flock*, Austin pointedly explains that management of a flock was "never a 'white man's job,'" and that a white man hired in that position was one of "the impossibles" (62). A sheep owner who would hire unskilled white men to take care of his flock, as Muir's employer obviously did, brands both himself and his hirelings as incompetents—boomers after a fast buck, not sheep people. Real shepherds, Austin carefully explains, usually began as children and were taught by parents who came from a long line of shepherds (51–54). Muir did not come from a long line of skilled husbandmen familiar with tending animals and the land. His father was not a farmer or land steward but a shopkeeper, even though he owned (and ruined!) two farms after immigrating to the United States. Many immigrants who tried to farm without knowing the ancient skills found the labor killing, and they often wore out and ruined farms.

In contrast to Muir, Austin claims no personal experience herding sheep. Instead of presenting herself as an authority, she presents herself as a simple reporter asking questions and listening to shepherds' stories told around their campfires. At her best, Austin practices the humble techniques of journalism and storytelling, meticulously gathering facts and stories from many different points of view rather than relying on her own knowledge. In fact, Austin probably possessed a deeper personal understanding of the rural culture than Muir. She had "grown up in a farming country, of farming kin" (*Earth* 227), then spent two years homesteading on the borders of California's old Tejon Ranch and fifteen in the Owens Valley, living for almost two decades among shepherds and beside what they called "the Long Trail," which wound through the Sierra (*Flock* 12).[13] She also wrote her book as she experienced the events it details, not forty-two years later. She knew and respected the shepherds she wrote about and tried to represent their culture from the inside.

A close reading and comparison of Muir's private papers and published work reveals many inaccuracies and contradictions. Perhaps partly motivated by his own embarrassing inability to learn shepherding skills and handle what he considered a simple, unskilled job, Muir publicly cursed sheep for their "reckless ravages" and called them "ruthless denuders" or "hoofed locusts." However, his early private journal observations and descriptions of the San Joaquin

Valley contradict these published statements. By the time Muir first saw the valley, sheep had been grazing it for more than one hundred years; there were more than 300,000 in the valley in 1833 (*Flock* 7). Yet, thirty-five years later, in 1868, Muir described this sheep-ravaged valley as "the floweriest piece of world I ever walked."[14]

Austin points out that California's shepherds came from countries where sheep, flowers, steep mountain pastures, and crystal streams had coexisted, and probably coevolved, for thousands of years (*Flock* 32, 52). While Austin admits that "[y]ou will find proof . . . in the government reports" that sheep grazing can cause damage if shepherds are not given their own "fixed" pastures, she makes clear that the damage should not be blamed on the shepherds, who are just following orders, or on the sheep, who like all creatures "use the face of the earth to better it" (172, 206–10). "No doubt," she argues, "meadow grasses, all plants that renew from the root, were meant for forage" (100). Shepherds and sheep merely follow the same techniques practiced by good gardeners when they pinch back, prune, fertilize, and burn in order to produce more bloom and healthier plants.[15] She explains that what can appear to be destruction can actually be cultivation. Grazing through pastures in early spring as growth began and again in the fall after seeds had dropped, sheep made ideal gardeners for flowering plants. Defending even the sheep themselves as laborers, Austin observes that their prunings and droppings fertilized and strengthened the beautiful flowered meadows and asks, "Is it not the custom [everywhere] to put sheep on worn-out lands to renew them?" (170, 208–9).

Muir wanted to protect the Sierra as "pristine wilderness" to be used only for recreation and to develop the sensibilities of privileged middle-class "mountaineers." Austin valued the Sierra as a vital part of an ecological web necessary for sustaining life. Then and today, this problematic division between those who value land as a place for recreation and those who must make their living from it makes rural communities and their sympathizers defensive toward recreationists.

Austin also realized that imagining the Sierra as pristine wilderness ignored centuries of Native American land management. The open, sunlit, parklike quality of the Sierra that so attracted tourists had been fire-maintained as pasture, first by native people and then by immigrant shepherds. As White says, although "academic historians have produced a respectable body of work . . . that concentrates on how Indian peoples shaped the natural world they lived in . . . by and large, this literature has been dismissed. . . . Working people of mixed race can't carry the story line" that environmentalist writers favor, of a "first white man" coming to an "untouched paradise," or of "the wonder of a world before work" (175–76). Ironically, Muir wanted to protect the Sierra "wilderness" from the very people and animals who had made it what it was.

Austin, however, is not simply presenting a rhetorical argument about sheep grazing in *The Flock*. Her characterization of working people, her use of both symbolism and fact, her focus on storytelling and its democratic implications, and her creation of a journalistic persona all work together to achieve unity as an argument supporting the democratic principles of equality and government by consent of the governed. She uses her powerful allegory to illuminate human relationships: the struggles between shepherds are similar to animal or tribal wars over hunting territories or struggles between modern economic ideologies. When the land belongs to no one and its welfare is no one's responsibility, then every year, she argues, the "best contriver" will possess the best pastures. In the chapter titled "The Strife of the Herdsmen," Austin explains how shepherds, under orders from their employers and with their own traditional sense of responsibility toward the welfare of their sheep, are forced to match wits against each other, the forces of God, beasts, weather, and park rangers in order to feed their flocks. Desperate shepherds infringed on the national park and, she says, "came out boasting, as elated, as self-congratulatory as if they had merged railroads or performed any of those larger thieveries that constitute a Captain of Industry" (197).

Although this comment sounds close to social Darwinism, Austin's political views favored neither hierarchy nor socialism. Lawrence Clark Powell (1971) calls her a "Fabian Socialist," one supporting gradual social progress while avoiding direct confrontation with the state. However, in Austin's mind the allegorical "flock" was not a cohesive, socialistic, cooperating group, but a seething stew composed of highly independent individuals. A sentence found in *The Flock* seems to summarize her politics: "The flock-mind is less than the sum of the intelligences of individual sheep" (109). The rural people Austin portrays are not helpless innocents in need of protection from powerful, more intelligent capitalists. Instead she stresses that the "sheepmen had always the advantage in superior knowledge of the country, of meadows defended by secret trails and false monuments, of feeding grounds inaccessible to mounted men, remote, and undiscovered by any but the sheep" (198). Some shepherds, like Narcisse the Red, who appears as a red-tinged Mephistopheles character, enjoyed the game immensely (158). Austin believed in the struggle and was not asking to have rural people "protected" from the captains of industry. She never waivered in her faith that "common" people can and should take care of themselves. Nor, like the social Darwinists, did she believe that the "best people" always rose to the top. Her shepherds were in constant flux from the estate of owner to hireling, and this cyclic flux, she says, makes all shepherds philosophers (61).

Sheep have traditionally symbolized the humble human masses, and both Muir and Austin were well aware of that tradition.[16] A comparison of their respective descriptions of the "Lambs of God" at the allegoric, political level displays deeply opposing philosophies. Even Muir's earliest writing shows no affection or sympathy for the masses and their children:

> The mongrel manufactured misarranged mass of mutton and wool called a sheep band which I have tended lo these six weeks with a shepherd's care are now rapidly increasing in number by little thick legged wrinkled duplicates, unhappy lambs born to wretchedness and unmitigated degradation. ("Twenty" 46–47)

He never waivered from this position, which exposes a cultural bias toward both the lives of sheep and the lives of working-class people.

In contrast, Austin, with affection, humor, and respect, describes lambs as they struggle to adapt to the unique regional challenges of California's Long Trail:

> Young lambs are principally legs, the connecting body being merely a contrivance for converting milk into more leg, so you understand how it is that they will follow in two days and are able to take the trail in a fortnight, traveling four and five miles a day, falling asleep on their feet, and tottering forward. (*Flock* 25)

Allegorically, Muir's young "Lambs of God" are a burden on society, increase the burden on the nation's natural resources, and face a life of permanent and increasing poverty. In Muir's allegory, someone will have the unpleasant burden of taking care of the helpless female masses, who are rapidly breeding more and more ragged children. In contrast, Austin allegorically characterizes young lambs as the hope of the future. Quickly able to stand on their own feet, they totter forward, even when physically exhausted. Hers is a fiercely proud attitude toward the nation's youth.

Muir's numerous allegories published both before and after *The Flock* equate common sheep with the working class and wild sheep with the leisure class. Muir's wild sheep go "wading in snow, roaming through bushes, and leaping among jagged storm-beaten cliffs" while remaining clean and self-confident, wearing "a dress so exquisitely adapted to its mountain life that is it always found as unruffled and stainless as a bird" ("Wild Wool" 872). Muir's common sheep, on the other hand, are "poor, dusty, raggedy, famishing creatures," whose brains "must surely be poor stuff" (*My First* 64, 114).[17] Although Muir's unpublished journal often records a wildness in domestic sheep that he found uncontrollable ("Twenty" 6–7), his political rhetoric and published writing present them as plodding dullards. He characterizes wild sheep, like himself and fellow hikers, as "the bravest of all the Sierra mountaineers," self-reliant, intelligent, and independent. The animal "mountaineers" who climb the highest peaks are obviously superior to the commoners in the pastures below: "The wild sheep ranks highest among the animal mountaineers of the Sierra" ("Wild Sheep" 419); "the domestic sheep is expressionless . . . the wild is elegant . . . the tame is timid; the wild is bold. The tame is always more or less ruffled and dirty; while the wild is as smooth and clean as the flowers of his mountain pasture." Muir even credits wild sheep with the ability to appreciate beauty ("Wild Sheep" 421–22).

Muir's various allegorical attempts to create a hierarchy supporting leisure land-use politics drifts into pathetic fallacy when he claims that wild animals are "as free from disease as a sunbeam," never weary or sick, and that "nothing truly wild [is] unclean" (*My First* 68, 226). Nature, he says, never allows her wild animals "to go dirty or ragged" ("Wild Wool" 872). Muir's "happy" wild animals nibble mountain plants so daintily that they never crush a flower or mar a leaf ("Bears" 161), a view similar, perhaps, to the one modern environmentalists have about their own work. White observes that because environmentalists "do not have to face" what they alter, they have a tendency to imagine their work as benign. If they thought more deeply, he suggests, they might discover that "on a good day, [they] put the efforts of Paul Bunyan to shame" (184–85).

Muir sees no famine in the wild, "no stagnation, no death," not "one drop of blood," and he is sure wild animals never experience "a headache or any other ache amongst them" (*My First* 73, 96).[18] According to J. Moussaieff Masson and Susan McCarthy, however, the sentimentalized view that the natural world is "a place without war, murder, rape, and addiction" where "animals never lie, cheat, or steal" is "embarrassed by reality" (Masson and McCarthy 42).

In contrast, Austin's is the more clear-eyed vision. Her animals, both wild and domestic, realistically live in the valley of the slant-winged shadow of death. One reviewer observes that although Austin "stops for queer speculations on the development of the animal mind," she "does not sentimentalize about them: she makes the limits of instinct quite as clear as its scope" ("A Review" 17).[19] While Muir's wild animals leave no scar on the landscape, Austin's wear mazes of white trails which eventually converge at water. Her bighorns starve in their tracks, trapped in deep snow; predators lurk at water holes; hawks patrol every trail and flyway. Austin uses accurate and detailed natural history about real sheep to express her respect for the intelligence of both common animals and common people. She finds the natural laws that operate within flocks and between shepherds, dogs, predators, and sheep quite similar to the natural laws that operate within society and between races, classes, and genders. Prejudice, in Austin's mind, is actually ignorance. In *The Flock* she carefully explains sheep's complex social structure as a culture with intelligence, range of emotion, cravings, watch keeping, selection of leaders, and communication patterns.

She describes their recognition, exclusion, and finally acceptance of strangers. In his 1930 review of *The Flock,* Henry Chester Tracy says that the chapter "The Sun in Aries," about "lambing and the ways of lambs and ewes," contains "more pure authentic science of behavior in it than you will find in many passages of heavier reading" ("Mary").

In addition, Austin describes sheep adoption, kidnapping, and the intricacies of the flock mind, which, she says, is neither natural nor permanent. She notes that once a sheep is separated from the flock, the shepherd must go and find it because it will not return on its own: "[I]t is as if for them the flock had never been." Sheep may very well understand the arm signals and will of the shepherd, but they only grudgingly obey, feeling "a little resentful of the importunity of the dogs" (*Flock* 110, 119, 117, 127). Real sheep, Austin suggests, when studied deeply, the way shepherds study them, can help us understand our own political problems. Sheep are not stupid, easily controlled, or of one mind, although they do have a few idiosyncracies. Ecologically, they are part of a much larger whole. In order to sustain the complicated web we call life, her plants, soils, insects, water, and animals, whether wild, domestic, or human, all depend on one another—even the locusts.

As Kevin Starr notes in *Americans and the California Dream, 1850–1915* (1973), turn-of-the-century Californians were frustrated with corrupt government and ruthless monopolies engaged in a brutal, "greedy and unregulated" struggle (viii). During the time when Muir and Austin were writing, socialism was becoming a popular alternative among disillusioned urban workers. Read allegorically, these lines Muir deleted from the early draft of *My First Summer* show both a dislike and a fear of the masses:

> The sheep are behaving worse than ever because hungrier than ever. . . . They broke away suddenly as if a plan had been formed during the night like the plan of a mutinous crew on shipboard. I fancy too that they would have knocked us in the head ere they had left us if only they had been able for they seem to be as wicked & ungovernable as they possibly have the power to be. ("Draft" 93)

But Muir or his editors chose to delete this fear from the published version. The final version admits to no emotion other than pity. Muir appears as a kindly monarch, fearlessly in charge; the sheep are helpless and afraid without him: "Having escaped restraint, they were like some people we know of, afraid of their freedom, did not know what to do with it, and seemed glad to get back into the old familiar bondage" (*My First* 57). The original version reveals Muir's fear of the working class, while the edited version reveals a desire to maintain subconscious control of that class through the power of animal stories.

His private journal indicates that Muir found flock politics unfathomable

and verging constantly on complete anarchy, but by the time he published
"The Wild Sheep" in 1894, he was ready to claim that a domestic sheep "is only
a fraction of an animal, a whole flock being required to form an individual"
(425). Austin, carefully explaining complex social structures, argues that sheep
can think for themselves but simply find life less complicated when they select
and follow leaders. She claims that the "earliest important achievement of
ovine intelligence is to know whether its own notion or another's is most
worth while, and if the other's, which one" (*Flock* 109–10). Muir fears the genuine wildness he sees both in sheep and in the common masses, while Austin,
like Thoreau, believes that this real wildness will save the world. Like Thoreau,
she finds it lurking just below the thin veneer of domesticity and breaking out
when oppressed people or animals reach a point of desperation. At the end of
The Flock, she calls this natural wildness one of the "arrows" that inhabitants
of the wild must learn to sleep in the shade of in order to survive.

Muir's idealistic descriptions of wild predators again use hierarchical metaphors: "Perhaps no wild animal in the world is without enemies, but high-
landers, *as a class* have fewer than lowlanders" ("Wild Sheep" 18; emphasis
added). As Thomas Lyon has suggested, because the Sierra peaks substitute
for heaven, and the devil's tracks are seldom found above timberline, Muir's
mountaineers are seldom bothered by the devil (Lyon 16). Muir's "devil" refers to common humans, common sheep, dogs, predators, perhaps all animals
except celestial mountaineers. While Muir's predators remain sinful thieves,
they prey mostly on domestic sheep, which Muir finds acceptable as long as his
wild sheep are safe. This predator-prey relationship takes on even more ominous tones when allegorically juxtaposed against the ruthless California politics of the day. Was Muir in favor of predatory politicians and businessmen
preying on "common" people as long as his mountaineering friends and their
camping places were safe?

Austin's complicated view of the predator-prey relationship is again more
ecological and less judgmental. Her predators are not thieves, but simply animals following their natural behavior patterns.[20] She sprinkles her writing with
constant reminders that under the right circumstances we are all not only animals but thieves: "Times when there is moonlight, watery and cold, a long thin
howl detaches itself from any throat and welters on the wind" (*Flock* 93). She
argues that problems with predators are caused by close herding and relates
an incident at El Tejon, during the drouth of 1876, when fifty-eight thousand
starving sheep were turned loose in December to die. The staggering flocks
slowly disappeared into the bear-, cougar-, and wolf-infested mountains. The
next fall, when rains finally replenished the lowland meadows, fifty-three
thousand healthy sheep trailed themselves back down for the winter (235).
Sheep and predators have shared the same pastures since time immemorial,

and in Austin's mind sheep were never huddled, helpless masses, too stupid to take care of themselves. Nor, she says, do shepherds have any quarrel with predators:

> It is only against man contrivances, such as a wool tariff or a new ruling of the Forestry Bureau, that the herder becomes loquacious. Wildcats, cougars, coyotes, and bears are merely incidents of the day's work, like putting on stiff boots of a cold morning, [or] running out of garlic. (176)

Bears, she muses, often stroll harmlessly over sleeping shepherds at night or burn their paws trying to rob frying pans. "Or so it was," she states pointedly, "in the days before the summer camper found the country" (186). The grizzly disappeared in California in 1922, hundreds of years after the coming of sheep and shepherds, but not long after the coming of the summer campers.

On an allegorical level, Austin's common people had always been able to survive and make a living in spite of predators, but perhaps the summer camper would prove too great a foe. As Wallace Stegner once wrote, "Tourists can be as destructive as locusts" (*Bluebird* 55). History may prove campers even more destructive than hoofed locusts and more dangerous to rural areas than thieves.

In Muir's wildness hierarchy, common sheep were at the bottom; above them were domestic dogs and then wild predators; and above them all were wild sheep and mountaineers. Muir grants Carlo, his dog companion, only an intelligent nose and eyes, and says that he can "almost" understand a human. Patronizingly Muir instructs him to "be careful not to kill anything," and calls him "wise" only when he looks "sheepish and ashamed" and tries to get Muir to "caress him and show signs of forgiveness" (*My First* 154, 233). Carlo has to be helped down through the rocks and retreats behind Muir when they come close to a bear (35, 181). Muir's companion shepherd travels with a silly dog named Jack, who cannot keep his mind off sex long enough to herd sheep (62–63). Even Stickeen needs Muir for a leader and howls, cries piteously, and trembles in fear when forced to follow Muir across the glacier crevasse ("Stickeen" 92). Taken together, these incidents reveal a condescending disrespect toward animal intelligence.

In contrast, *The Flock* is full of heroic, intelligent dogs: dogs whose loyalty to the shepherd is legendary, dogs who carry on without the shepherd and kill coyotes without help, dogs who can pick a sheep from the herd when the shepherd speaks only the animal's name. Austin observes that sheep are "silly" regarding dogs and predators because they never seem to be able to figure out which predators are their friends. Yet when viewed against the complexity of the sheep-sheepdog relationship, this silliness may actually be a form of wisdom because some dogs will turn on the sheep (*Flock* 135–52). In a chapter called "The Go Betweens," Austin's allegory takes on another dimension when she describes the way shepherds have domesticated the predator to guard sheep against its own kind. Like ex-criminals who make the best police because they are not easily fooled, predators can make a living either by preying on sheep or by protecting them and dining on choice mutton killed, butchered, and served to them in a dish by the shepherd. Exactly who has trained whom is a question Austin doesn't answer.

If the two authors were indeed fighting a duel over grazing in Yosemite, Mary Austin lost the battle. Sheep bells no longer tinkle through high Sierra meadows. Muir's persona "worked" on the reader, and Austin's did not. Although critics consistently list *The Flock* as one of Austin's best books and say that her sheep have the "potency of symbol,"[21] the book is usually read as a charmingly outdated pastoral that inspires the reader to want to "lie under the sky with dogs and flocks, lulled to sleep by the 'blether' of ewes and the bark of distant coyotes" ("A Review" 17–18). By 1930, Tracy was already calling *The Flock* one of Austin's "least known volumes" (24); modern critics dismiss it as "a study of the ways in which the insistent claims of motherhood can inhibit one's distinctive voice" (Wyatt 87). In contrast, *My First Summer* has consistently remained in print. Muir's persona appeals to readers who want to imagine themselves inherently superior to the common masses. Although speaking somewhat softly, Muir claims king-of-the-mountain status among nature writers. He says *Walden* is a "mere saunter," and he "could not guess" why people regard Thoreau as a hermit (qtd. in Buell "Pilgrimage" 180). In 1888, Muir climbed Mount Rainier with a well-organized twelve-man expedition, complete with packhorses, yet he says blithely that he "did not mean to climb it, but got excited and soon was on top" (qtd. in Melham 123). On hearing Clarence Starr King praised for a daredevil climb of Mount Tyndall, Muir says, "When I climbed Tyndall, I ran up and back before breakfast" (qtd. in Brooks 46). As "true mountaineers," Muir and the reader stare down bears, glory in earthquakes, cling to swaying pines during thunderstorms, ride an avalanche down a mountain, crawl behind a waterfall, and even write with eagle feather quills using ink from giant sequoias. The most daring, physically fit Americans alive, Muir and the reader are also the most noble. In them the mountains produce leadership, spirituality, exceptional ethics, persuasive force—and humility? Muir's persona says, "Come along with me; only you and I truly appreciate this wilderness." Only Muir and the reader can name each plant. No one else, not even the tourist, appreciates the "glorious objects about them" (*My First* 104). Readers, vicariously identifying with Muir's superiority, do not see themselves as common tourists but as "true mountaineers" and naturalists.

In contrast, although never very humble herself, Austin assumes the persona of naive reporter, happily tagging along behind shepherds and giving them credit for extensive knowledge gained through their daily work as they climb into the meadows with the flocks. She pooh-poohs the idea of risk, saying that city dwellers are often incredulous that a person can "go about" these mountains "unhurt and unoffended by the wild" (*Flock* 265). The Sierra, she says, is a maze of sheep trails, footpaths, and shepherd camps. Tucked away at the edge of most large meadows are food, shelter, and firewood. Rural western hospitality traditionally welcomes anyone to these supplies (265). Even the distinguished Joseph LeConte, leading a group of hungry students, once robbed a shepherd of his dinner right off the fire, with Muir's help and blessing (O'Neill 30). The presence of shepherds in the Sierra took any true risk out of traveling light in Muir's day, a fact often overlooked by today's young hikers, who succumb to exposure and exhaustion trying to follow in Muir's footsteps, some of which may have been made only by his fictive persona (Bowen 164–65).

Readers who prefer to think of themselves as inherently superior to the "average" citizen are put off by Austin's persona because it humbles them. She insinuates that at least in the mountain pastures, working shepherds possess a certain kind of common sense and wisdom that wealthy, highly educated visitors or housebound readers on vicarious adventures lack. White's modern version of the argument says that "[w]ork once bore the burden of connecting us with nature," but today we attempt to make this connection through leisure, and "play cannot bear the weight" (174). Austin's persona seems to warn the reader to "[s]tay away and leave these mountain pastures to the people who have given their lives to them." And keeping people away was probably her intent. Even as a child, when Mary Austin was admonished by her mother not to "antagonize people" but to try to "draw people to you[,] Mary would reply stubbornly, 'And what would I do with the people after I have drawn them to me?'" (qtd. in Fink 33).

Perhaps Muir never considered "the cumulative effect of his own behavior" (Rowell 480): that by drawing people to the mountains through his books, he might have been the "worst enemy the wilderness ever had" (Bowen 163). Today, more than two million travelers stand in line to see Yosemite Falls each year. The "beautiful" well-kept gardens full of flowers, "grass up to a bear's hips," and "champagne water" that Muir encountered during that long-lost first summer with the sheep have been replaced by two hotels, four swimming pools, five grocery and general stores, five souvenir shops, two golf courses, six gas stations, a bank, a hospital, campsites for six thousand people, and a vast motel and parking lot complex (Bowen 166). The meadows are ribboned with deeply rutted backpacker trails, park police wear riot helmets, and campers must carry water purification kits. When society privileges leisure over work, White points out, "[n]ature may turn out to look a lot like an organic Disneyland, except it will be harder to park" (185). Ironically, according to Robert Bauer's presentation at a recent John Muir conference, Snelling, the little grazing community where Muir wrote his "Twenty Hill Hollow" journal, had a population of 315 in Muir's day and has a population of 315 today.

Ultimately, Muir won the political battle over Yosemite, but in my view Austin left him in the dust of the Long Trail (now, ironically, parts of it are called "the John Muir Trail"). Arguing on one level against banning shepherds and sheep from Yosemite, at a deeper level she was arguing against dividing people, animals, or places into hierarchies and classes. She defended indigenous working people and recognized the importance of ecological interdependence between places and all their inhabitants. Through sheep, both real and allegorical, she championed equality and government based on consent of the governed, and she believed cultures that remain in closest contact with natural rhythms and resources will prove sustainable.

How threatening *The Flock* may have been to California or national politics in 1906 is probably impossible to determine today, but Austin's later friend, President Theodore Roosevelt, who developed the national park system, appears to have been enough impressed by her arguments to send "a forestry expert to interview her" (Austin *Earth* 289). Permanent federal grazing leases, a method she recommends in *The Flock*, saying that it will help stop grazing abuses on public land (171–72, 209), were implemented and are still in effect today. These grazing leases recognize and support the needs of rural people who work the land in order to provide food for the rest of society, in opposition to environmentalists' view that rural people are inherently destructive. White argues that modern "[e]nvironmentalists must come to terms with work" (174). Austin and I argue that environmentalists must also come to terms with rural people and land, animal, and human hierarchies.

Chapter Five

The Indigenous Desert Cow

The line dividing I *and* Not-I, us *and* them, *or* him *and* her *is not (cannot) always (be) as clear as we would like it to be. Despite our desperate, eternal attempt to separate, contain and mend, categories always leak.*
Trinh T. Minh-ha (94)

Several years ago I sat in a cattlemen's association meeting and listened to the president encourage members to call for a ban on Edward Abbey's books. I wondered if we were thinking about the same author. Surely the president didn't want to ban *The Brave Cowboy* (1956), the story of a horseman's last stand against civilization; or *Fire on the Mountain* (1962), the story of an old rancher's last stand against federal forced taking of his land; or *Good News* (1980), the story of a future war between urban bad guys and rural good guys? Even *Desert Solitaire* (1968) contains an entire chapter describing Abbey himself working cattle.

The cattleman president seemed to object mostly to Abbey's *Monkey Wrench Gang* (1975), a book that is now blamed for inspiring the dismantling of windmills and destruction of water troughs. But that was never Abbey's intention. The characters in his book were actually trying to preserve "prime grazing land for sheep and cattle" (154). His book is about people trying to stop encroaching civilization; it is not a tirade against ranching. But Abbey is not totally innocent, either. In 1985, he did stand before a packed house in Bozeman, Montana, and deliver a blistering address, later published as the essay "Free Speech: The Cowboy and His Cow," attacking public-land grazing (*One Life*).

In defense of Abbey, Kentucky farmer and author Wendell Berry (1985) explains that Abbey constantly drew fire from special interest groups because he would not stay in bounds, would not support the ideology they thought he should represent. According to Berry, Abbey fans often say, "Well, he did *say* that. But . . . ," and then try to defend his latest stunt. As a cattlewoman, I find myself in exactly that position when I read that published Montana speech. Well, Abbey did *say* that

> western cattlemen are nothing more than welfare parasites. They've been getting a free ride on the public lands for over a century, and I think it's

time we phased it out. I'm in favor of putting the public lands livestock grazers out of business. (*One Life* 12)

But . . . Abbey's kindest words toward cows strangely appear in a book called *Slickrock* (1987), which he wrote as a Sierra Club publication. Why would he attack cows in front of a ranching audience and defend them to a Sierra Club audience?

Quite often Abbey's voice is confrontational. Literary critic Ann Ronald observes that his *Slickrock* essays are "openly propagandistic" and editorially were "reinforced by the Sierra Club's urgency to trumpet a battle call" (114, 121). This is an accurate observation regarding Abbey's desire to protect the southern Utah canyon country from development. However, Abbey may not have agreed that the National Park Service would do a better job of protecting those canyons than local people. In a book intentionally aimed at a Sierra Club audience, he also pointedly describes pastoral Native American cattle raisers, remembers he "got hungry and saw God in the form of a beef pie," and relates how he and backpacker–river rat friends wasted an evening rescuing a heifer from quicksand. He even bestows a closing benediction on the heifer: "I hope *our* heifer got out of there in time" (19, 21, 49–50; emphasis added). Knowing that *Slickrock*'s Sierra Club audience was actively opposed to public-land grazing, perhaps Abbey hoped to soften their political stance toward grazing without being too obvious and losing that audience.

In contrast to *Slickrock*, Ronald contends, Abbey's political views were "reined in" (119) by the Time-Life editors of *Cactus Country* (1973). But here, for a general audience, Abbey rants that cows were "once a major problem at Organ Pipe," were guilty of "overgrazing," "trampling the seedling cacti, stripping the soil of its natural cover," and that cattle caused mesquite invasion. He warns that when the grass is gone, first goats, then archaeologists will follow the cattle (70, 94–95).

Ten years later Abbey seemed to want to soften his earlier statements about grazing when he collected two *Cactus Country* chapters ("Down to the Sea of Cortez" and "The Ancient Dust") and three *Slickrock* chapters ("How It Was," "Days and Nights in Old Pariah," and "The Damnation of a Canyon") into *Beyond the Wall* (1984).[1] He did not select the cow-bashing chapters from *Cactus Country* for this collection, and he made two intriguing editorial changes in the original text. In *Cactus Country*, he observes that water trails indicate "visitation of *not only* the usual starving scrub cattle *but also* many of the more common desert mammals" (149; emphasis added). In *Beyond the Wall*, this has been changed to "visitation of the usual scrub cattle and other desert mammals" (145). Cattle are no longer singled out from "other desert mammals" by the use of "not only . . . but also." In the revised sentence, cows are just another desert mammal, and just as "common." A few pages later, in *Cactus Country,* Abbey says the area is "inhabited only by a few starving scrub cattle and wild animals" (154). In *Beyond the Wall* this is rewritten as "inhabited by starving cattle and *other* wild animals" (152; emphasis added). Adding "other" draws a new circle that is obviously meant to include cattle as wild animals.

Through the years, Abbey figured out that the best way to get action was by making people mad, and he worked hard to become a master at it. I would argue that Abbey's essay "Free Speech: The Cowboy and His Cow" is a desperate final attempt to prod rural westerners into action. He laments sadly in "Telluride Blues—A Hatchet Job" that cowboys "don't seem to like to fight so much anymore" but passively allow developers to "tear up good deer- and cattlecountry," ruin little towns like Telluride, or turn their "hayfields, ranches, homes, [and] small towns" into coal (*Journey* 108, 123, 171, 175).[2] One of his greatest frustrations, throughout his life, was the fact that people seldom reacted to his books as he planned. When he insulted them, they sometimes loved it, and sometimes his words were taken up as weapons and used against rural people.

On the surface, Abbey's writing often appears to be simple political journalism, but Edward Abbey wrote literature, not didactic eco-rant speeches. He used modern environmental issues and people figuratively, as plot and character, but he was after bigger game: world politics, religion, human and ecological ethics. As he searched the Southwest for signs and symbols to work into his prose, he found the cowboy and his horse the stuff of myth: too heroic, too tragic, too remote, too exotic, and too romantic. He found Sonoran Desert plants and animals too regional. The Gila monster, barrel cactus, wild burro, scorpion, tarantula, even the stately saguaro signified little more than fear, adaptability, spartan independence, or tenacity outside desert borders. Surprisingly, he did find one complex and overlooked world-class symbol in the Southwest—the humble cow.[3] I argue that Abbey found this complicated desert cow character, as well as many of his other themes, motifs, and symbols, in Mary Austin's *The Land of Little Rain.*

Like Austin, Abbey spent considerable time thinking about the boundaries between domesticity and wildness. He says the call of the loon is "that wild, lorn, romantic cry, one of the most thrilling sounds in all North America. Sound of the ancient wilderness, lakes, forest, moonlight, birchbark canoes" (*Journey* 41). Ronald calls it the "[s]ound of sacrality" (130). Yet both Abbey and Thoreau say almost the same thing about the domestic rooster. Abbey's version: "The call of the male chicken, if not so familiar, would seem to us like the wildest, most thrilling cry in all of nature" (*Road* 97). Thoreau's version:

> The note of this once wild Indian pheasant is certainly the most remarkable of any bird's, and if they could be naturalized without being domesti-

cated, it would soon become the most famous sound in our woods. . . . No wonder that man added this bird to his tame stock. (378)

Obviously familiarity has something to do with the loss of wildness and mystery that domestic animals have undergone.

While hiking Glacier National Park's "Peaceable Kingdom," Abbey passed six mountain goats, "grazing not fifty feet from the trail; indifferent to my presence," and five bighorn rams bedded down on the trail. He says that he "approached to within twenty feet, waved my arms and whistled; grudgingly they got up and let me through" (*Journey* 50). In contrast, when he waves his arms and a stick at "half-wild" cattle, who have forgotten whom they belong to, "they bolt suddenly for the trees, like deer" (*Desert* 84, 230). The cow's heritage is in fact wild, noble, and savage. Worldwide, the cow was once the proud symbol of wildness and danger, hunted in protected walled forests by only the richest lords. The modern cow descended from extinct wild ungulates like the African, Asian, and European aurochs (*Bos taurus primigenius* to *Bos primigenius primigenius* to *Bos taurus primigenius* and *Bos taurus brachyceros*). England and Scotland's legendary, long extinct, shaggy wild white cattle (*Bos longifrons*)—drawings of which look amazingly like white bison—were also ancestors, as were "forest bulls" (tauri sylvestres), Scandinavian mountain cattle called "fjallrus," India's endangered beautiful red gaur (*Bos gaurus*), and many more. The cow's family tree includes Caesar's urus, Indonesia's banteng, and the hairy wild yak (*Bos grunniens*). Even the European and Asian wisent (*Bison bonasus*), a small, light-colored buffalo, contributed its genes to the pool.[4] Shakespeare, alluding to the wildness in cows, said that they were bothered more by the breeze than by the tiger (*Troilus and Cressida* I.iii.48). Modern breeds have added blood from *Bos indicus* (numerous breeds cross with Zebu and Brahman), *Bison bison* (crossed with Angus is "Amerifax," crossed with Simmental is "Simmalo"). The "American Breed" democratically crosses Zebu, Charolais, Hereford, Shorthorn, and bison—all of which thoroughly mixes the hollow-horned, cloven-footed, humped, hairy, short- and long-horned wild cattle breeds.

One of the most interesting parallels between Austin and Abbey is their mutual tendency to characterize the desert cow as an indigenous wild animal. In *The Land of Little Rain* Austin writes that "the habits of an earlier lineage persist" in the desert's "half-*wild* spotted steers." She observes that since "a few *wild*-eyed steers" have come to inhabit her neighbor's field, many of the wild native plants are returning. She finds a "pungent trail where *wild* cattle crop" sagebrush, and notes that "western bred cattle" have learned to avoid loco weed while "strangers eat it and go mad" (*Land* 13, 49, 88; emphasis added). She claims that cattle retain the wild wisdom to move down out of the mountains before a snow. Sheep "never learned the self-induced hypnotic stupor with which most *wild* things endure weather stress," but "shut-eyed cattle" turn "tail to the wind in a patient doze" (*Flock* 125; *Land* 97, 99; emphasis added).

Austin is also careful to point out that cattle did not come into the Southwest via Europeans' east-to-west frontier thrust, reminding the reader that cattle herding was first introduced by the "free riding *vaqueros* who need no trails and can find cattle where to the layman no cattle exist" (*Land* 58). In 1610 the Virginia colonies imported cattle from the West Indies, but Native Americans wiped them out in 1622. A colony of Dutch settlers brought cattle to New York State in 1619, and four years after the *Mayflower* landed the first British cattle arrived in Massachusetts. However, one hundred years before this more famous eastern assault began, the cow had already migrated into the desert Southwest with the Hispanic explorer Hernando Cortés (1485–1547). By the time white settlers arrived from the East four hundred years later, the cow had become almost indigenous to the Southwest. One of the few major sources of protein that the desert has proven able to produce sustainably—or at least for more than five hundred years now—is beef.

In his essay "Down to the Sea of Cortez," Abbey also gives credit to the Spanish vaquero for the arrival of desert cattle in the Southwest. He calls overgrazing "the old story" and describes Mexican scrub cattle as desert wildlife with Abbey-like affection:

> Scrub cattle ranging through the bush galloped off like gnus and wildebeests at our approach. I never saw such weird, scrawny, pied, mottled, humped, long-horned and camel-necked brutes trying to pass as domestic livestock. Most looked like a genetic hash of Hereford, Charolais, Brahman, Angus, moose, ibex, tapir and nightmare. Weaned on cactus, snakeweed and thistle, they showed the gleam of the sun through the translucent barrel of their rib cages. But they could run, they were alive—not only alive but vigorous. I was tempted to think, watching their angular hind ends jouncing away through the dust, that the meat on those critters, if you could find any, might just taste better than the aerated, water-injected, hormone-inflated beef we Americans get from today's semiautomated feedlots in the States. (*Beyond* 138–39)

This description of cattle contains subtle admiration both for the hardy Mexican cattle and for the hardy people who survive on so much less than the overstuffed, industrialized, north-of-the-border variety.

Anglo ranchers actually enjoyed only a very brief historical moment in the Southwest. A few years after Arizona became a state, government agencies ousted all residents along the U.S.-Mexican border, including the cow, and replaced them with state and national parks, national monuments, military reservations, proving grounds, and national recreation areas. When Abbey takes "A Walk in the Desert Hills" across this same southern Arizona desert where the cow first touched hoof, he seems happy the place is free of cow dung and says, "I give thanks again for the United States Air Force" (*Beyond* 19). However, I can't quite take him seriously. Perhaps no one knew better than Abbey that every inch of the U.S.-Mexico border area was once someone's home and some cow's pasture, and that it now belongs mostly to the government against which he thought true patriots should be willing to defend their country.

As Abbey walks along, with building irony he notes that "[o]nly one animal remains conspicuous in this region, by its absence—the cow" (*Beyond* 19). "[N]othing human" lives here or ever did (27). A few pages later, as his need for water has become critical, he says, "There has got to be water at Gray's Well—a rancher named Henry Gray once lived there—and if there isn't I'll die, and what of it?" (39). And what of the fact that Abbey probably once looked after that very windmill when he worked as a cowboy on the Henry Gray Ranch (*Cactus*)? Even Anglo ranchers have been "dispossessed," writes cultural geographer Paul Starrs, "by a government opposed to grazing partly because it was a Hispanic practice" (4). In one of Abbey's last books, *One Life at a Time, Please* (1988) he says, "Here on this international boundary, in this neutral zone, one's actual citizenship makes little difference" (151). Government agencies have displaced Native Americans, Hispanics, Anglos, and cows equally. I believe Edward Abbey, the hiker-curmudgeon-anarchist, would trust cattlemen of any race to maintain windmills in the desert, but would have no faith in government employees to perform the same critical task.

Although he was often under fire as a racist (for comments such as, "Stop every *campesino* at our southern border, give him a handgun, a good rifle, and a case of ammunition, and send him home" ["Immigration" in *One Life* 44]), Abbey actually demonstrated great respect for other cultures. For example, he dismisses the Peace Corps as "a typical piece of American cultural insolence" (187), and refuses to subscribe to the condescending idea that Mexican people need our "help." The cow symbolically reveals his genuine respect for those who can live, adapt, and thrive in his beloved desert—a place the white male author was tough enough to visit only with a backpack full of imported food and water. He implies that North Americans should be asking the countries they like to refer to as the "Third World" for help in learning to live lighter on the land.

The cattle breeds listed in the preceding passage represent an Americanized genetic hash of world countries: England, France, India, Scotland, North America, South America, Asia, and Africa. Their hides come in red, white, yellow, black, and brown, but do not correspond to the skin colors of humans found in the same area. Wild spotted mixed-breed cattle, usually symbolic of the "hybrid vigor," some would say "superiority," of crossbred animals and people, appear in the work of numerous mixed-blood western writers, from Leslie Marmon Silko's *Ceremony* (74–81) to J. P. S. Brown's *The Outfit*. As Susan Blumenthal points out, Silko's spotted cattle "are a cross between domesticated cattle and wild animals." They "are not animals from traditional Pueblo mythology or storytelling tradition. . . . Silko created them to represent the hybridization of Indian culture" (369). Abbey created his own spotted cattle for a similar reason, although it could be argued that neither author created the spotted cattle since the desert *corriente* did and do exist. Abbey did, however, resist Austin's and Silko's tendency to idealize and romanticize indigenous people and carefully tried to balance any praise he might give with plenty of insults.

Ann Ronald notices that although John Muir and Austin have many characteristics in common, Austin is "different from Muir, . . . and more like Edward Abbey in the significance she gives to human beings in nature's scheme" (143). After Ronald's comparison, and perhaps even inspired by it, Abbey himself wrote an introduction to a 1988 Penguin edition of Austin's book *The Land of Little Rain*. Although many interpret this introduction as being full of typical Abbey insults, he actually pays Austin grand tributes. What higher compliment could he give than to point out her "sharp and bristling personality, which attracted many, annoyed many others," and which paralleled his own? He observes that, like himself, she was "never afraid to take up unpopular causes." Abbey knew what it felt like to suffer ad hominem attacks from critics who concentrated on his many divorces and obnoxious personality while they ignored his actual work.[5]

Abbey admits to having read only one of Austin's books, *The Land of Little Rain*, and that one only twice: "the first time forty years ago, during my own student days in the American Southwest, the second time the day before yesterday, for the purpose of writing this introduction." Sometimes, however, Ed Abbey lies, stretches the truth, or phrases a sentence in such a way as to imply one thing and mean another. Seeming to simply refer to Austin's tale about a desert muleskinner who is addicted to the desert (*Land* 6–7), Abbey writes in his introduction, "Like many others, old Salty thought he hated the land of not much rain. He *believed* that he hated it. But every time he tried to leave, he soon returned" (*Land* xiii). "Old Salty" could easily represent Abbey himself. In his introduction he almost publicly admits that Austin's book, her ideas, and her use of a bristling gender-specific persona had been important inspirations to him. Also, at least twice between his student days and 1988, when he wrote his introduction to *The Land of Little Rain*, the salty old curmudgeon Abbey did return to "the land of not much rain" to pay it tribute. He mentions the book in *Desert Solitaire*, written in 1968 (239); and one chapter in *Cactus Country* (1973) opens with an Austin quote from it: "None other than this long brown land lays such a hold on the affections." The quote introduces a chapter called "The Real Desert," in which Abbey talks about Native Americans raising cattle; his view of two hundred miles of nothing but grassland crawling with bald-faced cows; his finding the "remains of a maggot-swarming, dehydrated cow"; and his evident knowledge that he would not be stepped on when he threw his sleeping bag down "across a cattle path" (20–24). Perhaps Abbey read sentences and chapters from *The Land of Little Rain* almost daily, like a Bible, but only twice "read it through."[6]

Abbey's books overflow with Austin's images, themes, political ideas, and religious allusions. Detail after detail—lone junipers, animals, indigenous people, cactus, black rocks, heat, mines, and the desert as an animistic force—appear in the work of both authors. It could all be coincidence, of course, because both were writing about the desert Southwest, but a few key passages seem too close to be coincidence. Austin's badger is "a pot-hunter and no sportsman" (*Land* 56); Abbey's father was "a pot-hunter and no sportsman" (*One Life* 33–40). Austin warns the reader always to trust animal trails in the desert when searching for water, no matter what the map says (10); Abbey also trusts the animal trails instead of his map (*Beyond* 18). Both authors observe how the desert influences life there: "nothing rots" (*Land* 4; *Down* 165), both trees and people prefer to live spaced well apart (*Land* 33; *Journey* 39), and both animals and humans endure the heat by burrowing underground in earth houses (*Land* 10, 107; *Journey* 72). Even some of Austin's sentences reappear in Abbey's writing: Austin calls memory "the light that never was"; Abbey watches a thunderstorm bathed in "the light that never was" (*Land* 31; *Confessions* 348).[7] Agreeing with Austin's feelings toward summer campers, Abbey also makes it clear that he is "certainly no mountaineer" (*Journey* 209).

Paralleling Austin's views toward wilderness and national park politics, Abbey's writing often deals with humans who for one reason or another have been kicked out of Eden, banned from their wilderness homes. He also reminds us that "[t]he American Indians had no word for what we call 'wilderness.' For them . . . the wilderness was home" (*Down* 237). In *Slickrock* he pointedly asks his Sierra Club audience, "What would it be like to *live* in this place?" (62; emphasis in original). "The Carson Productions Interview" is straight talk and not literature. During the course of the interview Abbey said that "the newly-approved Tellico Dam . . . has destroyed the habitat not only of the famous little fish known as snail darter but also forced 341 farm families off their land" (Balian 59). National parks, wildlife refuges, gunnery ranges, dams, and wilderness areas are still throwing the less powerful out of Eden: Native Americans, Hispanic settlers, ranchers, farmers, women, children, and cows. Edward Abbey did not approve. Instead, he hoped that someday cities would be smaller and more scattered, and that across the desert "blue-eyed Navajo bedouins will herd

their sheep and horses" (*Desert* 127). Someday, he hoped, we will be able to accept humans in paradise where "wilderness is not a playground but their natural native home" (*One Life* 28).

Like all wild animals, and ideal humans, Abbey's cows risk their lives for
their territories, often freely choosing the most awful brush- and prickly pear–
choked canyon, an island available only by swimming, or canyons subject to
flash floods and carpeted with quicksand. Abbey further blurs boundaries between wild and domestic when he concludes that wildness is a state of mind,
not genetically imposed (*Desert* 84–85; *Journey* 192; *Beyond* 75). Abbey did
not want to see cows or anything else kicked out of paradise because of some
imaginary dichotomy between wild and domestic. As Wallace Stegner says, "I
have known enough range cattle to recognize them as wild animals; . . . they
belong on the frontier, moreover, and have a look of rightness" (*Sound* 151).

Although Abbey's books are full of critical comments about agribusiness and
overgrazing, he carefully attempts to distinguish between agri-*business* and
agri-*culture* (the family farm or ranch), and he staunchly defends the latter.[8]
For example, in *Desert Solitaire* he lists ways to impose a "dictatorial regime"
on the American people. The first step, he says, is to concentrate people into
cities; the second:

> Mechanize agriculture to the highest degree of refinement, thus forcing
> most of the scattered farm and ranching population into the cities. Such a
> policy is desirable because farmers, woodsmen, cowboys, Indians, fisher-
> men and other relatively self-sufficient types are difficult to manage un-
> less displaced from their natural environment. (131)

Juxtaposing "Thus I Reply to Rene Dubos" in *Down the River* (1981) with
"The Second Rape of the West" in *Journey Home* (1977) and David Remley's
recap (1985) of the true story behind *Fire on the Mountain* reveals Abbey's
complex views on farming and ranching, views that support sustainable communities, rural people, and rural work.[9]

Using another tactic possibly inspired by Austin, Abbey uses gendered animal stories to help draw attention to the wild/domestic dichotomy. The cow is
always female in Abbey's writing.[10] The toilet truck driver in *The Brave Cowboy* describes middle-aged women as "domesticated cows" (93). In *Black Sun*
(1971), Ballentine asks why he should buy a cow (referring to women) when
he can get all the milk he needs (referring to sex) through the fence (50). A
very drunk Abbey, evidently preferring women with hips, observes that cow-
girls accompanying their men into an Arizona bar are "heifers" who "couldn't
calve a salamander" (*Road* 165). Cows are dumb enough to drown or bog down
in quicksand (*Beyond* 100, 102; *Journey* 190–93; *Desert* 92). Abbey and a friend
will eat cows but don't want to drink after them (*Desert* 163). True to his "dra-

matic persona," he shows affectionate concern only for a young (and, we can safely presume, pretty) heifer who has gotten her helpless little self stuck and needs to be rescued (*Beyond* 72–75). Theorist Trinh T. Minh-ha contends that both "[l]ady and whore were bred to please" (97). We might easily add the domestic cow. Abbey might add men.[11] Today, the cow crosses genders. On the one hand, she conjures a domestic female image: an overweight, middle-aged, bawling, slow, slothful, not too intelligent stomper of stream banks, dropper of dung, drawer of flies, and slinger of sagging udders. On the other hand, she represents the shameful, overgassed, shit-encrusted symbol of manifest destiny, overgrazing, overproduction, overconsumption, overeating, and the over-bearing, booted and spurred white males of the American West—an image strangely similar to Abbey's obnoxious persona.[12]

Science adds even more symbolic baggage to Abbey's gender-specific cow. Scientists classify bison and cattle into separate genera (*Bos* and *Bison*), although they can mate as only closely related species can. The difference between them? One rib: bison have fourteen on each side, and cows, of course, have only thirteen! The bison conjures in the American imagination a very male image: the patriarchal harem ruler. Perhaps because the cow is one rib short, like Eve, she is somehow "less of a man" than the noble bison. Like Eve, she also carries the blame for all our sins on her innocent shoulders. In Abbey's essay "Big Bend," the cows have been banished from "Cow Heaven" (*One Life* 135). One of the essays written for the Sierra Club portrays the same situation: "not a house in sight, not even a cow or horse. Eden at the dawn of creation" (*Beyond* 57). Deer, which Abbey calls "a giant rodent—a rat with antlers" (*One Life* 17), are allowed in the Garden, but not cows: "Everywhere deer sign, nowhere the faintest trace of man. We have stumbled into a miniature Eden" (*Journey* 199).

Abbey touches on another volatile subject when he investigates the tangled human-animal food chain.[13] Historically, he notes humorously, even noble Native Americans ate some animals into extinction (*Black* 56; *Beyond* 156; *Journey* 148–49). He wonders whether today's humans could or should give up agribusiness-produced wheat and return to eating chuckwallas (*Beyond* 156), or whether we could eat pinyon nuts "fast enough to keep from starving to death" (*Desert* 253).[14] He realizes that returning to slash-and-burn agriculture or a hunter-gatherer society may not be a utopian solution: "[U]ntil the coming of the white man the natives spent half their lives on the edge of starvation. Famine was common" (*Beyond* 190).[15] My own well-fed personal friends—Crow, Northern Cheyenne, Sioux, Paiute, Navajo, and Apache cattle ranchers—laugh and shake their heads no when I ask if they would like to return to the good old days (Nelson "Ranching" I and II).[16] When Abbey demands that a Native American drinking buddy tell him why his people exterminated all those mastodons, camels, and tree sloths, the Indian shrugs and answers, "We were hungry" (*Black* 56).

On another track, Abbey questions whether eating plants is wiser or more moral than eating meat. With frank satisfaction in his offensiveness, he brags about gluttonous river trips on which he and friends "stuff[ed] faces and stomachs" (*One Life* 118), and boasts about gorging on huge bloody slabs of dead cow meat, derisively referring to vegetarian meals as "pussy food" (*Down* 33, 45). Again writing for the Sierra Club, Abbey humorously stresses the idea that he perceives "no moral superiority in the position of the ethical vegetarian who . . . uproots harmless carrots, mutilates innocent turnips, violates cabbages and plunders fruit trees to keep body and soul conjoined" (*Cactus* 115). He enjoys taunting his readers with the fact that vegetarians, like the cow and the chuckwalla, can be "big, fat, ugly, [and] remarkably stupid" (*Road* 74, 84), while most meat-eating predators are thin and wily. With tongue in cheek, he says that plants probably feel pain and scream (*Journey* 207), that they have "hearts" and could be considered "friends" (*Beyond* 46, 144).

In *Beyond the Wall*, however, Abbey's dichotomy-blurring and hierarchy-rejecting voice takes the subject of food more seriously, as indeed world hunger deserves. Ronald notes: "Turning an idea from side to side, he balances one alternative against another. He poses an idea, then abandons it, suggests its opposite, then rejects them both" (97). He thinks about eating grass (*Desert* 252) but decides that the "sere, brown, short, tough native grasses that are the best cattle feed in the world" do not make good human food, and that land "too arid for conventional farming . . . will still support a beef-growing industry" (*Journey* 170). In Alaska, where plant life is scarce, his humorous argument with a vegetarian has a serious undertone: "Every time we eat a cow, I remind him, we save the life of a moose, two caribou, four mule deer, or eight char squared. . . . Whose side are you on, Jensen?" (*Beyond* 174–75). More seriously, he also subtly notes that humans who eat huckleberries steal food from grizzlies, that eating mushrooms competes with deer (*Journey* 39, 49), and that meat production "sacrifices" (*Down* 116) can be juxtaposed against vegetable production sacrifices:

> Like many rivers these days the San Juan is bound for practical ends, condemned by industrial agriculture to expire in a thousand irrigation ditches, transmogrified from living river into iceberg lettuce, square tomatoes, celery, onions, Swiss chard, and radishes. . . . Like fish, chickens, cows, pigs, and lambs, the rivers too are penned and domesticated and diverted. . . . Don't think about it. Nobody else does. Except animal liberationists. And vegetarians—those murderers of zucchini! those bean sprout killers! (*Down* 127)[17]

Although Abbey jokes about murdering plants, he also seriously challenges the vegetarian prejudice against eating meat: "To speak of 'harvesting' other living creatures . . . as if they were *no more than a crop*, exposes the meanest, cruelest, most narrow and homocentric of possible human attitudes toward the life that surrounds us" (*One Life* 39; emphasis added). Abbey believes that interdependent food sources form ecosystems and webs, not pyramids and chains. Eating lower on the food chain is simply one more form of elitist human classification.[18] Instead of a hierarchy, he argues, a spider chewing on a mosquito full of human blood or bacteria feasting on human flesh indicate a complicated and unsympathetic web with humans at the top *and* bottom (*Journey* 35; *Road* 134).

As his investigation into the food chain becomes more complex, Abbey suggests that all animals are potential "overgrazers." Porcupines gnaw bark from pinyon pines, and deer eat "themselves out of house and home." Ants have "denuded the ground surrounding their hill," bees are "gluttonous," a juniper clutches "at the rock on which it feeds," and even the wind eats rocks (*Desert* 25–30). A dust-to-ancient-dust cycle is completed as Abbey describes rocks with lips and teeth.[19] He concludes, as deep ecologists preach, that "even a rock is a being" and philosophically returns to the cow: "Only a fool, milking his cow, denies the cow's reality. Be true to the earth, said Nietzsche" (*Road* 128). Abbey's world, like Austin's, is entirely animistic, so he offers no easy solutions: "There seems to be no alternative to eating, much as one might prefer a more ascetic manner of life" (*One Life* 116).[20]

Setting a thought-provoking and symbolic example, Abbey claims that he wants to be reincarnated as a croaking, obnoxious, carrion-eating buzzard. The first words in praise of the buzzard Abbey ever read must have been Austin's essay "The Scavengers" in *The Land of Little Rain*. In it, she observes that buzzards are despised for their imagined lack of cleanliness and that our European-inspired morals and distaste for certain jobs or foods reappear as a distaste for certain animals and animal behaviors; therefore, we despise housekeepers, garbage collectors, and undertakers.[21] In Austin's stories, buzzards, vultures, and condors often help find lost people.[22] "The vulture merits respect for his bigness and for his bandit airs," she says, "but he is a somber bird, with none of the buzzard's frank satisfaction in his offensiveness" (19). She praises scavengers for providing an unappreciated but important service by taking out the trash and keeping the desert clean—except for tin cans, which she scorns as the worst "disfigurement" found in the desert (22). So, Abbey, with frank satisfaction in his offensiveness, probably enjoyed exasperating her ghost when he wrote about tossing his beer cans all over her nice clean desert—just like a dang man.

Abbey does not want his reincarnated self to go hungry, so he must also consider what a buzzard eats. Again, he was quite familiar with Austin's observation that "[i]n mid-desert where there are no cattle, there are no birds of car-rion" (5).[23] As he tramps around the desert Southwest, he notices that a lone buzzard might be found pecking at a roadkill rabbit, but the gathering and feasting of the clan mainly occurs around dead cows: "Arizona is where the vultures swarm like flies about the starving cattle on the cow-burnt range" (*Journey* 147). In Mexico he finds even more scavengers: "Above the cattle the vultures swarm like flies, attracted by the sight and smell of dying meat" (*Down* 149). And with a positive slant: "The inevitable vultures soaring over-head reminded us, though, that somewhere in this brushy wilderness was life, sentient creating, living meat" (*Beyond* 139). The scavengers remind him again that in the desert, the cow represents sustainable protein.

Seldom studied as a serious symbol in the sophisticated 1990s, the cow is no stranger to the nature-writing canon. In *Teaching a Stone to Talk* (1983), Annie Dillard fondly recalls her own cowperson days:

> I liked . . . the way the animals always broke loose. . . . [T]wo people and a clever cow can kill a morning. . . . You laugh for a while, exhausted, and si-lence is restored; the beasts are back in their pastures, the fences are not fixed but disguised as if they were fixed, ensuring the animals' temporary resignation; and a great calm descends, a lack of urgency, a sense of hav-ing to invent something to do until the next time you must run and chase cattle. (131)

Dillard contemplates cattle throughout her Pulitzer Prize–winning pilgrimage at Tinker Creek. In the opening pages she crosses "the bridge that is really the steers' fence." She remembers the "old Hebrew ordinance" to sacrifice an un-blemished red heifer "which has never known the yoke." The priest must "burn her wholly, without looking away."[24] Looping through fecundity, food chains, and the horns of the altar, Dillard concludes that the pasture she has been walk-ing through is "the steers' pasture" (*Pilgrim* 13, 267, 263). Chasing cattle gives humans a purpose, and sacrificing steers or heifers puts food on the table, satis-fying two basic survival needs. The least we humans should do in return is acknowledge that the pastures belong not to us, but to the cattle who feed us. Native Americans worshiped their food source; we cuss ours.

When Henry David Thoreau explains his idea of wildness in "Walking" (1862), he does so through the cow. Wildness, he says, remains preserved under the "thick hides of cattle and horses." Occasionally we see "evidence that they have not wholly lost their original wild habits and vigor," and Thoreau rejoices that "horses and steers have to be broken before they can be made the slaves of men" (218–19). This semidormant wildness in cattle gives Thoreau hope that humans also retain the seeds of instinct. No matter how oppressed, reasons

Thoreau, the human spirit can never be truly broken. In "Wild Apples" (1862), Thoreau argues that the cow helps apple trees return to a wild state.

Certainly Abbey knew that the cow had been quietly marbling in streaks of literary fat from Greek myth through the Bible, from India to South America, from Aesop to Darwin, paradoxically representing god, monster, disguise, sacrifice, laborer, wealth, and poverty. Io, one of the mortal women Zeus loved, was changed into a white cow by his jealous wife. Cattle have been described as "craven images" (e.g., the golden calf) and as unclean and forbidden meat. Nomads whose herds of cattle "munch[ed] their way across the Sahara, Persia, Arabia, Morocco, Ethiopia" were feared, hated, and imagined as expanding "traditions of arrogance and destructiveness" (Shepard 17). "It might come as a surprise to many, then," Jeremy Rifkin declares, "that much of the religious experience of the West, from before recorded history until well into the Christian era, was dominated by bull gods and goddesses, the cult of the bovine" (19). Cow worship was and is a worldwide phenomenon. Yi-Fu Tuan notes that in ancient Upper Egypt, "the cow goddess of the sky (Hathor) was believed to have given birth to the sun" (*Dominance* 71). Peter Mark found cattle standing "at the summit of the hierarchy of animals" in New Guinea. Young men wear masks decorated with cattle horns during coming-of-age ceremonies, and cattle are sacrificed to ensure rain (50). When Abbey adopted the cow as a character in his desert writing, he tapped into a deep and complex worldwide symbol.

Richard Shelton (1985) quotes Abbey as saying that *Desert Solitaire* is "not primarily about the desert." But "[i]f *Desert Solitaire* is not primarily about the desert," Shelton asks, "what is it about?" (72). Maybe cows? Cows are everywhere in Abbey's writing: hiding in every slick-rock canyon, grazing along every free-flowing river, constantly drowning, tracking up and defecating in every desert, and ruining the imaginations of those who follow them around. It seems that Edward Abbey was periodically obsessed with cow images and metaphors. He calls himself a "sick calf" (*Down* 184), dreams of giving up the writing life to carve "the image, say, of a cow" into redwood logs with a hatchet, but luckily sells a manuscript for enough money "to choke a cow" instead (*One Life* 54–57). He writes about the cowbird and the cowtongue prickly pear (*Beyond* 112, 119), cowflies, and bullbats—"birds with a bovine bellow" (*Desert* 35, 208). In Glen Canyon, where Wallace Stegner found drowned sheep and deer (*Sound* 120), Abbey found drowned cows. With all these references to cows, Stegner could certainly never classify Abbey's books as "big hat, no cows" (*Bluebird* 136).

Of course, my argument that Abbey's cows are much more than an environmental issue and that he was influenced by Mary Austin's thinking may be based on coincidence, conjecture, and wishful research. When I read passages in his journal or watch him on film, I sometimes doubt my own conclusions. Sometimes he really does seem to hate cows. The narrator of the documentary film *Edward Abbey: A Voice in the Wilderness* says,

> Those who knew him only through his writing saw just one side of Ed, a side that he carefully concocted for his readers. To know the real Ed Abbey, talk to those who were closest to him. You'll soon discover that in reality Abbey was more real and more outrageous than any character he invented on paper. (Temple)

However, as a writer myself, I don't think any of my closest friends or family members have even the vaguest idea about what I try to do on paper. I often say on paper what I don't dare to say aloud. Sometimes I think that is why writers write. So, I believe there is also a side to Ed Abbey that he never felt obligated to apologize for or explain and that only his readers can ever know, as there was to Austin.

As a writer, hiker, and river rat who passionately loved the desert, and who also politically championed anarchy and personal freedom, Abbey often found himself sympathizing with conflicting perspectives. Critic Trinh T. Minh-ha, a nonwhite female theorist, describes her own similarly complicated position as a "triple bind": do her loyalties lie with her race, her gender, or some bigger entity? I think Abbey found himself in much the same dilemma and solved it much as Trinh[25] does: with a plural voice. Trinh describes her own writing voice as a combination between a capitalized "I" representing the all-knowing "Author" and a lower-case "i" representing herself situated in a specific community. Trinh's "I/i" voice carefully tries to speak for multiple positions (9). In "The Poetry Center Interview," Abbey admits that he created a voice in his nonfiction and gave that character his own name, and that "some people mistake the creation for the author" (Hepworth 42).

Abbey as cocksure, white male author is often prepared to shoot even God. Ann Ronald (1982) calls this "Cactus Ed" narrator his "dramatic persona" (66–67). Like Coyote, the traditional desert storyteller's character, Cactus Ed is obsessed with sex, ribald humor, and irreverence. Using Trinh's system, this voice can be represented with capital letters as "ED." But behind the bluster is a quieter, more serious "ed." This lowercase voice is sympathetic, other directed, unsure, and groping. Austin's dual personality and voice, which she explains as "I-Mary" (the confident, sometimes obnoxiously so, female prophet) and "Mary-by-Herself" (a lonely, groping child), could in the same way be represented as Mary/mary. Abbey, like Trinh and Austin, types his way between his blustering narrator and his groping human self as ED/ed. He is not ashamed of his own personality, heritage, or gender, yet he is not willing to assume a didactic dictatorship, or to bear the responsibility as a model for society. His thoughts are as good as the next person's, and he has a right to voice them, but he does not consider them superior, only equal. This ED/ed perspective gives him a very modern complex voice with ancient desert storyteller roots.

So. What is Abbey the complicated desert storyteller trying to do with his complex, contradictory, and symbolic cow? Again Trinh provides a way to begin to solve the riddle. She says "every discourse that breeds fault and guilt is a discourse of authority and arrogance" (11), and that the "language of Taoism and Zen, . . . which is rife with paradox . . . is 'illogical' and 'nonsensical'" to Western readers expecting rhetoric because "its intent lies outside the realm of persuasion" (16).[26] Abbey's cow essay, "Free Speech: The Cowboy and His Cow," is rife with paradox. It is illogical and nonsensical, and his intent lies outside the realm of rhetoric and persuasion. In the introduction to *One Life at a Time, Please,* Abbey says that the cow essay will "conclude its career as the nucleus of a book length essay in mythology and meat" (3), which it did. As usual, he exercises his democracy-based freedom of speech to the limit, attacking several "sacred cows" as he attacks every authoritative and arrogant discourse that breeds fault and guilt: feminism, environmentalism, political correctness, motherhood, science, and religion. Under the rubric of mythology and meat, Abbey discusses world religions, world hunger, capitalism, art, and an author's heavy responsibility to his race, his gender, and the bigger picture. Readers able to listen to the ED/ed voice will find layer after layer of politics, religion, philosophy, and ecology here—with no easy black-and-white eco-rant answers.

In one of the last chapters of the book, Abbey discusses another "nature" writer, Ralph Waldo Emerson, and in so doing tries to point his readers toward this deeper consideration of his own work:

> Emerson tried to discover for himself an original and meaningful relationship to the world, a personal viewpoint that would salvage his deeply religious sensibility and lend aid to his pressing emotional needs. Since Christianity could no longer serve these needs, he attempted to find a new synthesis through Germanic idealism, Hindu theosophy, Confucian ethics, poetic romanticism, and his inescapable background of rugged Yankee individualism. His version of philosophic idealism, which he called Transcendentalism—borrowing the term from Kant—was an effort to override or transcend these dualisms through the identification of Mind (always capitalized) with Spirit (likewise), and the equation of both with Absolute Spirit which in turn becomes another term for—the World, the Universe, the All-in-One. (*One Life* 211)

Applied to Abbey's own books, this interpretation can help readers plunge beyond a surface analysis of his Cactus Ed dramatic persona to his complicated and worldly ED/ed voice.

Abbey's political views toward the cow are not quite so clearly negative if the reader begins to listen to the ED/ed voice, cussing cows in one breath and respectfully calling them wild desert animals in the next. When Abbey "shouts his message," Ronald notes, "it is least likely to be taken seriously" (199). Trinh explains this as an author's disorienting tactic: "Never does one open the discussion by coming right to the heart of the matter. For the heart of the matter is always somewhere else" (1). When ED shouts his message, as in the cow essay, the reader can be fairly certain he is after something other than agreement; "the heart of the matter" is somewhere else. When ED shouts, he is often lying, trying to cause trouble, trying to make people think or fight back.

Edward Abbey had a larger audience in mind than members of Earth First! He did *say* that he wanted sacred cows kept out of his elk pastures (*One Life* 19), but . . . What better way to explain noncapitalist democracy to a Hindu reader than ED/ed's desire to be reincarnated not as a rich man but as a buzzard, a black-feathered untouchable,[27] one who must patiently wait for carrion. When ED calls public-land cattlemen "sacred cows," I believe ed wants the reader to find out just why India's strict vegetarians hold the cow sacred. Although suffering constant ridicule from modern agribusinessmen, India's cow is an ecological miracle. Its manure provides nonpolluting cooking fuel and fertilizer, keeping the rivers free of chemical fertilizers. It provides milk to the lowest and poorest castes, although they too must wait until a sacred cow dies of its own volition and becomes carrion before their children can eat. In a country where farmers can't afford, or perhaps wisely have chosen not to become dependent on, gasoline and tractors, the cow provides natural muscle to plow the fields, haul produce to market, and furnish transportation. Providing everything from plaster for the walls to raw materials for the untouchables' leather businesses, the cow actually makes India's teeming vegetarian population possible.[28] Abbey was aware of Thoreau's influence on both Gandhi and Tolstoy. In "Down the River with Henry Thoreau," he notes that

> Walden has been published abroad in every country where English can be read, as in India—God knows they need it there—or can be translated, as in Russia, where they need it even more. The Kremlin's commissars of literature have classified Thoreau as a nineteenth-century social reformer, proving once again that censors can read but seldom understand. (*Down* 73)

Obviously Abbey, also labeled as a twentieth-century social reformer, ranges beyond simple rhetorical jousting between environmentalists and ranchers in the American Southwest in his thinking and writing.

Although readers examine the works of Emerson, Dillard, and Thoreau for deeper meaning, they often regard Edward Abbey's nonfiction as simple environmental journalism, a disrespect that Trinh finds the minority writer struggling against today, and that Austin found the divorced woman struggling against at the turn of the century. When a writer is labeled as a representative of some out-of-favor, angry group, readers look not for literature but for rhetoric; and readers usually find what they are looking for. In the introduction to *Journey Home,* Abbey's voice booms, "I am not and never will be a goddamned two-bit sycophantic *journalist* for Christ's sake!" (xxii). Wendell Berry (1985) more softly says, "Mr. Abbey is not an environmentalist" (19). And I say, more softly still, Mr. Abbey's cow is not just a cow.

Chapter Six

"That One-Eyed Hereford Muley"

I am interested in exploring my personal ecology. I live from deer;
this voice has been fed from deer. I appreciate the fact that
I am made out of the animal I love.
Richard Nelson (Trimble 305)

I was sitting in a boring literature class one day, a shiny-faced, idealistic under-graduate, thinking about boys—only I had started calling them men. I was an animal science major, studying to become a ranch manager or a cowboy's wife, whichever came first.

My college sat on the side of a mountain, as many colleges do so that college professors can look down on the town from a lofty perch, and I was watching buzzards outside the classroom window, almost at eye level. The professor was asking us to decide whether Edward Abbey's narrative voice should be classi-fied as homodiegetic or autodiegetic—yawn.

The buzzards were putting me to sleep. Buzzards drift so aimlessly and effortlessly on thermals, especially in the hot rimrock desert country of West Texas. But just as my eyelids were drooping, the big black birds seemed sud-denly to change gears.

Instead of drifting, they began to circle with more of a purpose. Was a cow dead down there on Main Street? I wondered if they had put to sleep the old cowboy, Nicasio Ramirez, who always sat on the corner in the sun. As the cir-cle tightened, more and more buzzards appeared out of nowhere. First ten, then twenty; then I was watching a hundred, then a thousand buzzards circle right outside my classroom window. It was a once-in-a-lifetime sight!

I raised my hand.

"Sir!" I stammered excitedly, "The buzzards are gathering to fly south right outside the window! There are thousands of them!"

The professor frowned, told me to keep my mind in class, and went on about Abbey. I changed my major to English that day. The professor probably thought his lecture had inspired me, and he was right. I decided right there in that classroom, as the buzzards broke their circle and headed south, that *I* should be teaching Abbey.

One of my favorite images, one that appears over and over in Ed Abbey's books, is of a cowboy, riding along, spending his life and imagination looking at a shit-encrusted, fly-clouded, jouncing cow's butt. Chuckle.

Western movies always leave out the cowshit and horseshit; ever notice that? Shit just doesn't fit into the western myth. Buffalo chips might be useful as fuel, but not cow chips—well, maybe in India, but not in the American West.

People who don't believe in cowshit would not want to brand brammer calves—ever—not even with the toe of their boot over the spout. They wouldn't want to be hit by a cow tail when the yuccas are blooming, wouldn't want to shove an arm up a heifer's cervix to pull a calf, wouldn't want to climb into crowding chutes when spring grass is green, wouldn't like "mud" without rain, scours, flat rocks, scared wild cows. Yup, real cows do shit, and I've spent a lot of years staring at their southern ends. My imagination is probably ruined.

As a matter of fact, one of my fondest memories and best stories involves a hot, sleepy afternoon moving bulls, the world's slowest, most boring job. Bobbing in my saddle after a big dinner, I suddenly woke up to realize that the biggest bull had switched his tail over one of my bridle reins and clamped down hard, grabbing hold of the rein tightly. My horse, of course, wanted air—now. Luckily, being in Texas, I was using split leather reins instead of a looped Mc-Carty or rawhide reins and *romal*, so I quickly dropped the captured rein and let the wreck work itself out. When everything finally came loose and stopped, I was still horseback, no bones broken, and my bridle was still in one piece. My rein had simply slid through between the bull's tightly clamped tail and his butt. The green, sticky rein I rode with the rest of the day imprinted the cheap lesson forever on my memory.

Cowshit creates memories. When it appears between your sandaled toes, under hat brims, inside a torn shirt pocket, up a pant leg, gets into boots or eyes or hair, is imbedded between your teeth, or smeared all over your rope—usually you have just finished learning a cheap lesson. The cowshit sort of says, "And don't ever try that again."

I had a neighbor once who lived about ten miles down the dirt road toward town. Our groundwater had been polluted by oil fields (which was enabling the ranchers who owned the places where we worked to stay in the cow business). So I caught drinking water off my tin roof and stored it in a cistern. My neighbor, however, was horrified that I would drink birdshit. Her water came from a brown, muddy cow tank that turned green in the summer. Nobody ever got sick drinking after cows, she said, but birds she didn't quite trust.

I agreed. After a morning of flanking calves and gripping slimy tails, I seldom bothered to wash my hands before dinner. My healthy little daughter grew up having shit fights (starting out dry, ending wet) with her wild little country kid friends, and none of them ever missed a day of school because of illness. Playing hooky maybe, but sick—never.

But my camp was on a hill, with no muddy cow tank close by. And cows attract a lot of birds. There was never a time during summer when at least half a dozen vermilion flycatchers weren't diving around my yard. My trees bloomed with scarlet tanagers, summer tanagers, and orioles. Herds of deafening scissor-tails woke me up every morning long before daylight. So I had to drink bird-shit. Cowshit, as Wally McRae says, is just grass and water, but flies and water? Yuck.

So, you say. If I love cows this much, how can I read Abbey's condemning essay "Free Speech: The Cowboy and His Cow" and still love Abbey? He was a sexist, a drunk, an opinionated old fart—just like most of my closest friends. It is comforting to know how someone thinks.

When Abbey says that ranches today are tax write-offs for corporations, investment syndicates, and land and cattle companies (heavy on the land), and that "Western cattlemen are nothing more than welfare parasites"—I don't even wince. He's not talking about me. He makes a careful distinction between wage-earning cowboys and wannabes, between ranchers and instant rednecks, between nouveau westerners and old weather-beaten westerners, between pet horses and working horses, between cow ranching and elk or dude ranching, between inheritors and heritage, between the mythic American horseback knight (white hat) and the dumb working cowboy who stares at a cow's butt all day (black hat).

Overgrazing. Yeah, I winced at that, maybe even bled. Even though I don't feel too patronizingly protective toward plants—I've seen what they can do to mountains, cement, and asphalt—I still can't put overgrazing in the same humorous category as cowshit. So, for the past ten years, ever since a cowboy friend mailed me a dog-eared copy of Abbey's damn essay, I have been studying everything I can find about grass and grazing and historical land uses and predator-prey relationships and fire and Allan Savory and water tables and pampas grass and diversity and mass extinctions and mourning dove habitat and plate tectonics and soil composition and weather patterns and on and on and on and on.

When Abbey said domestic animals, like humans, will improve if hunted, was he talking to me?

* * *

I've been reading some great nature writers lately, trying to get ready for a new class I will teach this spring. I suppose, basically, that's what I try to write most of the time too. Sometimes I have cowboys riding through the scene, but they and I both know that the scene is the most important part.

I should be inspired as I read. That's the reason we ask students to read great literature: so that if they have the desire, they will know what to shoot for. But it isn't working. The more I read, the more inadequate I feel.

I could never describe spring better than Aldo Leopold does when he is on his hands and knees in the mud of the first thaw, searching for draba. I could never write the sublime better than Annie Dillard watching a bug eat a frog. Tolstoy has already described driving a team of horses through a snowstorm. The respect the hunter feels for the hunted has been done by Faulkner. Chekhov covered the conflict between subdivision and old land families. Willa Cather has given the land a nurturing and sensual male gender. Thoreau has already explained how cows help apples become wild apples, and Barry Lopez has shown us, sadly, that the wolf can never be a real wolf again.

So what is left for me to write? Has it all been said?

Finding a trail means that someone has already passed here safely, and sometimes that is important. I have traveled Abbey's road, and sometimes he has traveled mine. I fell in love two different summers while working at the Grand Canyon. I've been into the abyss. I've rafted the Rio Grande and ridden the Chisos trails. I've run my own cattle at the foot of the Guadalupes and in the desert beyond Boquillas Canyon. I've seen the far side of Mexico's mountains and glimpsed its wild cattle through the brush. I've pulled up my share of survey stakes and slept with the *griz*. I've drunk from some of the most remote and well-hidden water holes in the West. My dad, like Abbey's, was a pothunter, not a sportsman. My dad and brother twice won second place in the same varmint-calling contest Abbey cusses at the end of *One Life at a Time, Please.* But I'm not ashamed.

Ed Abbey writes about a mountain lion following him through Arizona's Arrivipa Canyon—a huge pile of slick rock. But years before Abbey ever saw that canyon, while wolves still roamed it, I gathered cattle and branded calves there. One misstep and a shod horse's hoof would slide straight down those slick rocks for a half mile. The pale, carefully worn trails that followed the levelest footing across the backbone of that sheer rock country were terrifyingly faint. The only way to gather it was to climb to that backbone and ride each rib. Someone either braver or dumber than I made those trails. But perhaps that same trailblazing cowboy would be frozen with fear if asked to teach a new college class that has never been taught before: no textbook, no guidelines, no trail through a volatile, controversial topic.

But perhaps the same motive pushed us both to travel unknown dangerous ground: the wildly beautiful canyons, and our cows, are at stake.

So. I think it's time someone stuck up for cows. They have been getting a lot of bad press lately. Cows supposedly produce methane gas, eat like locusts, cave in creek banks, compete with wildlife, drop disgusting "pies" around campgrounds, and just, in general, look stupid.

I've worked enough cows that sometimes even I have a hard time coming up with something nice to say about them. I've been stepped on, dragged, butted, pushed, kicked, smashed, knocked down, run over by, humiliated by, and hurt by the beasts, especially my feelings. I've also questioned their intelligence on many occasions. Baby calves are cute, true, but only for a couple of weeks.

So, in the process of trying to think of something good to say, I've been doing some research. In some parts of the world, cows are sacred. Mothers let their children starve to death while cows—potential food—roam freely through the house and garden. Sometimes the cow represents wealth and can be traded for a wife or used to impress the neighbors. According to Homer, the armor of one Roman soldier cost nine cows, while the more impressive armor of another cost one hundred cows.

Even Shakespeare knew his cows—always referring correctly to heifers, steers, and bulls. He also knew their habits ("About the sixth hour, when beasts most graze") and their predators ("As fox to lamb, or wolf to heifer's calf").

During the voyage of the *Beagle*, Charles Darwin discovered that certain insects—and therefore certain birds, and therefore certain predatory birds, and so on—are found only among cattle herds. He also discovered that cattle grazing and manuring changed the vegetation of the Pampas, but not necessarily for the worse. While the cattle kept the dominant tall, coarse, single-species grass at bay, less intimidating grasses and a much more complex variety of plants gained a foothold. A dominant species, in this case pampas grass, can take over an area without some kind of check. So, thinking like a mountain may include learning to respect plant predators too.

Perhaps the most sobering comment about the cow comes from a Scotsman writing in 1776, Adam Smith, in *The Wealth of Nations*. Smith says that Spaniards, when searching for a new country worth conquering, would ask about its abundance of gold or silver. On the other hand, the Tartars, a nation of shepherds ignorant of the uses of money, would look for a country abundant in cattle.

"Of the two," says Smith, "the Tartar notion, perhaps, was the nearest to the truth."

* * *

I've also been reading a book called *Of Sheep and Men*, by R. B. Robertson. I had already read *Of Wolves and Men*, by Barry Lopez, and I always like to look at several viewpoints before I make a decision. *Of Sheep and Men* is set in the beautiful grass-covered Scottish border highlands, where sheep have been grazing for eight thousand years. It always shocks me when I read a book about people who live halfway around the world and I realize that I know them.

The book describes the life, customs, and intricate subtle culture of the "herds" who tend the sheep. It's filled with cryptic little one-sentence gems like, "What exactly the herd does on the hill is as scantily reported as the happenings in the office, and often for the same reasons." When pressed by the author as to what he hoped to find when he set out to look over his hills, the herd would simply answer, "I'm hopin' to find nothing."

At one point, a New York lawyer shows up in the Highlands. He cunningly weaves his way into the hearts and confidences of the normally cautious and secretive herds by pushing their emotional buttons. Although the herds publicly swear that they are broke, the lawyer finds out about the tremendous amount of money that changes hands in the sheep and wool business. He is taken to a million-dollar highland ram sale, where he learns the "behind the scenes" and "under the table" secrets. Under the pretext of wanting to know why older wool smelled different from modern wool, he manages to get inside and is actually shown around a Highland wool factory. He claims to be interested in local color when in reality he is pumping the herds for priceless information. On his departure, the "ignorant" herds quickly disperse to buy a few shares of textile stock on the New York Stock Exchange.

Although sheep and their herds have a reputation for peace and docility, Robertson advises against trying to make war on them. It seems that the Roman Ninth Legion once crossed the border with an armored division of seven thousand soldiers to try to take the Scottish hills. The entire division simply vanished off the face of the earth. Not a helmet, wagon wheel, or grave has ever been found. Or so the story goes.

The author also advises against asking directions from local herds, because they know only two distances: "a wee bit" is from five feet to five miles, and "a good long way" is from five miles to somewhere close to infinity. Robertson also cautions against expecting to find the serene wisdom of pastoral shepherds in the Highlands, for the herds are

> as erratic in their thought and as anxious to change their minds in order to agree with everything you say to them as the border herds' wives are dogmatic and anxious to disagree with you before you have fully expressed your meaning. We have not yet decided which attitude is the most infuriating.

One chapter of the book deals with Robertson's frustrations in trying to collect "characters," either to photograph or to tell stories. "[T]he trouble with collecting characters," he finds, "is that characters who are willing to be collected are not real characters at all." They soon turn out to be either "scroungers or drunks, drunkenly grinding an ax which becomes blunter each time they put it to the whetstone."

So, Robertson offers a foolproof way of knowing whether or not one is dealing with true characters: find a place that seems deserted and spin a gold coin in the air. If the silence deepens, there might be someone worth listening to about. But if you are immediately surrounded by a clamoring throng of old and young, fighting to sell you something or elbow others away from the central position in front of your camera, you are not dealing with real characters.

When a herd dies, a handful of wool is put in the coffin with him so the Lord will know on the Day of Judgment that the man was a herd. The Lord is, of course, expected to take this into consideration when assessing the man's sins.

In still another dang book, Jeremy Rifkin's comical tirade against cows, *Beyond Beef: The Rise and Fall of the Cattle Culture*, the bull is described thus:

> The bull has always reminded us of our maleness—he represents generativeness, ferocious power, domination, and protection. He is the most territorial of beasts, passionate and aggressive, the embodiment of fertilizing power. The bull is pure unrestrained energy. A formidable force, he is fearless, unreconcilable, and purposeful.

Rifkin is hilarious. The bulls I've known spend 99.9 percent of their time napping. They have no problem restraining their energy, and I've never seen them protect a single thing. Because of their size and weight, bulls do have power, but they seldom have it under control. Most of the fence posts they knock over get knocked over while they are fighting with each other or scratching an itch, not when they're trying to get somewhere. Fighting bulls are such a joke: dust, bellering, crashing horns—but at best only skinning up each other's foreheads, hardly even drawing blood. No eyes get poked out, no guts are ripped open, nobody dies; they just like to make a lot of noise when they walk. The biggest, most muscle-bound ones are usually sterile. During breeding season, you can always find at least three of them bunched up together taking a nap while cows fifty yards away are riding each other. Passion, if they have any, lasts less than a minute.

I had a neighbor once who ran for Texas governor. He liked to hold million-dollar Brangus bull sales for his oil-field friends. One year, one of his big, black, million-dollar bulls kept getting into the heifer pasture on a neighboring ranch that I helped take care of. Me and a partner were trying at the time to get into the cow business ourselves. We knew that the horned Hereford outfit we were working for wouldn't want to keep those half-Brangus, half-Hereford calves. So we made a deal with the boss to buy all the half-breeds. The pasture held five hundred heifers, a handful of young seven-hundred-dollar Hereford bulls, and this million-dollar fence jumper. Figuring it would be a good cross—horned black baldies—maybe we weren't quite as diligent as we should have been about keeping ol' Hormone on his own side of the fence.

Genes are independent little no-see-'em critters who must have a sense of humor. Brangus are five-eighths Angus and three-eighths Brahman. I always thought it strange that muley (meaning hornless) black Angus come from cranky Scotland while nervous, gray or white, scary-looking horned Brahmans come from gentle India. When the two are crossed, the humorous little genes in the Angus blood whip off everybody's horns and turn everybody black, and the tricky little Brahman genes give everybody big ears and humped-up shoulders. Crossing them back onto Herefords, we knew, would calm down some of the silliness. The new cross would have a toned-down version of their daddy's ears and big shoulders, and his black hair color, but they'd have their mamas' hustle, good sense, hips, and white (baldy) faces; and the horns would come back. Don't ask me why.

Cattle people fight and argue and try to scientifically "prove" which breed is better, but cows are not much different from humans. For every blonde-headed hero there are dozens of black sheep in the family, and there's more difference within a breed than between them. It just boils down to what color you like or whether or not big floppy ears will freeze off or white tits will sunburn in your country. Peel off the hide and they all produce T-bones, hamburger, and chuck roasts. They all taste like beef—although a horned Hereford tastes a little better.

Or so I've heard. I'm not sure I've tasted any other breed. I've seldom eaten the fattened-up feedlot version either. There was always a broken-legged steer or a prolapsed heifer that needed to be ate. I always felt sorry for Longhorn breeders if they had to eat their tough old cripples, too, and thanked God and Mr. Kokernot that we raised tender Herefords, who didn't really need feedlot finishing.

To bring this wandering self- and Hereford-promotional story to a close, ol' Hormone produced only three black baldy calves. So much for passion, virility, aggression, fence jumping, and million-dollar price tags.

Comedian Rifkin also describes the cow:

The cow is one of the most gentle and sublime of creatures, the embodiment of patience. Her enlarged udders are available for all the world to suckle. She is nurturer and nourishment, the giver of life. She is self-contained, peaceful, a serene image, grounded and tranquil. The cow is purity, and represents the forces of benevolence and good in the world.

That one is especially funny. It's obvious that Rifkin has been looking at too many four-color calendars of cows and doesn't really know the meaning of "sublime." It's also obvious that he has never tried to milk an old desert range cow. First of all, she doesn't have "enlarged udders." Second, even with two stout horses, two stout ropes, and two stout cowpersons who know their business, it might not happen. Cows don't let down their milk unless they want to, and a bawlin' old cow, slingin' snot and stretched out on her side in the rocks and cactus, probably doesn't want to. Unless you smell like a calf, you won't get any milk, and even then you'd dang well better smell like *her* calf. She's sublime, alright. You'll never see a Hereford milk cow. Those black-and-white refrigerator magnets and salt-and-pepper shakers ain't cows. I don't know what they are.

* * *

On the Chihuahuan Desert where I have lived for the past thirty years, grass is short, bunched, and dust colored. Passers-through sometimes can't even see it. Visibility improves at sundown when the late evening light bathes the land in fuzzy gold. Except for the grass, this desert is like all deserts: hot, dry, and mute. Here green is not garish like fifties neon, but grayed, faded, and brittle. In the best of years, native gramas stay green only about two weeks. People who love this country prefer their grasses in khaki. Our blue is not royal but sun-bleached, like faded denim. No lipstick company would copy desert reds unless their customers wanted dignity instead of attention. Desert colors are not aggressive. They don't compete, don't shout. They steal your heart with a whisper.

The ground is rocky, rainfall sporadic, water sources tiny—the grass desert's three greatest assets. If any one of these factors were changed, this country would fill with something else: farms, industry, cities, and golf courses. Wide fifty-mile flats are broken by mountains but not mountain ranges. Even mountains in this country prefer to live scattered. Sometimes one, sometimes two, seldom more than four or five are bunched together. A local lion trapper calls them "islands." He says they keep our lion's gene pool viable by forcing dispersing kittens to make lengthy migrations.

Some call our mountains ghost mountains and say that at night they go away to play with other mountains, but I can see the mountains even at night. We also call the lions ghost cats. Except for trappers and hunters, you have to believe in mountain lions rather than see them. I believe. Trapper friends have shown me their tracks, their scat, their scrapings. A pretty good tracker myself, I can't find their sign or read it without help from a lion hunter, although I once found a dead deer covered with lion trash less than a mile from town. And once, I think I heard one growl at my dog. In northern California, in that half-light of gray dawn, maybe I saw one trotting easily with a little band of deer. When my presence became known, one of the gray animals, who seemed to be trailing a long tail, streaked away from the deer herd. It stopped just at the break of a hill to look at me when I whistled—typical coyote behavior, but normally not lion behavior according to the experts. As Hawthorne would say, my eyes could have been playing tricks in the half-light. Maybe I imagined the tail. Maybe at least one lion stops for a whistle like a coyote.

Mountain lions are very territorial. Where mountains occur in belts of wide, timbered ranges and prey is more abundant, lion territories are smaller. Lions don't seem to like open country, so a mountain island sometimes becomes home to only one lion, and by claiming the mountain, he or she may claim two hundred square miles or more. A male passing through may smell a female's territory markers and discover she is in heat. When more than one male shows up, the results are often similar to Saturday night at the bar—the first comer whips or kills the intruder, or vice versa. Studies done in Big Bend National Park show that one lion may claim the same territory for generations, sometimes until the patriarch or matriarch becomes sterile. More happily, before the race dies out, an aggressive teenager will kill and replace an aging mother or an aging male, or a hunter will do the same job. But time, heat, and distance frustrate the efforts of lion hunters. A few minutes after sunrise, scent trails evaporate. Ghosts.

When survival depends on limited food supplies, kittens may die of starvation. Prey bases are precious. Dispersing kittens and ragged grandparents sometimes end up in town, living for a while on pets, until the local newspaper editor looks up from his morning coffee and spots tawny fur in the apple tree. I find few mountain lion stories in Native American collections, but in the grass desert everyone has a lion story. One enterprising young lion followed a dog through a pet-door entrance at the back of a local restaurant, killed the dog in the kitchen, and dragged it back out the pet door and into the rocks to eat and cover with litter for later.

But few lions end up on the open flats except when passing through. Local ranchers capitalize on this knowledge by raising colts—a lion delicacy—in the flats. One border rancher who likes to test boundaries is raising a small band of sheep in his open flat country—just to prove he can attract eagles again and defy environmentalists. He blames the lack of eagles on their protection. He says the sky here used to be full of eagles until local sheepmen were put out of business. With no prey base, the eagles disappeared. So, he wants to feed eagles again, and somehow he thinks that will make "those damn environmentalists" mad.

For thirteen years I lived on a big ghost-mountain ranch whose scent markers enclosed more than 220 square miles, most of it fenced only by rimrock and canyon. When gathering cattle in this country, we would find the same cow in the same place year after year. The ranch raised horned Herefords, and although they never drew blood, they hooked and horned each other unmercifully until some kind of status quo was reached, even inside corrals. Cows in my country become very territorial. Ideal country to a cow is flat. Although cows seldom kill one another, they are cruel when defending their territories. Old cows, young cows, lame cows, cows with any kind of weakness, even if it's just lack of courage, are pushed to the fringes. Like wolves, the alpha males and females eat first and best. But like wolves, they also babysit each other's kids. Also like wolves, cows are very careful where they step. Rocks make their feet sore. One can follow their meandering soft, dusty water trails for miles and never find a pebble. Wolves loved to trot down those soft trails too—it was one of their downfalls.

The cows that hold the territory along the streams that run through the flats are the most aggressive, but I always liked best the ones who ranged up on the rocky points with the lions. Seems like they always had the best calves and the longest horns, but maybe I just wanted that to be true because my territories too were always easy to defend because no one else wanted them. I like horned cattle. I believe that if you take away their horns, they become stupid and help-less. They can't defend their territories, and they can't protect their calves. It's the same with women.

But I also remember an old one-eyed Hereford muley who didn't fit the stereotype. In her honor, I would like to speak a word for absolute freedom and wildness.

* * *

A partner and I once bought some old cows that local ranchers were selling. When a rancher sells an old cow, he thinks she won't make another winter and he wants to sell her before she crumbles. We thought we might be able to buy these old cows cheap, squeeze one more calf out of them, and get ourselves a start in the cow business.

We also leased country the ranchers didn't want. It was too rough, too re-mote, too prone to losing its water sources in dry years. The place was called "Dry Canyon." Ranchers sometimes discover a piece of country within their territories where water dries up too often, where cow teeth wear out too fast, or where calf numbers are low because bulls can't handle the steep terrain well enough to get around and breed the cows. Sometimes, when country never makes a profit and some honest, hardworking kids come along who want to try to put together something of their own, a benevolent rancher might lease that bad country. Bankers will also sometimes loan money to hardworking, proud people who will somehow pay back their debts. And as the old ranchers, the banker, and the kids all know—gambling sometimes works.

So, we leased Dry Canyon, put down our scent markers, and we had a plan. Healthy young heifers were too expensive, and Dry Canyon too remote, to husband them through their first calf. Prime cows were impossible to buy at any price, so we carefully selected and bought the twenty best grannies we could find. We had also leased some state park land that would make a good holding pasture and had enough grazing for about a month. The park needed the grass "mowed" a little to keep the fire hazard down. The grannies could re-cover their strength there after their calves were shipped. We could hold them on that country and wait for good cool fall weather to trail them into Dry Canyon. Dependable cool weather in the desert sometimes doesn't come until December.

Dry Canyon was in great shape to receive them. Grass was good, and every pocket had caught a little water. We planned to drop the grannies on the rim that looked off into Big Aguja Canyon and gradually move them, as water sources dried up on the rim, down toward the most dependable water in the bottom of Dry Canyon, saving that grass until last.

We knew the drive in would be hard on them, up and down steep mountain trails, no water until the end. But once we got them to the lease, all the drives from then on would be mostly downhill as they got heavier and heavier with calf. They wouldn't have to—and we knew they couldn't, no matter what—climb back out until they were much thinner, with their calves walking on their own feet. It wouldn't be easy for the old ladies. But it was a good gamble.

We had the grannies preg-checked by a vet to ensure that each carried a spring calf. We wouldn't need a bull. If the venture worked, we'd have the old cows to sell at a better price, hopefully, than we gave for them, and their calves too. We'd pay back the bank, borrow less money next time, and make another gamble until we could get a start. My partner and I were a little younger than the ranchers who were selling the old cows. We figured we could make longer circles horseback and we still believed in our own immortality.

All the cows were good native horned Herefords, except one. She came from a ranch we neighbored and seemed in good shape except for being hornless and one-eyed. She had evidently had an operation for cancer eye—which consisted of digging out the bad eye with a pocketknife and sewing the bloody hole shut. Bad eyes are common in white-faced Herefords, especially the ones that live in desert country where sunlight is intense. Because she had a defect, and no horns, the horned cattle hooked her constantly.

The trail to Dry Canyon is only one cow wide. Steep rock walls rise and fall on each side, making cowboying difficult. We couldn't afford help. Even friends expect day wages and a meal, and this was horse-killing country. Four of us took on the job. My daughter's grandpa, over seventy years old, rode point to keep them on the trail. We didn't figure he would need to stop any runaways. The most patient rider, my little daughter, rode drag. We knew she would lolly-gag along, happily sucking on her saddle strings, looking for birds and letting the cattle string out long and slow. Some people like a wide herd, but cows don't get as hot or as tired when allowed to trail one another in single file. The other two riders, myself and my partner, would ride swing, climbing up and down the cliffs at the sides of the herd, trying to keep the cattle strung out and trailing. But we soon discovered that two riders could ride along in front and chat, and two could ride along in the rear and chat. The old one-eyed cow, because the others picked on her, struck the lead and never stopped. The others simply followed, trying to hook her in the butt.

The one-eyed cow's habits became more interesting as the winter wore on. When we gathered the grannies to move them to the next water hole, the old muley was already there. She had new salt and water trails well marked for the followers. As the herd moved in, she moved out, and sometimes one or two went with her.

Toward spring, we started finding dead cows and dogie calves. Although the grass held, the old cows were struggling too hard in the rough country, and the water was drying up fast. We found one cow down, still alive, but covered with black lice. Her calf, still nursing, had a ring of black lice around his white nose. I thought about Barry Lopez's theory about the "conversation of death." I wondered if the old cow had sacrificed herself to the lice for the sake of the herd, since none of the others was infested. Mother Nature has no sympathy for the weak. Someone called me Mother Nature once when I said anybody dumb enough to break a leg ought to be left there to die of thirst. We picked up the calf and shot the cow.

On the morning of the last move to more water, we rose in the dark and trailered our horses to the end of the road. The sky was turning gray as we stepped into our saddles, and the March wind had already started to pick up. When I headed into Dry Canyon I always tried to be prepared for emergencies. I knew we would be without food, water, or help for many hours. Most of the cowboys I have known never carry food or canteens. They never carry first-aid kits. Not because of any foolhardy attempt at heroics, but because if the day is going to be long enough to need food and water, then the horse doesn't need to be carrying one more ounce of weight. If the animal that is doing all the work can't drink or eat, reasons the cowboy, then the human the animal is packing around sure doesn't need anything. Horses should always eat and drink first.

I knew that nobody happens down the trail in Dry Canyon. No photographers, no artists, no backpackers, no rangers, nobody. We were on our own. In my pocket was a tiny jar of Carmex, relief against the painful, bleeding chapped lips I knew would come after eighteen hours in the saddle on a hot, wind-whipped March day. Real cowboys grow mustaches to protect themselves from chapped lips. I can't seem to grow one.

Around my neck I had tied a cotton bandana that sorta matched my shirt. I hoped my partner would think it was just a dumb female fashion statement. I am cowboy enough to disdain the cotton bandana under normal conditions. In winter and fall, my neck rag is silk, like it ought to be. But I knew I would need no warmth today. River rafting had taught me the cooling effects of a cotton bandana soaked in water and tied dripping around my neck. I thought that trick had saved my life at least twice. Dry Canyon had also taught me that bones break, oak brush limbs and yucca puncture, horseshoes come off, and bandages are hard to come by. So I thought the bandana would be an inconspicuous first-aid kit for both me and my horse.

Perhaps my immortality had already begun to crack.

The rest of my safety precautions were common cowboy gear. I wore high-heeled boots so my foot wouldn't slip through the stirrup in case my horse fell. I wore leather leggins to turn the brush from my largest veins and arteries. I wore a long-sleeved shirt and a broad-brimmed Navajo creased hat to turn the sun. I looked at the starry, cloudless sky and chose not to pack my slicker, which would just tear up anyway in Dry Canyon's brush. I wore tight-fitting cotton jeans that would not bunch up in wrinkles to rub the insides of my knees raw, and I wore no belt to catch on the saddle horn and tie me to a horse I might want to get away from. You can sometimes tell what kind of horses people ride by whether or not they wear belts.

And I was riding a new horse. As we mounted and started up the steep jeep trail that led into Dry Canyon, the wind tore at my hat. I tightened the stampede string that kept it in place to act like a helmet to protect my feeble brain in case a limb or a rock tried to get me. But the wind was strong and getting stronger. I knew it would be an all-day battle to keep the hat in place, and I knew I might need both hands to keep my horse under—not control, but maybe distraction. So I rode back to the truck, threw my hat in the cab, and tied the cotton bandana around my hair to keep it out of my face. My head was now exposed to more danger than I usually risk, but I figured I would just lose my hat anyway when it sailed off into one of the deep canyons. If I got into a storm with my new horse, a real likely time for trouble would be when I grabbed too fast for a wind-loosened hat and was off-balance and one-handed.

My partner wears a hat with a much smaller brim, tightly curled on the sides, and has very little hair to keep it pulled down over. He never leaves his hat behind, but he did lose it once, and got terribly sunburned. I found it a couple of weeks later by following what I thought would be the wind's trail. I was right and the hat lay right where I expected it to be: due east, at the foot of the first dry creek bank where it could hide from the wind. That also happened one March.

Riding a new horse is like no other experience. My skin tingled with awareness. My eyes and ears and all six senses searched ahead for trouble while I pretended to be lost in thought and relaxed. I knew the wind would pick up my long-fringed leather leggins and throw them at my horse's neck. So, nonchalantly, I fiddled with them and flipped them around, first one and then the other, getting my horse used to the booger, as I chatted with my partner. Up ahead, somewhere in the darkness, I heard the wind hit the dry leaves of a live oak and shake it like an Indian rattle. Live oaks do their fall shedding in the spring for some reason. Had we been beside the tree at that moment, I'd have jumped with fright and startled my horse. Charlie Siringo used to claim that cowboys rode horses so much that they, too, would shy at a windblown piece of paper when they walked down a sidewalk in town. I've always believed it's the other way around, that cowboys taught horses to shy at paper.

It's like riding over a covey of quail and have them hit the air under you, or a big jackrabbit jumps out of her shade. The horse sees those sights in his home pasture daily but becomes frightened because the rider tenses for action and the horse doesn't see the danger that its rider has evidently seen. There was a bright purple prickly pear patch in the East Pruitt pasture that every horse in my string shied at. Those same purple cactus were everywhere, so it must have begun when I became startled in that spot for some reason. The next time we passed it, the horse remembered and became tense. Then, expecting the horse to get tense, I'd tense in that spot. Then, forgetting which horse got nervous there, I'd tense up no matter which one I was riding, and so it went until every horse I rode knew that particular purple cactus patch. Anyway, I mentally prepared myself to remain calm when the wind rattled a live oak beside me today. There were no live oaks in this horse's home pasture.

The blowing dust and tiny rocks were already getting into my hair, eyes, and nose. This would be a black booger day. I cleared my throat repeatedly, puffed my cheeks full of air and shook my head violently, expelling wind to drive out the dust like an escaped balloon—pretending to cuss the weather. If I had had any money in my pocket, I'd have been jingling that too. I kept up this coughing, cursing, leggin-flipping frenzy until the wind finally hit a tree next to me and my horse didn't bat an eye.

After the first long uphill pull, my horse's head began to swing easily between the slack reins of my *mecate,* and neither wind nor snapping leather fringe seemed to worry him enough to expend more energy than necessary. Perhaps because of the weather, the climb, and the early hour, the horse knew this was going to be a long, long day and he better save his energy. So, he finally convinced me to relax and save mine too.

Many hours later, when we got our wobbling old grannies to the expected water hole, it was dry. We pushed on to the next—also dry. We were in trouble. Could the old cows live to reach the last water hole on the rim of the canyon, and if they lived to reach it, would there be water? Would any of them still be alive the next time we came back? This was too much stress on old cattle. The gambling odds had suddenly shifted. Stumbling, staggering, stringing saliva with every agonized step, the old ladies inched their way toward the last water hole. I cussed, jerked on the reins, and drove spurs into my horse unmercifully. He traveled too fast. He pushed too hard. I had to keep circling him to keep him backed off the old cows. The more I tried to slow him down, the more antsy he became. I cussed. I jerked him around. I don't think I've ever treated a horse worse. My own frustration, knowing we had lost the gamble, was coming out in the horse. His neck and shoulders were covered with white lather. I think I wanted him to buck me off, hurt me, give me a reason to quit.

We didn't make it. When we reached the last water, the old cows just stood and drooled. The country rose in a circle almost straight up from the water hole—yearling country. We looked around and figured we'd find most of these old cows lying right where they stood the next time we rode in. But, as we sat there, letting our horses drink and avoiding each other's eyes, I noticed the old one-eyed cow slip off over the rim and down a deer trail. She was pushing on to the more permanent water and grass in the canyon below. I marked the spot in my memory. We might need that trail.

Back in civilization, another six hours later, we heard that winds had been clocked at over a hundred miles per hour in the mountains that day. A roof had blown off at the airport, and trees had blown down on the college campus. I had forgotten all about the wind.

By spring only ten cows and fifteen calves remained alive. One of them was the one-eyed muley. She had raised a good calf, and she led us back out. I made up my mind that when shipping time came, I'd insist on running her one more year.

But I didn't. We cut our losses and finally, years later, repaid the debt. We gave up the Dry Canyon lease and never went back. But maybe we should have. That country made good horses. It raised my daughter horseback and taught me to look at a one-eyed cow with respect, something my more expensive college education never did.

* * *

But I wouldn't call that old one-eyed cow wild, exactly. I've known some cows who were so wild they couldn't be gathered. Constantly pursued by some of the West's finest cowboys, those phantom cows lived long, wild lives, were never branded, and learned not to leave tracks. (My lion-runnin' friend, Roy McBride, always interrupts my story here to correct me and say that they did leave tracks. But I remind Roy that only he could see them. For the rest of us, there were no tracks.) I've seen mule deer in Texas, shot at every deer season, and often by poachers in between, who didn't run from an approaching pickup, horse, or foot traveler. But nobody in a pickup and few people horseback ever catch a glimpse of renegade cattle. Foot travelers better hope they don't.

I have worked cattle in places where, when I heard a twig snap, I had only a few tense moments in which to decide whether to run for my life or give chase. Some of those old, wild, sharp-horned, brush-popper cows came out of a manzanita thicket like a freight train, aiming for my horse's belly. I've helped pull weak cows out of deep mud where they had bogged down, only to have them turn and try to kill me for my efforts. Thoreau in his sissy-sounding nineteenth-century words calls it "sportiveness in cattle" and says it is usually "unexpected." They'll nearly all try to kill you, though, so you start expecting it; then you are disappointed if they don't.

Cows are often called stupid when they step on a cowboy's foot, when they take his horse away from him, when they blow snot down his neck while he's trying to brand their calf. They are called stupid when they get old, smooth-mouthed, and stiff-jointed and refuse to get on the truck that will permanently take them away from their pastures. They are called stupid when they silently lose a tracker in noisy, slippery shale, or lie down and disappear behind a foot-high bush. They are called stupid when they outhear, outsee, and outsmell their tracker. I've heard college-educated cowboys humbly admit to being out-smarted by a stupid cow.

Although ranchers "protect" cows in order to raise every calf, the cow is quite capable of taking care of herself. Even in the heyday of the wolf, dinners of baby calf were few. According to my friend Roy, wolves had much better success with weaned yearlings. Antelope and deer with young fawns often bed down with horned mama cows. I know one Montana rancher who has so much faith in his own ornery cows that he voluntarily makes a home for Yellowstone's problem grizzly bears who can't get along with tourists. "I seldom have trouble with trespassers," he says with a sly grin.

Maybe the number of times an animal has killed a man should determine wildness? The cow beats the *griz* a hundred times over. I once knew a crippled cow, down and paralyzed from calving, who still almost killed a cowboy. As he tried to help her drink from a bucket, she hooked him down, then pounded, slashed, and scraped him through the brush and rocks for several long minutes before he was finally able to crawl for his life. As Thoreau would say, she was "not yet subdued to man."

I've helped pull calves from wild heifers, down and dying trying to deliver a backward calf, who would jump up and run off, leaving their calves unlicked because they smelled like a human. Like all wild animals, cows react to changes in weather, showing restlessness and nervousness when a storm is brewing. I've seen three hundred heifers sniff the breeze off a blue norther, throw number nines in their tails, and stampede. Or, as Thoreau would say, they were "running about and frisking in unwieldy sport" as they "shook their heads, raised their tails and rushed up and down a hill."

Thoreau enjoyed seeing his neighbor's cow break out of her pasture early in the spring and boldly swim the river like the buffalo. I've seen cattle hump up with their snow-covered backs against the wind, like buffalo, and wait patiently for the three-day thaw they seemed to know was coming. I've seen them break ice for a drink. Bison will sweep snow away with their heads in order to find feed, but cows prefer to let the wind do the work and will drift until they find a windswept mesa. History is full of tales of abandoned cow herds left to die in a blizzard and found alive with new calves the following spring. Of course, that happened in the days before fences stopped cows from drifting. And sometimes the snow comes just too deep and neither cows nor bison nor caribou make it.

Like all animals, cows have to be taught to eat hay or feed cubes. This doesn't come naturally. On some big desert ranches where cows are never taught, a drouth can wipe out an entire herd. I've seen antelope learn to come to the feed ground to eat. Friends Bill and Sherry Dugan used to feed hay to the Yellowstone elk every winter using sleighs and their big workhorses, yet I've known wild cows who refused to eat and starved themselves to death once corralled.

In Arizona, near Mayer, the winter of sixty-six or sixty-seven, I helped drag hay, one bale at a time behind a snowmobile, to little bands of cows found trapped under pine trees where they had tramped out their own deep snow prison. They were so hungry and desperate they were eating each other's tails, yet some wouldn't eat the hay I brought to them. These were the wild cows that no one ever saw in normal weather. That winter many Navajos also starved, and antelope stood next to helicopter-dropped hay and refused to eat it. Lulled into carelessness mild winter after mild winter, Arizonans were unprepared. I would bet Arizonans are unprepared today.

In spite of their wildness, classic cow characters to compare with Hemingway's marlin, Faulkner's bear, or London's dog-wolves are nonexistent, even in cowboy literature. This surprises me because everyone I know has a story about some bull, some cow, some heifer, some steer, or some calf. A few characters show up in cowboy poetry: Bruce Kiskaddon's "Long Eared Bull," "The Cow and Calf," "A Calf's Troubles"; and Gail Gardner's "The Sierry Petes," which casts the devil as a maverick steer. A few show up in Australian books.

I can think of only one good cow character in cowboy fiction: J. P. S. Brown's old maverick steer, Sun Spot. Brown characterizes the steer in such a way that I know the steer—how he likes to nap on south-facing slopes to warm the white spot on his side, how he has managed to evade capture, where he drinks, where he eats. The cowboys, of course, catch him, and, of course, turn him loose.

The only thing I don't like about Brown's portrait is the name. I've never named a cow. Cows are not pets. The "too familiar" relationship between person and pet seems disrespectful somehow. I'm sure an animal rights person would say not giving names to animals is simply distancing yourself from what you will kill and eat, but milk-pen calves and the steers who are kept up and put on feed for slaughter usually do get named and petted. Instead, I think not naming an animal is a form of respect. Naming an old range cow just seems like something the cow wouldn't like. She's not a human and she's proud of it. I got to know a lot of them quite well, but I always called them respectfully "that old high-horned cow who hangs out at Last Chance" or "that old one-eyed Hereford muley."

* * *

Buffalo and deer were sacred animals to the native people who depended on them for meat. Considering them spirits, gods, other nations, the native people respectfully and reverently tried to live a sacred life in order to be worthy of the sacred meat. Altars, talismans, prayers, dances, feasts, fasts, games, and celebrations—many religious rituals surrounded the killing of the buffalo.

Old age in nature is cruel. No longer able to digest the native grasses, lame, infested with parasites, sexually impotent, often excluded from the herd, an old buffalo faces slow starvation. Overpopulation in nature is also cruel. Calves are left on the birthing ground or kicked off too young. Fertility slows down and stops because of malnutrition, and again, slow starvation is nature's final leveler. The buffalo understands that the opportunity to become meat is a gift from the Great Spirit. Like a bride, though, meat should be taken only by a worthy hunter.

Today my people do not worship their Hereford buffalo. My people eat, worthy or not, without ritual. Few of my people pray at all over their food, and those who do never mention the Hereford buffalo. After this selfish prayer, my people eat the sacred meat without reverence. My people call the Hereford buffalo stupid, slow, and dirty. My people do not want to share the cool shade of the sacred trees, do not want the Hereford buffalo to eat the sacred prairie grasses and drink the sacred water which the Great Spirit gave to them.

In an essay called "The Hunter," Larry Littlebird of Laguna Pueblo tells stories about winter meat. He begins:

> It is fall. There is a special clarity in the way light appears at this time of year. And it gives my memory a sense of another time, a time when my young eyes can see beyond the haze and the world stands out, still, brilliant, and defined. In the fall, all talk and thoughts turn to hunting. As the stories of the deer and the hunter unfold detail by detail, in my child's mind, images of the deer appear and take shape.

His words give my memory, too, a sense of another time, and bring into focus an old picture of my daughter. It is fall. She is a small girl-child, wearing tiny leather boots made from the sacred hide of the Hereford buffalo. She wears a tiny leather belt, tiny leather gloves, tiny leather chaps, tiny silver spurs with tiny leather spur straps, and a great big cowboy hat with a great big feather from a red-tailed hawk stuck defiantly in the leather hatband. Her medicine.

She stands with her face close to the faces of the silent young animals that have been loaded onto cattle trucks. She watched as many of those animals were born. She watched them play in the sacred prairie grass as sacred white-faced babies. She gently painted their castration and branding wounds with *tecole* to keep them safe from screwworms. During the ordeal, she petted their curly white foreheads, trying to calm their fears as they struggled to be re-united with their mothers. My daughter's hands have touched their soft, clean red and white hair. Her feet have touched the soft earth trails their feet have made, showing her the route to water, off the mountain, through the catclaw. In my daughter's veins runs the red living waters from their ancestors' meat. In my daughter's long hair shines the health of their ancestors' fat.

She knows these sacred animals have always shown respect for all other nations. They have shared the sacred pastures equally and eaten only the prairie grasses the Great Spirit gave them. They have shared the sacred water with all nations. They have begun no wars but ended many. Today they have been given the gift of becoming meat so their own nation can continue to prosper and will not starve, and so my daughter's people too can continue to prosper and will not starve. She knows this is all part of the Great Spirit's plan.

But she wonders if her people deserve this sacred meat. Will her people re-member to sing the songs, dance the dances, tell the stories, and say the prayers? My little daughter looks into the liquid brown eyes, fringed with long soft white lashes. The calves look quietly through the slats of the cattle truck into her blue eyes. My little daughter weeps.

Conclusion

Collapsing the Wild/Domestic Dichotomy

Having worked for ten years in a designated wilderness area (back-country patrol and scientific fieldwork) I found that my sense of place as wilderness diminished as my familiarity increased. The loss of that "wild" feeling was a bit like the loss of innocence: I might sigh, but I wouldn't want it back.
C. L. Rawlins

Mary Austin and I both lived in the West and came to know some of its desert places intimately. As a storyteller myself, I recognized Austin's power immediately and understood that it was coming through her animal stories, since my own life among animals has helped me see deeply into Austin's writing. Animal stories operate on a mythic, psychological level, especially today because our lives have become so distanced from animals. Usually branded as juvenile, however, animal stories are seldom studied seriously by literary scholars. Domestic animals especially have been ignored.

Perhaps the first step in reimagining domestic animals should be to illuminate the ways they have been stereotyped in American literature, just as early feminist critics did for women. This effort on behalf of domestic animals would parallel the feminist project, which, as Cheryll Glotfelty explains, contributed to

> the vital process of consciousness raising by exposing sexist stereotypes—witches, bitches, broads, and spinsters—and by locating absences, questioning the purported universality and even the aesthetic value of literature that distorts or ignores altogether the experience of half the human race. (xxiii)

Austin and I would also question the universality and aesthetic value of literature that distorts or ignores the experience of half the animal world as well, and possibly for gender-related reasons. Domestic animals have been portrayed as oppressed, passive, ignorant, destructive, and sexless while wild animals are portrayed as free, pugnacious, smart, nondestructive, and virile. Like all binary oppositions, these stereotypes do not hold up under scrutiny either as metaphor or as reality.

Glotfelty also advises modern ecocritics to study "the environmental conditions of an author's life—the influence of place on the imagination—demonstrating that where an author grew up, traveled, and wrote is pertinent to an understanding of his or her own work" (xxiii). I believe all research is influenced by personal experience, so perhaps my animal-immersed life has enabled me to find meaning in Austin's animal stories that other critics have overlooked. Because I began my education in a one-room rural school, I bristle along with Austin at denigration of rural education and communities. Karen Langlois, for instance, finds Austin "[h]indered by her inadequate academic background" (157). This is another pervasive stereotype that is easily challenged. Although Iowa farmers are often mocked as midwestern illiterates, in reality Iowa has led the nation in both literacy rates and SAT scores every year but one since testing began (U.S. Department of Education 1993, qtd. in Reynolds 474). Recognizing the failure of big-city schools to provide quality education, a 1997 article in *Orion* magazine calls for reruralization of education (McKibben). David W. Orr, asking his thought-provoking question "Is Environmental Education an Oxymoron?" answers that "it is sobering to note that the only people who have lived sustainably in the Amazon rain forests, the desert Southwest, or anywhere else on earth could not read (which is not to say that they were uneducated)" (149).

Several Austin critics also denigrate the time she spent in small towns. Melody Graulich claims that Austin rejected "the conformity of the midwestern small town with its repressive religions, its anti-intellectualism, and its rigid gender roles," and notes that a female character in Austin's *A Woman of Genius* is " '[h]emmed and pinned in' by the book's villain[,] the 'social ideal' of small-town America." Although acknowledging that Austin "associated the West with liberation," Graulich still believes that Austin was oppressed by the small town: "If Wallace would not leave the stultifying small desert towns, she would go alone" (Afterword 387; Introduction 4, 11–12, 15). John P. O'Grady also sees Austin as hampered by the "artistically stultifying environment of remote mining towns"(126). Yet most Austin critics also agree that the quality of her writing peaks in *The Land of Little Rain* (1903), *The Basket Woman* (1904), *Isidro* (1905), and *The Flock* (1906)—the writing she produced while living in that "stultifying" place. Austin and I argue that rural places are inspiring and quite compatible with living lightly on the land.

Austin's genuine respect for her neighbors, their stories, and their various cultures would have deepened her awareness of animal metaphor, symbolism, and psychic power. Her animistic sense of place and her affection for the smallest of the "furry people" would have broadened this awareness into full and meaningful insight. As she says of herself, "Without apparently having any choice about it, progress has meant for [me] a series of forward flashes, long spells of concentrated observation, patient, even anguished inquiry, and suddenly thunder, lightning, rainbow, and the sound of wings" (*Earth* 217). Austin would have listened to animal stories constantly while living in a rural culture in which storytelling revolved around hunting stories, work, and close observation of animals on a daily basis. She wrote in order to create new American myths, and she discovered that the best way to accomplish that task was through animal stories. Consequently, she created powerful animal characters.

Recognizing that gender bias was causing the West to be misrepresented in American literature, Austin reasoned rightly that wilderness and wildness were falsely imagined human constructions. In actuality, she observed, humans learn not exotic freedom but real domesticity from "wild" animals: homemaking, territory claiming, food storing, working, raising and educating young, forming various social groups, making or following trails. Using animal stories she places women in the "wilderness," in the West, in history, literature, and religion. Through animal stories she attempts to give value to women who were neither virgins nor mothers, to value women's stories and women's work, to imagine women as strong and capable leaders, and to portray women as being capable of making choices about their own lifestyles.

In addition, she uses animal stories to reimagine the western male as gentle, nurturing, and humble, with the right to perform and enjoy domestic work. She finds wildness in both genders and domesticity in both, just as she finds wild animals very domestic and domestic animals very wild. Both Greek myth and Native American stories portray father sky and mother earth as partners, not rivals or combatants. But, as Leslie Fiedler explains, pagan goddess worship was replaced and suppressed by Christianity's extreme patriarchy. The goddess archetype resurfaced as the Virgin Mary, but was further repressed by Protestant religions. Frighteningly, it reappeared once more in the Puritan imagination as the witch, and perhaps again in modern times as Gaia. Austin believed that until humans reconcile father sky with mother earth as partners, these warring archetypes will not rest in our psyches.

Austin uses animal stories to argue against all linear, dualistic, or hierarchical thinking in general, reversing those animals who usually represent the common, the primitive, or the unbeautiful with their more glamorous counterparts. Through sheep, coyotes, cows, and buzzards, she encourages respect for the masses, the racially other, the old, the eccentric, the traditionally "illiterate cowhand" (Stegner *Sound* 256), and "ignorant" rural people. Austin also uses animal stories to argue against hierarchies based on false measures of intelligence or language.[1]

In order to write the kind of literature that would dissolve hierarchies and better represent democratic thinking, Austin needed a new genre. Decades ahead of deconstruction she was blurring boundaries between literature and folklore, hoping "all the literature will be the possession of all the people, and the distinction between 'popular' and real literature will cease to exist" ("Non-English"

611). She also wanted to blur distinctions between formal literature and women's gossip, between literature and storytelling, between literature and music, between prose and poetry, between fiction and nonfiction, between adult and children's literature, and even between human and animal discourse. Her most successful books follow a strange new narrative formula that Faith Jaycox calls "genre defying" and Carl Bredahl labels "divided narrative." She was a champion of noncanonical works almost before an American canon existed, and she credits the Negro, the Hispanic, and the Native American with the production of music and literature that is "not only expressive of life as it is being lived among us, but at the same time spiritually satisfying" (Austin "Regional Culture" 476). Austin believed that literature could be a powerful tool for reform, but also that, like government and religion, sometimes literature itself needed reform.

I wish I could close this book by simply reprinting Barry Lopez's beautiful essay "The American Geographies," in which he weaves a tribute to those who truly know their homes. He calls "the packaging and marketing of land as a form of entertainment" something "sinister and unsettling," and says it distorts even further the complexities of place in the public imagination, creating "a ground on which experience is imposed" rather than "from which experience grows." He says that

> to really come to an understanding of a specific American geography, requires not only time but a kind of local expertise, an intimacy with place few of us ever develop. There is no way around the former requirement: if you want to know you must take the time. It is not in books. (118)

Yet fourth-generation land managers who have watched their places suffer through drouth and flood, freezing and thawing, hail and wind, who have also watched the healing and blooming that come after good rains and sunshine, are forced to comply with the book. Lopez says that "while American society continues to value local knowledge as a quaint part of its heritage, it continues to cut such people off from any real political power." This is as true "for small farmers and illiterate cowboys as it is for American Indians, Native Hawaiians, and Eskimos" (124). I would apply all he says about place to animals as well. The more one really knows wild animals, the more domestic they seem. The more one knows domestic animals, the wilder they seem. And the same is true of people. The best cooks, most fastidious housekeepers, and worst gossips I have ever known personally were cowboys and hunters.

Austin also uses animal stories to explain that becoming at home in a place is a long, sometimes painful, subtle process. "In the long run," she states cryptically, "the land wins" ("Regional Culture" 474). She recommends studying animals as they adapt to new places. Although Austin never used Foucault's word *subjectivity,* she was asking serious questions long before he did about the ways experience shapes a people. "When all these combined influences of climate and landscape line and occupational rhythms and class adjustment and religious faith have worked upon a given people long enough to have their effect dominate over the effect of any previous set of influences," she says, "we have a native culture" (AU 625). She also asks rhetorically, "[W]hat is a race but a pattern of response common to a group of people who have lived together under a given environment long enough to take on a recognizable pattern?" ("Regionalism" 97). She believes that in the best regional American literature "the region must enter constructively into the story, as another character, as the instigator of plot" ("Regionalism" 104–5). The desert is a great leveler. Everyone needs protection from the sun: birds must shade their eggs instead of keeping them warm, plants keep their brains underground, the shepherd weaves a "little screen of twigs" to protect his head, flowers and women both fade quickly (*Land* 5, 4, 58, 79, 66). Using the image of a hawk and a sparrow sharing a strip of shade during the hot "white truce of noon" (*Land* 6), Austin portrays a desert capable of forcing even the lion to lie down with the lamb—at least at noon. Yet her theories, which Mark Schlenz calls "semiotic regionalism," cannot be reduced to simple geographical determinism. Instead of cause and effect, Schlenz says, Austin stresses dialectics between place and people, historical and biophysical (65). Rather than the desert simply determining lifestyle, basket makers, *curanderos,* irrigators, miners, cattle and sheep, horse and burro—and all animals—contribute toward maintaining the desert both physically and spiritually.

It is difficult to say whether American geographers, critics, or poets began the trend toward focusing on smaller and smaller places like one particular farm (Frost, Leopold), one particular river or pond (Twain, Thoreau), one island (Jewett), one fictitious county (Faulkner), or one particular desert community (Austin). But as the literary focus became grounded in smaller places, American literature both improved and became more universal. Austin's own writing makes an excellent example for the influence of place. Her first words about the coyote, written when she first arrived in the desert Southwest, are flat and trite: "During the night the coyotes came close up to the camp and howled, and growled, and barked, and shrieked like so many demons. There seems to be no limit to the hideous noises these animals can produce" (*One Hundred* 10). As she lived with them, however, coyotes grew tremendously, both realistically and spiritually, in her imagination:

> The coyote is your true water-witch, one who snuffs and paws, snuffs and
> paws again at the smallest spot of moisture-scented earth until he has

freed the blind water from the soil. . . . I have trailed a coyote often, going across country, perhaps to where some slant-winged scavenger hanging in the air signaled prospect of a dinner, and found his track such as a man, a very intelligent man accustomed to a hill country, and a little cautious, would make to the same point. (*Land* 10–11)

Austin found that the environmental water and grazing issues of her day were often controlled by media rhetoric that created a false wild/domestic dichotomy inspired by and reflected in American literature, which ranked both places and animals into hierarchies. She recognized the power relationships between European and East Coast writers and critics, and western people, between urban and rural; and she understood how those relationships, as expressed in literature, had encouraged colonization of the West, its animals, resources, and people. Her animal stories are attempts to rewrite the myths and defend rural communities from truly big business, tourist development, and urban takeover.

The same situation now threatens the modern West, which is why investigating Austin's work is crucial work for ecocritics. Bruce Weaver traces the insidious rhetorical patterns involved in removing rural people from their homes in his essay " 'What to Do with the Mountain People?': The Darker Side of the Successful Campaign to Establish the Great Smoky Mountains National Park." That campaign lasted almost twenty years, during which time "men of stature" used modern public relations techniques to convince the voting American public that the Smokies were "uninhabited" pristine wilderness, even though a minimum of four thousand people lived within the proposed park boundaries. As the campaign progressed, representations of the mountain people escalated from "quaint" hermits to gun-toting, dim-witted ravagers of the land. Finally, they became inbred liars, ignorant troublemakers, and bootleggers who should be rooted out for their own good. The park's urban upper-class promoters, who stood to reap millions in tourist dollars, were represented as fighting unselfishly to preserve trees and wilderness while the generally poor mountain people were represented as greedy capitalists. Weaver concludes his very detailed investigation with an ominous warning: "We can only hope that contemporary environmentalists do not fall prey to the same misconceptions that forged the words and deeds of the promoters of the Great Smoky Mountains National Park." But that same rhetoric is once again rampant all over the West. Yes, what *shall* we do with the mountain people?

In a paper delivered at a meeting of the New England American Studies Association, Kent Ryden argues that it is

workers in nature—fishermen, loggers, farmers, miners, and the like—who achieve the most intimate, detailed knowledge of nature: not a mystical,

spiritual kind of knowledge, but one born of experience, of necessity of assessing and adapting to or reacting against the particular physical proper-
ties of earth and wind and water and flesh in a specific time and place; not
the result of uplifting leisured visits to the natural world, but of immediate, difficult, daily, full-body immersion in that world; a knowledge of
force and slope and texture and resistance that is carried in the memory,
joints, and muscles. ("Ethics")

Ryden grants that "this sort of knowledge does not necessarily result in responsible environmental behavior," but does believe that respecting this kind
of knowledge as legitimate will help "break down barriers between parties who
are conventionally aligned on opposite sides of environmental debates." He argues further that

[o]ut of environmental knowledge gained through work rather than
through leisure and literature, perhaps, can come a sort of environmental
wisdom and responsibility, yet one that does not bring with it a corre-
sponding desire to sweep working people off the landscape completely.
("Ethics")

Austin used animal stories to argue that the wilderness always had been and
always should be treated as a home, not a playground. Her writing inspired Edward Abbey, who also attempted to defend rural people—and/or to make them
angry enough to defend themselves—through animal symbolism. But Austin's stories didn't work during her day, Abbey's didn't work during *his* day,
and they don't seem to be working today. Perhaps literary criticism can better
expose the myths that are playing rural people against environmentalists while
developers and government bureaucracies grab the land and water.

Austin also argues through her animal stories that wildness and domesticity
are cyclic. Wild animals can choose to become domestic, and domestic animals
can become wild. Hunting causes tame animals to run and hide, while nostalgia
and imagination cause "civilized" people to revert to and adopt "primitive"
ways, through dress, pretense, romance, and summer camping. However, instead of condemning this hunger for animal contact and domestic wildness,
Austin encourages it. Unlike almost all other nature writers, Austin's goal is to
understand her neighbors, not reform them. Only through the humble act of
listening to each other, returning to the land and listening to the plants and animals that have been able to adapt to its rhythms and make a sustainable living
there, can we continue to rejuvenate and improve our society.

I have no answers to the environmental problems we face. My hope with
this book is simply to expose some of the myths that may be responsible for di-

viding the people who should be working together to solve the problems. As William Howarth advises, we who love the natural world must get over the us/ them dichotomy (69). I might suggest—as David Abram, Ray Hunt, and Tom Dorrance suggest—that we apprentice ourselves to animals, accept them again as teachers. Academics must learn to respect the kind of knowledge that does not come from books. Austin believed that we have only scratched the surface of what animals might be capable of teaching. Where but in the animal world can we find the answers to some of society's worst problems: overpopulation, pollution, racial prejudice, war? Where but in the animal world can we find examples of true multicultural democracy in all its complexity and contradiction?

I might suggest a ceremony, the kind Paula Gunn Allen says will "fuse the individual with his or her fellows, the community of people with that of other kingdoms, and this larger communal group with the worlds beyond this one" (249). I might suggest more intermarriage between "illiterate cowboys" (although most of the cowboys I know have college educations, and quite a few have doctorates and law degrees) and "environmentalists" (although most of the ones I know are descended from farmers and ranchers and love to ride horses). I might suggest feeling a stewardship toward all nature—not just the "beautiful" but the cracks in the sidewalk and the edge of the asphalt too. What grows there? Does it bloom? Who eats it? We need to learn to live again with the flies, rats, snakes, and wolves—and maybe even with fatal diseases. Only animals can teach us to trade the poverty of affluence for the affluence of poverty. Only animals can teach us to stop demonizing our food and begin to worship it, and to live our lives in such a way as to be worthy of that food. Only animals can teach us that in the end, all organisms need a predator, whether it be a mountain lion, a human, or a virus.

This book is, of course, as it should be, inconclusive, contradictory, and incomplete. Theologians, psychologists, anthropologists, sociologists, and historians will all find a gold mine in animal stories. I have only hinted at Austin's animistic plants, water, clouds, and dust. She questions the dichotomy between wild and domestic through all natural beings, animate and inanimate, and suggests multilayered, ecosystemic relationships between them. Austin's work will produce fertile ground for research into food taboos, water symbolism, wind, and black rock, topics that will lead to world religion, class struggles, government by consent of the governed, and sustainable economics. I predict that Mary Austin will become the American Shakespeare for ecocritical research.

Respectfully, I would like to give Austin the last word and quote in full one of the last pieces of writing she ever produced. Her last wish was not to be enshrined in the Huntington Library, critiqued as America's greatest author, worshiped as a female prophet, or housed in a heavenly golden castle.

WHEN I AM DEAD

This is what I shall do
When I am dead.

When the hot wind frets not
Nor the sharp sleet;
When weariness wears not my heart,
Nor stones my feet;
When the fire's spell is unbound
And I faint no more for bread;—
How well I know what I shall do
When I am dead!

I shall take a white road
On a warm last-lighted hill,
Where saffron-shod the evening goes,
Where the pale gilias unclose
And the flitter-moths are still.

I shall take a high road where the flock scent lingers
In the browsed sage and the blue, bush-lupin fingers,
I shall find a by-road by the foot changes
Till I come where the herders' fires
Blossom in the dusk of the grape-colored ranges.

And I shall sit by the bedding fires
With the little, long armed men,
Elcheverray and Little Pete and Narcisse Julienne—
For what can come when sense decays
They being even as I, and all of us being dead—
And the dull flesh fails,
But that man is one with his thought at last
And the Wish prevails?

So it shall be day as we will,
With a burnished blue hot sky,
And a heat dance over the open range
Where tall pale guidons of dust go by.
Or it shall be dark, as we choose,
At the lambing pens under Tremblor Hill
With the mothering mutter of the ewes,
And a wind to which the herd grass cowers,

While the dogs edge in to the watching fires
And darkly the procreant earth suspires.

So it shall be when Balzar the Basque
And the three Manxmen
And Pete Giraud and my happy ghost
Walk with the flocks again.

Notes

PROLOGUE: THE RURAL STORYTELLER

1. John and Susie are actually composites of several people to whom I feel a great deal of gratitude. They know who they are.

2. *Tecole* is a nasty, sticky concoction of pine tar and insecticide that is painted on branding wounds to prevent screwworms and other flies from laying eggs which hatch into maggots. The worst job on a branding crew is painting on *tecole*.

INTRODUCTION: ANOTHER TROUBLESOME DICHOTOMY

1. Homes and fuel quickly took their toll on the forests, however, and by 1626 the colonies had already passed ordinances to regulate the cutting and sale of trees (Nash *Readings* xi).

2. We are gradually finding out that even in the wildest parts of the Amazon rain forest, the flora is not natural but planted, harvested, moved, and managed by the local people (Posey).

3. See Blackburn and Anderson, *Before the Wilderness;* and Hurt, *Indian Agriculture in America.*

4. For a similar reading of Thoreau's essay, see Fritzell (105).

5. Ray Hunt, universally acknowledged as one of the best modern horse trainers, says it well: "I never rode a broke horse but then maybe I'm a sorry hand" (5). See also Tom Dorrance for more elaboration of horsemanship based on a horse's free choice and willing cooperation. These authors provide convincing arguments that horses are never actually "broken."

6. Leo Marx notes also that Thoreau uses the word *pasture* to encompass wild nature (246).

7. Cultural geographers also began talking more and more about the role of imagination in constructing places when Max Oelschlaeger argued that wilderness was an idea governed by economic and political ideology, and Neil Evernden pronounced nature itself a social creation.

8. For critical responses to Cronon's collection of essays, see Sessions; essays in Soule and Lease; O'Grady "Thinking"; and Cohen "Trouble."

9. A study enumerating the number of times the average working scientist was quoted in subsequent studies by other working scientists found that both Thoreau and Muir were cited more than 4 times a year; the average scientist was cited 8.2 times per year (Buell *Imagination* 363).

10. For an excellent summary of the presumed extinction of giant Canada geese and their subsequent rediscovery, see Kline (49–51).

11. Ankney's study won Ducks Unlimited's 1997 Conservation Achievement Award in the "Professional/Technical" category at the 62nd North American Wildlife and Natural Resources Conference.

12. Although Brown does not give the source he is questioning, Dagget's book gives a favorable description of Jelks's property. While they agree on most points, the two authors appear to contradict each other when Brown claims "taller and browner grass" for the Audubon property while Dagget claims taller grass on Jelks's property: "When we reached Jelks's ranch, the first thing that became obvious to everyone was that the grass, which had barely reached above our sneakers on a similar dry mesa top on one of the preserves, reached above our belts here" (Dagget 39).

13. Ammon and Stacey blame livestock grazing for destroying grass habitat and forcing birds to nest under brush cover. Again, I think this is demonizing livestock grazing rather than simply stating the results of their study. Also, although not backed up by a scientific study, I have personally observed rare and colorful tanagers, vermilion flycatchers, and scissor-tailed flycatchers nesting only near heavy concentrations of fly-producing livestock. Food supply is more important to nesting success than habitat. Anyone who wants to experiment with this concept can adopt any vacant city lot. Don't mow it, don't fertilize it, don't water it, and see what it will grow.

14. Numerous cultural geographers discuss aspects of this idea, including Michael Hough, Wes Jackson, Donald Meinig, Yi-Fu Tuan ("Topophilia"), John B. Jackson, Kevin Lynch, and Winifred Gallagher.

15. See David Mazel's excellent paper "American Literary Environmentalism as Domestic Orientalism."

16. See Jones; Tracy references; Keiser; Wynn "Mary Austin"; Young; Ruppert "Discovering"; Rudnick; Hoyer references; and Albertine for investigations regarding Austin's numerous interests and ties to Native American cultures. In addition, Benay Blend is currently working on a reevaluation of Austin's cultural appropriations.

17. See Young; Pearce; Work; Ruppert "Mary"; O'Grady *Pilgrims*; Scheick; and "Mary (Hunter) Austin, 1868–1934" for numerous stylistic or autobiographical comparisons, both pro and con.

CHAPTER ONE. WALKING ANCIENT DOMESTIC TRAILS

1. I have shot at, intending to miss, numerous coyotes in order to scare them when they stopped running at the sight or smell of a human. I didn't want them to become easy targets for someone who did want to kill them. Park rangers in Big Bend National Park have also been forced to shoot mountain lions with bird and rat shot in order to sting and scare them away from people. The protected lions were so fearless that encounters with people were becoming uncomfortably frequent.

2. For a modern example of this same kind of display of wealth through importation of exotics, see Mungall and Shefield.

3. In this way the West continues in its role, as described by Frederick Jackson Turner, as an eastern colony. In Turner's famous address about the so-called closing of the frontier, he posits that "American history has been in a large degree the history of the colonization of the Great West." The idea was to keep the West from being settled (i.e., to keep it as public land) in order to keep the power in the East. He thought the East feared that westerners "would become hordes of English Tartars" (199, 224).

4. Although normally overly complimentary toward all Native American tribes, Austin seems to imply in this story that Navajos were a predatory and thieving people. She also compares them to predators in another story, saying that Navajos seldom have a home "in the area," and they "pretend to despise all people who live in fixed dwellings" (*Trail* 292). This attitude may reflect animosity between Navajos and the Pueblo people who were close friends of Austin's, although according to Leslie Marmon Silko, some of the Pueblo people and the Navajo were friends (*Storyteller* 210).

5. Henry Chester Tracy notes that because *The Trail Book* is "[d]isguised and segregated as 'juvenile,' [it] is likely to escape notice." He argues that there is an "elemental force here that goes deeper than folk tale form and myth construction. . . . The grip of the old lost life is upon it" (*The American* 247). In *Earth Horizon*, Austin explains that *The Trail Book* was meant to be a collection of "prehistoric trail stories each one illustrating one of the pre-Columbian cultures. I meant them to be factual . . . [but my] publishers missed the point of them completely" (316).

6. For an excellent interpretation of Austin's female guides and trail symbolism, see Melody Graulich's introduction to *Western Trails*.

7. In the Tejon Notebook, she writes that the water birds remind her of the Greeks: "I like seeing the birds—wading birds whose names I do not know stretching out their wings in the early morning. They looked like people, in loose garments, strange Greek looking people, transformed into birds and liking it" (AU 267, 10th page).

8. For an excellent introductory survey, a collection of critical essays on American and Canadian literature, and a collection of the animal stories discussed, see *The Wild Animal Story*, edited by Ralph Lutts. The book would make an excellent text for a college course on animal stories.

9. Worse than a thieving wolf is a dog that slips from grace. Sometimes even well-fed pets that lie on the porch during the day sneak off in packs of town dogs to ravage nearby ranches at night. A story by Ernest Thompson Seton tells of a sheepdog who faithfully guarded his master's flocks by day and killed neighbors' sheep by night. Austin and Seton were close friends and correspondents, Austin being one of the people Seton asked to write a letter of recommendation for him when he was becoming a U.S. citizen.

10. Since figuratively the wolf is also often representative of the male womanizer or rapist, this story also operates humorously on several male-female levels.

11. See William Logan's excellent lyric tribute to *Dirt: The Ecstatic Skin of the Earth*, which elevates soil into the literary realm it deserves. David Wallace attempts to do the same for manure in his essay "The Dungheap."

12. See also William Howarth for an explanation of Darwin's theories (78).

13. Wendy James reports that the Uduk tribe of Africa believes monkeys are degenerate humans descended from a brother and sister who ran off into the bush (201). The

Uduks' "primitive" ideas sometimes seem plausible. The common misconception that a "smarter" human somehow evolved from monkeys is a phenomenon science has never claimed or witnessed. Degeneration through inbreeding, on the other hand, is common. Also, actually measuring human intelligence against monkey intelligence may prove embarrassing to humans.

14. John Ruskin, writing in the nineteenth century during the heyday of romanticism, describes two kinds of "pathetic fallacy." One, "willful fancy," is so obviously untrue that the writer would never expect a reader to actually believe it. The other form he describes as caused by an excited emotional state like love, joy, or mourning, which makes the author "more or less irrational." The key to successful figurative language, declares Ruskin, is truth.

15. J. J. Clarke, in *Voices of the Earth*, warns that

> while the removal of old animistic "superstitions" about hidden purposes and driving spirits within nature has enabled us to subject nature to rational understanding and control, it has also meant the loss of a sense of the sacredness of nature and has encouraged us to treat it as a dead object which can be used for our purposes with impunity. It has also helped to engender a materialist and determinist philosophical climate which has contributed to our sense of alienation from the world of nature. (6)

According to Clarke, scientific myths simply replaced older myths, but they are myths nonetheless. Roy Willis, in *Signifying Animals*, describes two of these new science myths. One imagines the natural world as a vast and "immensely complex machine" from which all traces of spirit and mind have disappeared and in which complete domination of nature will come with scientific knowledge. The other he describes as the Holy Grail myth, which promises the "restoration of a lost wholeness and plentitude." Both versions, he says, cast the scientist as hero and the natural world as a "field concept" (xxvi).

16. Larry Littlebird's "The Hunter" is an excellent example of a Laguna story in which the teller slyly points out the similarity between pig and deer tracks to children (545–48).

17. Some linguists even theorize that humans learned to speak by imitating animal sounds. See the "bow wow theory" as explained in Mario Pei's "Animal Voices" (20–25).

18. See Hunt and Dorrance for highly respected testimony that horses are capable of this kind of understanding and communication. In addition, border-dwelling cowboys often claim quite seriously that some horses speak only Spanish, and some only English, although some are bilingual.

CHAPTER TWO. GENDERING THE WILD AND DOMESTIC

1. Jung's works include *Symbols of Transformation* (1912), *Psychological Types* (1921), *Archetypes of the Collective Unconscious* (1934), *Psychology and Alchemy* (1944), and *Psychology of Transference* (1946). An in-depth comparison of these two thinkers would make an excellent dissertation.

2. Insanity or madness, and the lack thereof in shepherds, is a recurring theme with Austin's human characters and would make an interesting study.

3. The reason animals in Native American stories frequently shape-shift into human form may be a subtle refusal to anthropomorphize such human-only problems as insanity. Thus shape shifting may actually be a more realistic form of storytelling than sentimental anthropomorphism.

4. Stephen Budiansky argues in *The Covenant of the Wild* that many domestic animals probably freely chose to live with humans.

5. London said that with *White Fang,* he intended a "complete antithesis" of *The Call of the Wild.* "Instead of devolution or decivilization of a dog," he planned to describe "the evolution, the civilization of a dog—development of domesticity, faithfulness, love, morality, and all the amenities and virtues" (qtd. in Labor and Leitz xv).

6. An interesting essay by Edmund Leach, "Anthropological Aspects of Language: Animal Categories and Verbal Abuse," discusses gendered connections to wildness and animals concerning taboos, obscenities, foods, abuses, and sexual and excretory body parts and functions. The categories are often organized as binary oppositions.

7. Kolodny also asserts that as part of the Edenic wilderness myth, agriculture became associated with loss of freedom and manhood because of its archetypal connections to female goddesses. In analyzing the Great Mother archetype, Erich Neumann finds that "the sociological school of anthropologists correlates the Great Mother with agriculture and the economic dominance it gave to woman." In Egypt, she "appears as a cow goddess and mistress of the herd . . . [or] bearing sheaves and surrounded by leaping rams, rules over the fertility of vegetation and cattle." Strangely, however, this female deity is also traditionally imagined as "goddess of the hunt," and when she appears in animal form may be either wild or domestic: cow, swamp bird, ewe, lioness, fish, or mermaid (268–78).

8. From 1576 to 1614 various animals were "excommunicated," "prosecuted," and "executed," mostly by the Catholic Church, for various "crimes" against man or nature. The animals included pigs, locusts, weevils, dolphins, grasshoppers, snails, dogs, rats, gadflies, cows, sheep, goats, asses, mules, mares, and horses (Evans 324–28). People explained what they could not understand as witchcraft, so highly trained animals, sick animals, or rebellious animals were often brought to trial as witches themselves, not just as familiars. These persecutions may also have stemmed from a Christian attempt to root out deeply imbedded animal worship.

9. See also David Brown's provocative essay "Rambo: The Desert Big Horn as Masculine Totem," as well as Henry Harrington's analysis of it in "Looking at the Desert Bighorn."

10. See Richard Slotkin for an in-depth study of the single, aggressive male in literature.

11. Austin once shared a shelter with a lone male antelope during a rainstorm (*Earth* 194).

12. Antelope also frequently graze and bed down with horned cattle while raising their young, the cattle protecting both their own calves and the antelope fawns from predators.

13. J. Wilkes Berry says that Austin's male characters are regularly presented as "childish, oafish, or villainous," and her women are "drab, dispirited, and male-dominated" ("Characterization" 119). One wonders if critics read the same books.

14. For an interesting case study about how language education affects children from homes where dialects are spoken, see Caffilene Allen's "First They Changed My Name." The author says she was taught to hate her mother and her culture, but love her teacher and Standard English. Only now, many years later, is she beginning to regain a sense of pride in her heritage.

15. Male mountain lions do not help tend the kittens, nor do males hunt sheep in packs. Unless traveling with unweaned kittens, even female lions are solitary hunters. The female raises her young alone (McBride).

16. Austin herself mastered this skill (*Earth* 247), and to my father's shame, so did I.

17. Several critics have noticed that Austin obviously opposed the idea that the West had been shaped by individualistic, self-reliant, and aggressive personalities (Rudnick 19). According to Norwood, "Mary Austin knows that her culture requires a certain defeat of pride before it can accept the requirements of life in the wilderness" ("Heroines" 334).

18. Graulich observes that Austin "became a prominent feminist theorist, articulating what would become major concerns of the feminist movement" (Introduction 14); however, I would still like to see clarified and emphasized the fact that Austin's work and philosophy predate by many years most of the "new" feminist ideas credited to Virginia Woolf. Austin herself felt that because she was a westerner, her ideas were ignored by the critical power centers ("New York").

CHAPTER FOUR. HOOFED LOCUSTS OR WILD ECO-SHEEP?

1. For critical reviews linking Austin's novel *The Ford* with California water politics, see, for instance, Blend, "Mary Austin and the Western Conservation Movement."

2. In *John Muir and the Sierra Club,* Holoway Jones posits that "the role of the Southern Pacific in the establishment of the California parks is one of the most provocative conservation questions yet to be exposed by the historian." His book includes an intriguing summary, including maps, of the battle for Yosemite. Noel Perrin suggests,

> It's a coincidence, but a nice coincidence, that the year in which [Muir] began to describe the Western mountains as wonderful places, sacred ground, God's outdoor temples, was the same year [1869] in which the transcontinental railroad was completed. (20)

3. In 1878 Muir was writing with a kindly attitude toward shepherds:

> Back among the hills, and in almost every town and hamlet, there are shepherds, tradesmen or laborers, who, while working hard for a bare livelihood, yet zealously pursue some branch of natural history . . . hungering and thirsting after knowledge for its own sake. (Qtd. in Kimes 21)

But later, after the political battle for land had become a heated power struggle involving the giants of railroad, California government, and San Francisco development, and after Muir himself had married into a wealthy California fruit-ranching family, he ridiculed the ignorant, ill-mannered sheepherder. This statement may have appeared when Muir's glaciation theories, which he began to publish around 1872, were being attacked by Josiah Whitney as the simple ideas of a sheepherder.

4. The Austin Collection in the Huntington Library also contains a clipping of an article written by Muir entitled "The Hetch-Hetchy Valley: A National Question" and published in *American Forestry*, vol. 16 (1910), further evidence that Austin followed Muir's work.

5. In this article, Norwood also argues that Austin was "unsympathetic" to the national parks and sympathetic to the shepherd. Eleven years later, however, Norwood changed her mind. The later, ecofeminist statement appears in *Made for This Earth* (279).

6. For a concise overview of Bakhtin's complex theories and a complete bibliography of his work, see Donald Marshall (39–41).

7. Jan Dizard reviews a modern version of this same situation in *Going Wild*. Once a small farming community, the Quabbin was dammed to provide a water source for Boston and somehow became an "accidental wilderness."

8. White says he has "phrased this issue so harshly not because I oppose environmentalism (indeed, I consider myself an environmentalist)" but precisely because he thinks environmentalism must play a key role in addressing many political issues. I, too, have chosen to present my argument "harshly" and blatantly biased toward Austin's views. I believe the rural viewpoint has been stifled for so many years that an angry tone is justified. As Austin well knew, rural people have had no voice in either literature or politics. Their voices need to be heard and respected by today's environmentalists.

9. Information about the missing journal appears in the introduction to the microfilmed John Muir Papers; "Twenty Hill Hollow" is in reel 23 of the John Muir Papers; the working draft of *My First Summer* is in reel 31.

10. In 1890 Muir had been forced to defend his reputation with a letter to the editor of the *Oakland Daily Evening Tribune* that ran under the lengthy title "John Muir in Yosemite. He Never Cut Down a Single Tree in the Valley. Twenty Years Ago He Was Employed by Mr. Hutchings to Saw Lumber from Valley Timber" (Kimes 50). But this may not have been quite truthful. As an example of the many discrepancies between Muir's private and published works, in the early draft of *My First Summer*, Muir describes cutting down silver firs to build a sheep corral—but the passage was struck before publication ("Draft" 51).

11. Shakespeare's Cordelia was also struck dumb when asked to compete with the greased tongues of her flattering sisters. King Lear realized too late that the latter were simply after his fortune, and that Cordelia could not express her more genuine love in mere words.

12. In "Pahawitz-na'an" she also writes about Paiute shepherds (*Mother*).

13. Hoyer also notes that Austin frequently traveled to Round Valley to "visit the Birchim family, who operated one of the largest sheep ranches in the Owens Valley" ("Weaving" 139).

14. Limbaugh and Lewis, reel 1, letter dated July 19, 1868. ·

15. Numerous scholars back up Austin's views. The "pristine" Yosemite wilderness had been heavily managed by Native Californians before European shepherds arrived, but signs of management are not always obvious to the inexperienced (Blackburn and Anderson; Solnit *Savage*; Nabhan; Snyder 92). Although Solnit credits Indian people with the "park like atmosphere," she never mentions shepherds and calls other early settlers "squatters." Forest managers in British Columbia are now paying sheep producers to control weeds and brush in new tree plantations (Glimp et al.). Reducing trees and brush to grass produces more water, not less, as Muir claims. Watershed managers in Massachusetts's "Quabbin" are finding that they must cut trees in order to maintain water regeneration and that oversized deer populations "have been munching" young hardwoods and softwoods, "virtually all of them, down to the ground" (Dizard 11, 25, 36). Suppression of fire in the Sierra has led to "the brushy understory that is so common in the Sierra now" (Snyder 137). In addition, scientists in Great Britain have found sheep grazing beneficial to buttercup and early spider orchid (Frost 1981, and Hutchings 1987, summarized in West 8).

16. Both would have been familiar with the numerous Christian stories, and even the Buddha held a sheep tibia in his hand while creating animate beings (Szynkiewicz 75).

17. Glotfelty, analyzing women's backpacking handbooks, finds that one guide even draws a silly distinction "between (bad) dirt and (good) soil, and argues that dirt is found in the city and in houses, but that in the wilderness one finds only good soil" ("Femininity" 448).

18. In a recent review of the excessively anthropomorphic best-seller *The Hidden Life of Dogs*, critic Jonathan Raban notes the book's claim that dogs become faithful to their mates, noncompetitive, serene, and happy as they gradually return to a wilder state. The dogs "wilt under the burden of their goodness, diminishing in reality as their morals improve" (38). The same is true for Muir's wild animals—they wilt and diminish in reality.

19. As already argued, many of Austin's contemporary male authors did not let facts about animals stand in the way of their animal stories. Around the turn of the century, many nature writers began to assume a savage persona and took more and more liberties when recounting their knowledge of the wild and wild animals. This competition for wildness began to wear away the credibility of the genre. It climaxed in 1913 when Joseph Knowles stripped naked and walked off into the forest in a cold drizzle in front of a fleet of newspaper reporters. He supposedly lived off the land, lured a bear into a pit, clubbed it, and made himself a coat. Knowles wrote a book that sold 300,000 copies before his comfy cabin stocked with canned goods and clothes was discovered. Nature faking became such a lucrative business and political tool that even Roosevelt publicly demanded a return to truth. Top-selling authors of the day Ernest Thompson Seton, Jack London, and John Burroughs came under attack for nature faking. Many others, including Muir, should have been scrutinized more closely. For a survey of this interesting competition between writers to lead wild lives, intimately know wild animals, and write of wild topics that eventually ended in a literary scandal, see Lutts's *Nature Fakers*.

20. See Austin's short story "A Shepherd of the Sierras" (1900) for very early kind words toward predators.

21. Editors of *Twentieth-Century Literary Criticism* make this claim, as do numerous critics quoted therein. The quote comes from the same collection: Vernon Young, "Mary Austin and the Earth Performance," 31.

CHAPTER FIVE. THE INDIGENOUS DESERT COW

1. Although *Slickrock* also contains a few negative cow statements, Abbey chose to republish only the chapters with kind words. The one negative sentence that appears in the selected chapters was edited out: "At that time I did not realize that what looked so open and free was, even then, tied up in cattle grazing permits, defacto property of the local ranchers" (22).

2. Abbey may be making a similar prodding statement when he implies in the essay "God's Plan for the State of Utah: A Revelation" that fictitious angelic representatives of God were "not familiar with" the Sahara Club, obviously a pun on the Sierra Club (*Journey* 105).

3. This is not to say that the cow was the only symbol Abbey used. See Carl L. Davis's "Thoughts on a Vulture," David E. Gamble's "Into the Maze with Edward Abbey," and Jerry A. Herndon's "Moderate Extremism: Edward Abbey and 'The Moon-Eyed Horse'" for discussion of a few others. Obviously more could be listed: the lone juniper, buzzard, and red bandana come to mind.

4. Like all theories dealing with very ancient history, experts disagree to some extent on wild cattle lineages. For numerous interesting arguments and photographs, see Darlington 50; Cross 105; Rouse; *Our Magnificent Wildlife*; Whitehead; and Harting.

5. Many of Austin's land-human relationships have been interpreted as representative of relationships between herself and men. Melody Graulich comes to a similar conclusion: "She devoted a good deal of attention to love, marriage, and divorce, but she found no remedy" (Introduction 16). William Scheick suggests that by anthropomorphizing the desert to fit her own "terrible" life, Austin does a disservice to the Southwest. Marjorie Pryse, in her excellent introduction to a collected volume including both *The Land of Little Rain* and *Lost Borders*, writes: "The desert herself enters every story as a character and story trails lead to an oasis of emotional and spiritual nourishment." Yet, this insightful beginning does not lead to nourishment. Pryse interprets Austin's "unfulfilled" life as "thirsty," and her interest in Indian women as "sympathy" because "Austin knew what it meant to be excluded in childhood, to be viewed as 'other,' to be scorned and mistreated by the men she cared about" (xvi). But Austin never imagined the desert as barren or unfulfilled. Critics who expect to find thinly veiled allusions to Austin's barren life are still imagining the desert as a wasteland. Austin did not. And neither did Edward Abbey. Fred Lewis Pattee, in a brief mention of *The Land of Little Rain* in a 1930 survey of female novelists, *probably* describes Austin's female desert the way she would have wanted it described. In Austin's work, he says, "the Desert is the principal character, alive, sinister, lovable, death-dealing, irresistible, beautiful" (45). Although

autobiography and biography can be illuminating, in both Abbey's and Austin's cases it has hindered analysis of their work and bogged it down in ad hominem arguments surrounding their lives. Besides, as D. H. Lawrence argues humorously, "[t]he proper function of a critic is to save the tale from the artist who created it" (2).

6. I'm not so sure Abbey didn't read every word Austin ever wrote, and even her critics' comments. In 1986, two years before Abbey wrote his introduction to *The Land of Little Rain*, Austin critic David Wyatt claimed that John C. Van Dyke's book *The Desert* was published two years after Austin's book (93). Abbey, perhaps anxious to correct the error, states in his introduction that "Van Dyke's almost-forgotten book" was published first (*Land* ix). Abbey is, of course, correct. Van Dyke, an eastern art professor, published *The Desert* in 1901. In it he describes the Southwest as a colorful, artistically balanced visual spectacle of rock and sand, devoid of life and people. Describing the desert as art, Van Dyke compares the saguaro to a Moslem minaret, a Doric column, and a Greek temple column—anything but a living being that "keeps its brain underground," as Austin was prone to say about desert plants (*Land* 4). Two years later, perhaps even in response to Van Dyke's book, Austin seemed almost in a frantic hurry to put life back into the desert. Van Dyke's book would have struck Austin as an easterner's view of the desert, portraying it as an empty, beautiful wilderness—a great place to visit and escape life's problems, but not a home. In Austin's book the desert is a home, not objectified art. Every nook and cranny teems with plants, animals, and eccentric human characters as she challenges Van Dyke's image of the desert as beautiful but barren. The tension created between Austin's idea of the desert as home and Van Dyke's idea of the desert as art interested Edward Abbey throughout his writing career.

7. Note also that this phrase appears in Abbey's journal entry dated July 20, 1988—probably immediately after he had just reread *The Land of Little Rain* in order to write his introduction, which was published the same year.

8. For excellent clarification between agribusiness and the family farm or ranch, see "Failure of the Agrarian Utopia," in Henry Nash Smith's *Virgin Land;* or "Horse-Drawn Tools and the Doctrine of Labor Saving," in Wendell Berry's *The Gift of Good Land* (1981). Numerous perspectives and references also occur in Abbey's work: *Brave; Fire; Good; Road* 107, 137, 164, 196; *Desert* 131, 141; *Journey* 163, 234–35; *Down* 43, 95; *One Life* 63–66, 154–55; as well as in an interview by Solheim and Levin (90).

9. Among Austin's collected papers is an article entitled "Agriculture and Moneyculture," which reminds the reader that historians have traced the fall of both Greece and Rome to the fall of their agricultures (AU box 131, folder 1).

10. For some interesting Abbey comments on feminist writing, see "The Future of Sex: A Reaction to a Pair of Books—Brownmiller's *Femininity* and Steinem's *Outrageous Acts*" in *One Life at a Time, Please.*

11. While Austin's confrontational female voice and female-gendered stories are more politically correct and socially acceptable today than Abbey's, in her own day, as he points out in his introduction to *The Land of Little Rain*, "[s]he was an active feminist at a time when that particular cause entailed risk and trouble" (x). Even her "friends" called her "God's Mother-in-Law" behind her back or said they would "spare" visitors from having to deal with her. After Austin's death, Elisabeth Egenhoff laments,

in one of the desert communities, it was proposed that a fountain be erected to her memory—a low pool, where even the smallest creature might come to drink—the town officials summarily refused, so selfish, cruel, and mean was she thought to have been. (202)

Today Abbey's virile male voice invites the same kind of hostility.

12. In "Agua Dulce" in *Stories from the Country of Lost Borders,* as the Mojave stage passes a Paiute village, which Austin muses has "a look of home," the stage driver speaks his thoughts: " 'There's some,' said the driver to the desert at large, 'that thinks Indians ain't properly folks, but just a kind of cattle.' " The driver, it turns out, once loved an Indian woman, and so disagrees with the statement (197). Austin, equally valuing animals and people, may have disagreed with the statement on one level and agreed on another. I think it highly probable that Abbey also read *Lost Borders.* Cattle are often used symbolically to represent low- or working-class people.

13. Both authors were serious students of a desert sense of place and asked questions such as, How did the land influence those living there? How did plants and animals adapt? How could people actually live in and off of desert lands? Austin's essay "Regionalism in American Fiction" (1932) may be the most important literary criticism ever written on sense of place. In it Austin presents what she calls the "four great causatives" of regionalism: climate, housing, transportation, and employment. Austin was arguing that landscape unconsciously influences the rhythms of American Indian songs and poetry several years before D. H. Lawrence met her and coined the phrase "Spirit of Place" in 1923. If Abbey didn't read Austin's thoughts on regionalism, he at least wrote them. But he would have added one more "great causative" to Austin's list: food.

14. In Austin's day, Native Americans were often called "savage" based on their food choices. She explains simply: "As for food, that appears to be chiefly a matter of being willing" and goes on to list typical Indian foods without judgment: yucca, carrion, offal, thorns, potato peelings, roots, freshwater clams, chuckwallas, desert turtles, seeds, berries, and mesquite pods (*Land* 4, 17, 19, 24, 61, 35).

15. Austin also points out in her two parallel stories "The Basket Woman—First Story" and "The Basket Woman—Second Story" (*Basket*) that returning to a hunter-gatherer society is not a utopian solution and that native people often starved. In *The Land of Little Rain,* Austin almost constantly talks about the Indians' struggle to find food in the desert.

16. See also Iverson.

17. As I have already argued, Austin was a staunch defender of sheep grazing. She implies a similar attitude toward privileging vegetable crops over animal crops when she complains that California's "publicity" literature is aimed at attracting "real estate investors, prospective orange-growers and vine-yarders," lumping them all into one equally villainous category (*Earth* 229).

18. Paul Shepard, bashing agriculture in general, argues,

The cereals are wind-pollinated annuals, shallow-rooted, ephemeral, without soil-forming virtues, and their association with flowering forms or pollinator insects is minimal. By supporting large, minimally nourished human populations and by their destructive effects on the environment when grown in cultivated uniformity, the cereals are truly the symbol and agent of agriculture's war against the planet. (25)

19. Abbey's numerous references to rocks with lips and teeth can be found in *Beyond* 156; *Road* 119; *Brave* 112; and *Down* 45, 148.

20. In *The Land of Little Rain*, Austin relates that Shoshones considered the mourning dove a friend because the bird announced the presence of desert springs and yet hunted them for food at those same springs (34). Hoyer explains that the mourning dove in the Christian religion often signifies the Holy Ghost, and that in this passage Austin "implies that the Shoshones in effect hunted the divine" when they hunted the doves at the springs ("To Bring" 11). Modern humans go to great lengths to justify the taking of life in order to eat. To animals and native people, it is simply a sacred part of life.

21. Ironically, through the carrion-eating birds Austin produces almost a total reversal of color symbolism; the blackest birds come closest to performing those jobs attributed to angels: watching over, rescuing, taking the "miserable dead" to heaven (*Land* 18, 57), and keeping the earth clean and sweet smelling. In "Mamichee" Austin symbolically questions whether or not angels might be black when a white African condor helps Christian ladies find a starving child. Differences between good and evil are largely a matter of perspective. Killing, stealing, and scavenging can be forms of nature's necessary cycles. Bredahl calls it a "holistic response to one's world" which includes "even death [as] part of the process rather than enemy" (57).

22. Austin argues, "if you go far [enough into the desert] the chances are that you will find yourself shadowed by their tilted wings. Nothing so large as a man can move unspied upon in that country, and they know well how the land deals with strangers" (*Land* 5). Although too late, buzzards find and lead rescuers to Timmie O'Shea, who is lost in the desert without water (*Land* 18). In "The Merry-Go-Round" buzzards help an Indian woman find a lost white boy (*Basket*). In another story about searching for lost gold in the Arizona desert, Austin uses a condor narrator because the condor probably followed all the people who ever looked for gold. The big black bird would have been the last to see them alive, but because condors are not interested in gold, he keeps the secret (*Trail* 243–66). Abbey humorously advises desert visitors to try to forget about the vultures circling overhead (*Journey* 87).

23. Although condors are today associated with the California coast, in the 1800s they ranged from British Columbia to Baja and as far east as Arizona. In prehistoric times they were found in Nevada and across the southern United States all the way to Florida (Terres 957; Paul Ehrlich et al. 24). Condors (*Gymnogyps californianus*) are the largest carrion-eating birds found in North America. When Austin describes "vultures," she may be talking about condors, as Hoyer notes, although he makes the claim based on white wing patches ("Dancing" 206). Black vultures also have white wing "patches," but Austin refers to the bird's "bigness" (*Land* 19). Since black vultures are smaller than buzzards (turkey vultures), she is probably talking about condors. My theory is that after Indians stopped slaughtering thousands of bison at one time by driving them off cliffs, and cattlemen designed ways to prevent huge cattle die-offs during drouths, and

all garbage was buried, the condor was no longer able to find enough food to continue its existence. Food supply is more crucial than habitat. *The Audubon Society Encyclopedia of North American Birds* seems to agree, stating that threats to condors are "shooting; secondary poisoning of condors from feeding on dead coyotes poisoned in control work; and loss of cattle ranches (where condors feed on dead livestock) to housing and other changes in land use" (Terres 957).

24. Austin also uses the red heifer symbolically. In "Jimville—A Bret Harte Town" Austin refers to red earth being "as red as a red heifer" (*Land* 40). Another "red heifer," which appears in *The Land of Little Rain* as a sacrifice, is a "red" Indian woman who had been a "sacrifice" to a miner. He left her when he struck it rich, she died in "Squaw Gulch," and the miner who rescued her baby went back to the gulch where he found her and discovered the Billy Boy (40–42).

25. Trinh is considered her surname.

26. Like Emerson, Thoreau, Dillard, and Abbey, Austin goes beyond Christian religion and mixes in the "lotus-charm" of Eastern religions, Aztec and Hopi snakes, a Yaqui Campo Santo, African blood drinking, and Hindu sacred cows. Henry Smith observes, "She has a religion deeper than organized churches, a politics beyond parties and governmental machinery, an ethics untrammeled by the letter of codes, and a confidence in America independent of the bitter froth or the childish self-sufficiency of the moment" (26). The same could be said of Edward Abbey.

27. Austin's words, too, seem to inspire thoughts of India when she describes vultures waiting to feast on dying desert cattle:

Death by starvation is slow. The heavy headed, rack-boned cattle totter in the fruitless trails; they stand in long, patient intervals, they lie down and do not rise. There is fear in their eyes when they are first stricken, but afterward only intolerable weariness. . . . Their even-breathing submission after the first agony is their tribute to its inevitableness. It needs a nice discrimination to say which of the basket-ribbed cattle is likeliest to afford the next meal, but the scavengers make few mistakes. One stoops to the quarry and the flock follows. . . . The buzzards have all the time, and no beak is dropped or talon struck until the breath is wholly passed. . . . [A] wolf at the throat would be a shorter agony than the long stalking and sometime perchings of these loathsome watchers. Suppose now it were a man in this long-drawn, hungrily spied upon distress! (*Land* 18)

28. For an excellent explanation of the practical reasons behind the Hindu sacred cow, see "Mother Cow," in Harris.

CONCLUSION. COLLAPSING THE WILD/DOMESTIC DICHOTOMY

1. In an unpublished manuscript, Austin even outlines Shakespeare's debt to folklore, saying he wrote from an "absolute democracy of spirit," and it is therefore "even more fitting to celebrate Shakespeare in America than in the country which produced him" (AU 142).

Works Cited

Abbey, Edward. *Abbey's Road*. 1979. New York: Plume, 1991.

———. *Beyond the Wall*. New York: Henry Holt, 1984.

———. *Black Sun*. 1971. New York: Avon, 1982.

———. *The Brave Cowboy*. 1956. New York: Avon, 1992.

———. *Cactus Country*. New York: Time-Life Books, 1973.

———. *Confessions of a Barbarian*. New York: Little, 1994.

———. *Desert Solitaire: A Season in the Wilderness*. 1968. New York: Simon, 1990.

———. *Down the River*. 1981. New York: Plume, 1991.

———. *Fire on the Mountain*. 1962. New York: Avon, 1992.

———. *Good News*. New York: E. P. Dutton, 1980.

———. Introduction to *The Land of Little Rain*, by Mary Austin. 1903. New York: Penguin, 1988.

———. *The Journey Home*. New York: E. P. Dutton, 1977.

———. *The Monkey Wrench Gang*. 1975. New York: Avon, 1976.

———. *One Life at a Time, Please*. New York: Henry Holt, 1988.

———. *Slickrock*. Layton, Utah: Peregrine Smith, 1987.

Abram, David. *The Spell of the Sensuous*. New York: Vintage, 1996.

Albertine, Susan, ed. *A Living of Words: American Women in Print Culture*. Knoxville: U of Tennessee P, 1995.

Alcock, John. *The Masked Bobwhite Rides Again*. Tucson: U of Arizona P, 1993.

Allen, Caffilene. "First They Changed My Name." *MS*, January–February 1994: 25–27.

Allen, Paula Gunn. "The Sacred Hoop: A Contemporary Perspective." In Glotfelty and Fromm 241–63.

———. *Studies in American Indian Literature: Critical Essays and Course Designs*. New York: MLA, 1983.

Ammon, Elizabeth M., and Peter B. Stacey. "Avian Nest Success in Relation to Past Grazing Regimes in a Montane Riparian System." *Condor* 99.7 (1997): 7–13.

Ankney, C. Davison. "An Embarrassment of Riches." *Journal of Wildlife Management* 60.2 (1996): 219–23.

———. "Sky Carp and Tundra Maggots." *Range*, Winter 1997: 34–36.

Austin, Mary. *The American Rhythm*. New York: Harcourt, 1923.

———. AU. See "Mary (Hunter) Austin Collection."

———. *The Basket Woman: A Book of Fanciful Tales for Children*. Boston: Houghton, 1904.

———. *Children Sing in the Far West*. Boston: Houghton, 1928.

———. *Earth Horizon: Autobiography*. 1932. Afterword by Melody Graulich. Albuquerque: U of New Mexico P, 1991.

———. *The Flock.* Boston: Houghton, 1906.

———. "The Folk Story in America." *South Atlantic Quarterly* 33 (1934): 10–19.

———. *The Ford.* Boston: Houghton, 1917.

———. "The Ford of Crevecoeur." In *The Mother of Felipe and Other Early Stories* 131–41.

———. Introduction to *The Path on the Rainbow,* ed. George W. Cronyn. New York: Boni and Liveright, 1918. xv–xxxii.

———. *Isidro.* Boston: Houghton, 1905.

———. *The Land of Journeys' Ending.* New York: Century, 1924.

———. *The Land of Little Rain.* 1903. Introduction by Edward Abbey. New York: Penguin, 1988.

———. "The Little Coyote." *Atlantic Monthly,* February 1902: 249–54.

———. "A Lost Dog." *Catholic World,* August 1909: 625–35.

———. "Mamichee." *Catholic World,* May 1910: 182–97.

———. Mary (Hunter) Austin Collection. Huntington Library, San Marino, Calif.

———. *The Mother of Felipe and Other Early Stories.* Ed. Franklin Walker. San Francisco: Book Club of California, 1950.

———. "New York: Dictator of American Criticism." *Nation* 3 (1920): 129–30.

———. "Non-English Writings II: Aboriginal." In *The Cambridge History of American Literature,* ed. William Peterfield Trent, John Erskine, Stuart P. Sherman, and Carl Van Doren. New York: Macmillan, 1945.

———. *One Hundred Miles on Horseback.* 1889. Introduction by Donald P. Ringler. Los Angeles: Dawson's Book Shop, 1963.

———. *One Smoke Stories.* Boston: Houghton, 1934.

———. "Regional Culture in the Southwest." *Southwest Review* 14 (1929): 474–77.

———. "Regionalism in American Fiction." *English Journal* 21 (February 1932): 97–107.

———. "A Shepherd of the Sierras." *Atlantic Monthly* 86 (1900): 54–58.

———. *Stories from the Country of Lost Borders.* Ed. Marjorie Pryse. New Brunswick: Rutgers U P, 1987.

———. *The Trail Book.* New York: Houghton, 1918.

———. *Western Trails: A Collection of Short Stories.* Ed. and introduction by Melody Graulich. Reno: U of Nevada P, 1987.

———. "When I Am Dead." *New Mexico Quarterly* 4 (1934): 234–35.

Bahn, Paul. "Horse Sense, or Nonsense?" *Antiquity* 54 (1980): 139–42.

Balian, Chairmaine. "The Carson Productions Interview." In Hepworth and McNamee 58–61.

Bauer, Robert. "Rediscovering Twenty Hill Hollow." Paper presented at the California History Institute, John Muir in Historical Perspective conference, Stockton, Calif., April 18–21, 1996.

Belanger, Luc, and Jan Bedard. "Role of Ice Scouring and Goose Grubbing in Marsh Plant Dynamics." *Journal of Ecology* 82.3 (1994): 437–46.

Berger, Joel. *Wild Horses of the Great Basin: Social Competition and Population Size.* Chicago: U of Chicago P, 1986.

Berger, John. "Why Look at Animals?" In *About Looking*. 1980. New York: Vintage, 1991. 3–28.

Berry, J. Wilkes. "Characterization in Mary Austin's Southwest Works." *Southwestern American Literature* 2 (1972): 119–24.

Berry, Wendell. "A Few Words in Favor of Edward Abbey." In Hepworth and McNamee 9–19.

———. *Another Turn of the Crank*. Washington, D.C.: Counterpoint, 1995.

———. *The Gift of Good Land*. San Francisco: North Point, 1981.

Blackburn, Thomas C., and Kat Anderson. *Before the Wilderness: Environmental Management by Native Californians*. Menlo Park, Calif.: Ballena P, 1993.

Blend, Benay. "Building a 'House of Earth': Mary Austin, Environmental Activist and Writer." *Critical Matrix* 10.1 (1996): 73–89.

———. "Mary Austin and the Western Conservation Movement, 1900–1927." *Journal of the Southwest* 30 (1988): 12–34.

Blumenthal, Susan. "Spotted Cattle and Deer: Spirit Guides and Symbols of Endurance and Healing in *Ceremony*." *American Indian Quarterly* 14 (1990): 367–77.

Bowen, Ezra. *The High Sierra: The American Wilderness*. Time-Life Books. Washington, D.C.: Time, 1972.

Bradford, William. *Of Plimouth Plantation*. 1856. Ed. Samuel Eliot Morison. New York: Random House, 1952.

Branch, Michael. "Ecocriticism: The Nature of Nature in Literary Theory and Practice." *Weber Studies* 11.1 (1994): 41–55.

Bredahl, A. Carl, Jr. *New Ground: Western American Narrative and the Literary Canon*. Chapel Hill: U of North Carolina P, 1989.

Brooks, Paul. *Speaking for Nature: How Literary Naturalists from Henry Thoreau to Rachel Carson Have Shaped America*. Boston: Houghton, 1980.

Brown, David E. "Out of Africa." *Wilderness*, Winter 1994: 24–34.

———. "Rambo: The Desert Bighorn Sheep as a Masculine Totem." In *Counting Sheep: Twenty Ways of Seeing Desert Bighorn*, ed. Gary Paul Nabhan. Tucson: U of Arizona P, 1993.

———, ed. *The Wolf in the Southwest: The Making of an Endangered Species*. 1983. Tucson: U of Arizona P, 1988.

Brown, J. P. S. *The Outfit*. 1971. Cody, Wyo.: MQM, 1995.

Brussard, Peter F., Dennis D. Murphy, and C. Richard Tracy. "Cattle and Conservation Biology—Another View." *Conservation Biology* 88.4 (1994): 919–21.

Budiansky, Stephen. *The Covenant of the Wild: Why Animals Chose Domestication*. New York: William Morrow, 1992.

Buell, Lawrence. *The Environmental Imagination: Thoreau, Nature Writing, and the Formation of American Culture*. Cambridge: Harvard U P, 1995.

———. "The Thoreauvian Pilgrimage: The Structure of an American Cult." *American Literature* 61.2 (1989): 175–99.

Bullock, J. M., B. Clear Hill, and J. Silvertown. "Demography of *Cirsium vulgare* in a Grazing Experiment." *Journal of Ecology* 82.1 (1994): 101–12.

Carrighar, Sally. *Wild Heritage*. Boston: Houghton, 1965.

Carson, Rachel. *The Sea around Us.* 1950. New York: Signet, 1961.

"Channel Islands Cattle Harm Native Vegetation." *National Parks,* January–February 1995: 18–19.

Chase, Alston. "Bison Herds and Yellowstone National Park." *New York Times,* April 26, 1997. Posted by Ralph Black on asle@unr.edu.

———. *Playing God in Yellowstone: The Destruction of America's First National Park.* New York: Harcourt, 1987.

Church, Peggy Pond. *Wind's Trail: The Early Life of Mary Austin.* Ed. Shelly Armitage. Santa Fe: Museum of New Mexico P, 1990.

Clarke, J. J. *The Voices of the Earth: An Anthology of Ideas and Arguments.* New York: George Braziller, 1994.

Clutton-Brock, Juliet. "The Flight of the Vole." *Times Literary Supplement,* January 5, 1996, 12.

Cohen, Michael P. *The Pathless Way: John Muir and American Wilderness.* Madison: U of Wisconsin P, 1984.

———. "The Trouble with Wilderness, Comment: Resistance to Wilderness." *Environmental History* 1.1 (1996): 33–42.

Colley, Ann C. "Edward Lear's Anti-colonial Bestiary." *Victorian Poetry* 30.2 (1992): 109–20.

Cronon, William, ed. *Uncommon Ground: Toward Reinventing Nature.* New York: Norton, 1995.

Cross, Joe. *Cattle Clatter.* Kansas City: Walker, 1930.

Dagget, Dan. *Beyond the Rangeland Conflict: Toward a West That Works.* Layton, Utah: Gibbs Smith, 1995.

Darlington, C. D. "The Origins of Agriculture." *Natural History* 79.5 (1970): 46–57.

Davis, Carl L. "Thoughts on a Vulture: Edward Abbey, 1927–1989. *RE Arts and Letters* 15.2 (1989): 15–23.

Devine, Robert. "The Cheatgrass Problem." *Atlantic Monthly,* May 1993: 40–45.

Dillard, Annie. *Pilgrim at Tinker Creek.* New York: Harper, 1974.

———. *Teaching a Stone to Talk.* 1983. New York: Harper, 1992.

———. *The Writing Life.* 1989. New York: Harper, 1990.

Dizard, Jan E. *Going Wild: Hunting, Animal Rights, and the Contested Meaning of Nature.* Amherst: U of Massachusetts P, 1994.

Dorrance, Tom. *True Unity: Willing Communication between Horse and Human.* Ed. Milly Hunt Porter. Tuscarora, Nev.: Give-It-A-Go Enterprises, 1987.

Douglas, Mary. "The Pangolin Revisited: A New Approach to Animal Symbolism." In Willis 25–36.

Eagleton, Terry. *Marxism and Literary Criticism.* Berkeley: U of California P, 1976.

Eastlake, William. "A Note on Ed Abbey." In Hepworth and McNamee 20–22.

Egenhoff, Elisabeth L. "Mary Austin: A Page from History." *Mineral Information Service, California Division of Mines and Geology* 18.11 (1965) 202 + .

Ehrlich, Gretel. *The Solace of Open Spaces.* New York: Penguin, 1985.

Ehrlich, Paul, David S. Dobkin, and Darryl Wheye, eds. *Birds in Jeopardy: The Imperiled and Extinct Birds of the United States and Canada Including Hawaii and Puerto Rico.* Stanford: Stanford U P, 1992.

Emerson, Ralph W. "Nature." 1836. In *The Portable Emerson,* ed. Carl Bode, col. Malcom Cowley. New York: Penguin, 1981.

Engle, Leonard, ed. *The Big Empty: Essays in Western Landscapes as Narrative.* Albuquerque: U of New Mexico P, 1994.

Erdrich, Louise. "Skunk Dreams." *Georgia Review* 47.1 (1993): 83–94.

Evans, E. P. *The Criminal Prosecution and Capital Punishment of Animals.* New York: E. P. Dutton, 1906.

Evernden, Neil. *The Social Creation of Nature.* Baltimore: Johns Hopkins U P, 1992.

Fiedler, Leslie. *Love and Death in the American Novel.* 1960. Rev. ed. New York: Stein and Day, 1966.

Fink, Augusta. *I-Mary: A Biography of Mary Austin.* Tucson: U of Arizona P, 1983.

Flores, Dan L. "Environmentalism and Multiculturalism." In *Reopening the American West,* ed. Hal K. Rothman. Tucson: U of Arizona P, 1998. 24–37.

Fritzell, Peter. *Nature Writing and America.* Ames: Iowa State U P, 1990.

Gallagher, Winifred. *The Power of Place: How Our Surroundings Shape Our Thoughts, Emotions and Actions.* New York: Poseidon P, 1993.

Gamble, David E. "Into the Maze with Edward Abbey." *South Dakota Review* 26.1 (1988): 66–77.

Gardner, Gail I. *Orejana Bull.* Prescott, Ariz.: Sharlot Hall Museum P, 1987.

George, Ronnie F. *Mourning Doves in Texas: Life History, Habitat Needs, and Management Suggestions.* Austin: Texas Parks and Wildlife, 1988.

Glimp, Hudson A., Donald G. Ely, James Gerrish, Ed Houston, Rodney Knott, Dan Morrical, Bok Sowell, Charles Taylor, and Robert Van Keuren. "Rangelands, Pasture and Forage Crops." In *Sheep Production Handbook.* Englewood, Calif.: American Sheep Industry Association, 1998. 103–28.

Glotfelty, Cheryll. "Femininity in the Wilderness: Reading Gender in Women's Guides to Backpacking." *Women's Studies* 25.5 (1996): 439–56.

Glotfelty, Cheryll, and Harold Fromm, eds. *The Ecocriticism Reader: Landmarks in Literary Ecology.* Athens: U of Georgia P, 1996.

Graber, David M. "Resolute Biocentrism: The Dilemma of Wilderness in National Parks." In Soule and Lease 123–35.

Grabo, Norman S. "Ideology and the Early American Frontier." *Early American Literature* 22.3 (1987): 274–90.

Graulich, Melody. Afterword to *Earth Horizon: An Autobiography by Mary Austin.* 1932. Albuquerque: U of New Mexico P, 1991.

———, ed. Introduction to *Western Trails: A Collection of Short Stories.* Reno: U of Nevada P, 1987.

Graulich, Melody, and Betsy Klimasmith, eds. *Exploring Lost Borders: Critical Essays on Mary Austin.* Reno: U of Nevada P, 1999.

Gripman, Abbie. "Turning a Vista into a Mess." *High Country News,* May 25, 1998, 4.

Guthrie, Stewart Elliott. *Faces in the Clouds: A New Theory of Religion.* New York: Oxford U P, 1993.

Harrington, Henry. "Looking at the Desert Bighorn: The Gaze in Nature Writing." *Southwestern American Literature* 21.1 (1995): 187–93.

Harris, Marvin. *Cows, Pigs, Wars and Witches: The Riddles of Culture.* New York: Random House, 1974.

Hart, E. Richard, ed. *That Awesome Space: Human Interaction with the Intermountain Landscape.* Salt Lake City: Westwater P, 1981.

Harting, James Edmund. "Wild White Cattle." In *British Animals Extinct within Historic Times: With Some Account of British Wild White Cattle.* Boston: Osgood, 1880. 213–47.

Hayles, N. Katherine. "Searching for Common Ground." In Soule and Lease 47–63.

Hecht, Jeff. "Back through the Nests of Time." *New Scientist,* August 28, 1993, 10–11.

Hepworth, James. "The Poetry Center Interview." In Hepworth and McNamee 33–42.

Hepworth, James, and Gary McNamee, eds. *Resist Much, Obey Little.* Salt Lake City: Dream Garden P, 1985.

Herndon, Jerry A. "Moderate Extremism: Edward Abbey and 'The Moon-Eyed Horse.'" *Western American Literature* 16.2 (1981): 97–103.

"Holiday Publications." *Dial.* 1903. In "Mary (Hunter) Austin, 1868–1934" 17.

Holzer, Harold. "Strangers and Pilgrims." *American History Illustrated,* November 20, 1985, 24–32.

Hough, Michael. *Out of Place: Restoring Identity to the Regional Landscape.* New Haven: Yale U P, 1990.

Howarth, William. "Some Principles of Ecocriticism." In Glotfelty and Fromm 69–91.

Hoyer, Mark. *Dancing Ghosts: Mary Austin's Synthesis of Native American and Biblical Mythologies.* Ph.D. diss., U of California, Davis, 1995.

———. "Prophecy in a New West: Mary Austin and the Ghost Dance Religion." *Western American Literature* 30.3 (1995): 235–55.

———. "'To Bring the World into Divine Focus': Syncretic Prophecy in *The Land of Little Rain.*" *Western American Literature* 31.1 (1996): 3–31.

———. "Weaving the Story: Northern Paiute Myth and Mary Austin's *The Basket Woman.*" *American Indian Culture and Research Journal* 19.1 (1995): 133–51.

Huber, S. A., M. B. Judkins, L. J. Krysl, T. J. Svejcar, B. W. Hess, and D. W. Holcombe. "Cattle Grazing a Riparian Mountain Meadow: Effects of Low and Moderate Stocking Density on Nutrition, Behavior, Diet Selection, and Plant Growth Response." *Journal of Animal Science* 73.12 (1995): 3752–66.

Hulme, Philip E. "Herbivores and the Performance of Grassland Plants: A Comparison of Arthropod, Mollusc and Rodent Herbivory." *Journal of Ecology* 84.1 (1996): 43–52.

Hunt, Ray. *Think Harmony with Horses: An In-Depth Study of Horse/Man Relationship.* 1978. Ed. Milly Hunt. Fresno: Pioneer Publishing, 1982.

Hurt, R. Douglas. *Indian Agriculture in America: Prehistory to the Present.* Lawrence: U P of Kansas, 1987.

Iverson, Peter. *When Indians Became Cowboys: Native Peoples and Cattle Ranching.* Norman: U of Oklahoma P, 1994.

Jackson, John B. *Discovering the Vernacular Landscape.* New Haven: Yale U P, 1984.

Jackson, Wes. "Wilderness as Saint." *Aperture,* midsummer 1990: 50–54.

James, Wendy. "Antelope as Self-Image among the Uduk." In Willis 196–203.

Jaycox, Faith. "Regeneration through Liberation: Mary Austin's 'Walking Woman' and Western Narrative Formula." *Legacy: A Journal of Nineteenth-Century American Women Writers* 6.1 (1989): 5–12.

Jones, Holoway R. *John Muir and the Sierra Club: The Battle for Yosemite.* San Francisco: Sierra Club, 1965.

Jones, Llewellyn. "Indian Rhythms." 1923. In "Mary (Hunter) Austin, 1868–1934" 45.

Kehde, Suzanne. "Walter Van Tilburg Clark and the Withdrawal of Landscape." In Engle 133–45.

Keiser, Albert. "The Indian Drama." 1933. In "Mary (Hunter) Austin, 1868–1934" 45.

Kimes, William F. *John Muir: A Reading Bibliography.* Palo Alto, Calif.: W. P. Wreden, 1977.

Kircher, Cassandra Lee. "Women in/on Nature: Mary Austin, Gretel Ehrlich, Terry Tempest Williams, and Ann Zwinger." Ph.D. diss., U of Iowa, 1995.

Kiskaddon, Bruce. *Rhymes of the Ranges: A New Collection of the Poems of Bruce Kiskaddon.* Ed. and introduction by Hal Cannon. Layton, Utah: Gibbs Smith, 1987.

Kline, David. *Great Possessions: An Amish Farmer's Journal.* Foreword by Wendell Berry. San Francisco: North Point P, 1990. 49–51.

Kolodny, Annette. *The Land before Her: Fantasy and Experience of the American Frontiers, 1630–1860.* Chapel Hill: U of North Carolina P, 1984.

———. *The Lay of the Land: Metaphor as Experience and History in American Life and Letters.* Chapel Hill: U of North Carolina P, 1975.

———. "Unearthing Herstory: An Introduction." In Glotfelty and Fromm 170–81.

Labor, Earle, and Robert C. Leitz III, eds. Introduction to *Jack London: The Call of the Wild, White Fang and Other Stories.* New York: Oxford U P, 1990. ix–xxii.

Langlois, Karen. "Marketing the American Indian: Mary Austin and the Business of Writing." In Albertine 151–68.

Latta, Frank F. *Saga of Rancho El Tejon.* Santa Cruz, Calif.: Bear State Books, 1976.

Laurence, David. "William Bradford's American Sublime." *PMLA* 102.1 (1987): 55–65.

Lawrence, D. H. *Studies in Classic American Literature.* New York: T. Seltzer, 1923.

Lawton, Harry W., Phillip J. Wilke, Mary DeDecker, and William M. Mason. "Agriculture among the Paiute of Owens Valley." In Blackburn and Anderson 329–47.

Leach, Edmund R. "Anthropological Aspects of Language: Animal Categories and Verbal Abuse." In *New Directions in the Study of Language,* ed. Eric H. Lenneberg. Cambridge: MIT P, 1964. 23–63.

Leeming, David Adams. *The World of Myth: An Anthology.* New York: Oxford U P, 1990.

LeGuin, Ursula K. "The Carrier Bag Theory of Fiction." In Glotfelty and Fromm 149–54.

Leigh, R. A., and A. E. Johnston, eds. *Long-Term Experiments in Agricultural and Ecological Sciences.* Oxford: CAB International, 1994.

Leopold, Aldo. *A Sand County Almanac: With Essays on Conservation from Round River.* 1949. New York: Ballantine Books, 1966.

Lewis, Martin W. *Green Delusions: An Environmental Critique of Radical Environmentalism.* Durham, N.C.: Duke U P, 1992.

Lewis, R. W. B. *American Adam: Innocence, Tragedy and Tradition in the Nineteenth Century.* 1955. Chicago: U of Chicago P, 1984.

Limbaugh, Ronald H., and Kirsten F. Lewis, eds. The John Muir Papers, 1858–1957 (microform). Alexandria, Va.: Chadwyck-Healey, 1986.

Littlebird, Larry. "The Hunter." In Slovic and Dixon 545–48.

Logan, William Bryant. *Dirt: The Ecstatic Skin of the Earth.* New York: Riverhead Books, 1995.

London, Jack. *The Call of the Wild.* 1903. In Labor and Leitz 3–88.

———. *White Fang.* 1906. In Labor and Leitz 89–291.

Lopez, Barry. "The American Geographies." In *Finding Home: Writing on Nature and Culture from* Orion *Magazine,* ed. Peter Sauer. Boston: Beacon P, 1992. 116–32.

———. "The Country of the Mind." In Trimble 288–303.

———. *Of Wolves and Men.* New York: Scribner's, 1978.

———. "Unbounded Wilderness." *Aperture,* midsummer 1990: 2–14.

Love, Glen A. "*Et in Arcadia Ego:* Pastoral Theory Meets Ecocriticism." *Western American Literature* 17.3 (1992): 195–209.

———. "Revaluing Nature: Toward an Ecological Criticism." In Glotfelty and Fromm 225–39.

Lutts, Ralph H. *The Nature Fakers: Wildlife, Science, and Sentiment.* Golden, Colo.: Fulcrum, 1990.

———, ed. *The Wild Animal Story.* Philadelphia: Temple U P, 1998.

Lynch, Kevin. *Managing the Sense of a Region.* Cambridge: MIT P, 1980.

Lyon, Thomas J. *John Muir.* Boise: Boise State College, 1972.

McBride, Roy T. "The Status and Ecology of the Mountain Lion (*Felis concolor stanleyana*) of the Texas-Mexico Border." M.S. thesis, Sul Ross State U, 1976.

McDonald, Kim A. "Scientists Rethink Anthropomorphism." *Chronicle of Higher Education,* February 24, 1995, A8.

McKibben, Bill. "Educating to Scale: The Wilderness Community School." *Orion,* summer 1997: 80–81.

McRae, Wallace. *It's Just Grass and Water.* Spokane, Wash.: Oxalis Group, 1986.

Manes, Christopher. "Nature and Silence." In Glotfelty and Fromm 15–29.

Mark, Peter. *The Wild Bull and the Sacred Forest: Form, Meaning and Change in Senegambian Initiation Masks.* New York: Cambridge U P, 1992.

Marshall, Donald G. *Contemporary Critical Theory: A Selective Bibliography.* New York: MLA, 1933.

Marx, Leo. *Machine in the Garden: Technology and the Pastoral Ideal in America.* New York: Oxford U P, 1967.

"Mary (Hunter) Austin, 1868–1934." In *Twentieth-Century Literary Criticism,* vol. 25. Detroit: Gale, 1988. 15–46.

Masson, J. Moussaieff, and Susan McCarthy. *When Elephants Weep: The Emotional Lives of Animals.* New York: Delacorte P, 1995.

Mazel, David. "American Literary Environmentalism as Domestic Orientalism." In Glotfelty and Fromm 137–46.

Meinig, Donald W., ed. "The Beholder's Eye." In *The Interpretation of Ordinary Landscapes: Geographical Essays.* New York: Oxford U P, 1979.

Melham, Tom. *John Muir's Wild America*. Washington, D.C.: National Geographic Society, 1976.

Mighetto, Lisa, ed. *Muir among the Animals: The Wildlife Writings of John Muir*. San Francisco: Sierra Club, 1986.

Milchunas, D. G., and W. K. Lauenroth. "Quantitative Effects of Grazing on Vegetation and Soils over a Global Range of Environments." *Ecological Monographs* 63.4 (1993): 327–67.

Mourt's Relation: A Journal of the Pilgrims at Plymouth. 1622. Introduction by Dwight B. Heath. Bedford, Mass.: Applewood Books, 1963.

Muir, John. "Bears." In Mighetto 161–75.

———. "The Hetch-Hetchy Valley: A National Question." In Austin Mary (Hunter) Austin Collection.

———. *John Muir: The Eight Wilderness Discovery Books*. Seattle: The Mountaineers, 1992.

———. The John Muir Papers, 1988–1957. See Limbaugh and Lewis.

———. *The Mountains of California*. 1894. Ed. Robert C. Baron. Golden, Colo.: Fulcrum, 1988.

———. *My First Summer*. Draft, pre-1911. In Limbaugh and Lewis, reel 31.

———. *My First Summer in the Sierra*. 1911. Ed. Edward Hoagland. Introduction by Gretel Ehrlich. New York: Penguin, 1987.

———. *Our National Parks*. 1901. In *John Muir* 457–605.

———. "Stickeen." 1909. In Mighetto 83–94.

———. "Twenty Hill Hollow Journal." 1868. In Limbaugh and Lewis, reel 23.

———. "The Wild Sheep." 1894. In *John Muir* 419–28.

———. "Wild Wool." 1875. In *John Muir* 871–76.

Mungall, Elizabeth Cary, and William J. Shefield, eds. *Exotics on the Range: The Texas Example*. College Station: Texas A&M U P, 1994.

Nabhan, Gary Paul. "Cultural Parallax in Viewing North American Habitats." In Soule and Lease 87–101.

Nash, Roderick Frazier. *American Environmentalism: Readings in Conservation History*. 3d ed. New York: McGraw, 1990.

———. *Wilderness and the American Mind*. 3d ed. New Haven: Yale U P, 1982.

Nelson, Barney. "Ranching on the Reservation, Part 1: The Crows." *Western Horseman*, April 1993: 94–97.

———. "Ranching on the Reservation, Part 2: Northern Cheyennes." *Western Horseman*, May 1993: 10–13.

Nelson, Richard. "The Gifts of Deer." In Trimble 304–24.

Neumann, Erich. *The Great Mother: An Analysis of Archetype*. Trans. Ralph Manheim. Princeton: Princeton U P, 1972.

Newman, J. A., P. D. Penning, A. J. Parsons, A. Harvey, and R. J. Orr. "Fasting Affects Intake Behavior and Diet Preference of Grazing Sheep." *Animal Behavior* 47.1 (1994): 185–94.

Norris, Frank. *The Octopus*. 1901. New York: Signet, 1964.

Norwood, Vera. "Heroines of Nature: Four Women Respond to the American Landscape." 1996. In Glotfelty and Fromm 323–50.

———. *Made for This Earth: American Women and Nature.* Chapel Hill: U of North Carolina P, 1993.

———. "The Photographer and the Naturalist: Laura Gilpin and Mary Austin in the Southwest." 1982. In "Mary (Hunter) Austin, 1868–1934" 39–41.

Norwood, Vera, and Janice Monk. *The Desert Is No Lady.* New Haven: Yale U P, 1987.

Noss, Reed F. "Cows and Conservation Biology." *Conservation Biology* 8.5 (1994): 613–16.

Oelschlaeger, Max, ed. *The Idea of Wilderness: From Prehistory to the Age of Ecology.* New Haven: Yale U P, 1991.

Oerlemans, Onno Dag. "The Meanest Thing That Feels." *Mosiac* 27.1 (1994): 1–32.

O'Grady, John P. *Pilgrims to the Wild: Everett Ruess, Henry David Thoreau, John Muir, Clarence King, Mary Austin.* Salt Lake City: U of Utah P, 1992.

———. "Thinking Is False Happiness." *Terra Nova* 1.3 (1996): 121–29.

O'Neill, Elizabeth Stone. *Meadow in the Sky: A History of Yosemite's Tuolumne Meadows Region.* Fresno: Panorama West Books, 1983.

Orr, David W. "Is Environmental Education an Oxymoron?" In *Ecological Literacy: Education and the Transition to a Postmodern World.* New York: SUNY P, 1992.

Our Magnificent Wildlife. Pleasantville, N.Y.: Reader's Digest Association, 1975.

Owens, L. B., W. M. Edwards, and R. W. Van Keuren. "Sediment Losses from a Pastured Watershed before and after Stream Fencing." *Journal of Soil and Water Conservation* 51.1 (1996): 90–95.

Parini, Jay. "The Greening of the Humanities." *New York Times Magazine,* October 29, 1995: 52–53.

Pattee, Fred Lewis. 1930. "The Feminine Novel." In "Mary (Hunter) Austin, 1868–1934" 45.

Pearce, T. M. 1965. From *Mary Hunter Austin.* In "Mary (Hunter) Austin, 1868–1934" 34–36.

Pei, Mario. "Animal Voices." In *What's in a Word? Language—Yesterday, Today, and Tomorrow.* New York: Hawthorn Books, 1968. 20–25.

Perrin, Noel. "Forever Virgin: The American View of America." In *On Nature: Nature, Landscape, and Natural History.* San Francisco: North Point P, 1987. 20.

Posey, Darrell Addison. "The Science of the Mebêngôkre." In *Finding Home: Writing on Nature and Culture from* Orion *Magazine,* ed. Peter Sauer. Boston: Beacon P, 1992. 135–148.

Powell, Lawrence Clark. "Mary Austin: *The Land of Little Rain.*" In *California Classics: The Creative Literature of the Golden State.* 1971. Capra P, 1982. 44–52.

Pryse, Marjorie, ed. Introduction to *Stories from the Country of Lost Borders.* New Brunswick: Rutgers U P, 1987. vii–xxxviii.

Pyne, Stephen J. "History with Fire in Its Eye." In Hart 105–12.

Quigley, Peter, ed. *Coyote in the Maze: Tracking Edward Abbey in a World of Words.* Salt Lake City: U of Utah P, 1998.

Raban, Jonathan. "The Hidden Life of Dogs." *New Republic* 210.9 (1994): 36–38.

Rawlins, C. L. E-mail message from crawlins@wyoming.com. Posted on asle@unr.edu, September 29, 1996.

Remley, David. "Fire on the Mountain." In Hepworth and McNamee 50–57.

"A Review of *The Flock.*" *Nation.* 1906. In "Mary (Hunter) Austin, 1868–1934" 17–18.

Reynolds, David R. "Rural Education: Decentering the Consolidation Debate." In *The Changing American Countryside: Rural People and Places,* ed. Emery N. Castle. Lawrence: U P of Kansas, 1995. 451–480.

Rifkin, Jeremy. *Beyond Beef: The Rise and Fall of the Cattle Culture.* New York: E. P. Dutton, 1992.

Ritvo, Harriet. "At the Edge of the Garden: Nature and Domestication in Eighteenth- and Nineteenth-Century Britain." *Huntington Library Quarterly* 55 (1992): 363–78.

Roberts, Jeanne Addison. "Animals as Agents of Revelation: The Horizontalizing of the Chain of Being in Shakespeare's Comedies." In *Shakespearean Comedy,* ed. Maurice Charney. New York: Literary Forum, 1980. 79–96.

Robertson, R. B. *Of Sheep and Men.* New York: Knopf, 1957.

Ronald, Ann. *The New West of Edward Abbey.* Albuquerque: U of New Mexico P, 1982.

Rosenberg, John D., ed. *The Genius of John Ruskin.* Boston: Houghton, 1963.

Rouse, John E. *The Criollo: Spanish Cattle in the Americas.* Norman: U of Oklahoma P, 1977.

———. *World Cattle.* Norman: U of Oklahoma P, 1970.

Rowell, Galen. "Along the High, Wild Sierra: The John Muir Trail." *National Geographic,* April 1989: 466–93.

Rudnick, Lois. "Re-naming the Land." 1987. In Norwood and Monk 10–26.

Ruess, R. W., and S. W. Seagle. "Landscape Patterns in Soil Microbial Processes in the Serengeti National Park, Tanzania." *Ecology* 75.4 (1994): 892–905.

Ruppert, James. "Discovering America: Mary Austin and Imagism." 1983. In P. G. Allen *Studies* 243–58.

———. "Mary Austin's Landscape Line in Native American Literature." *Southwest Review* 68 (1983): 376–90.

Ruskin, John. See Rosenberg.

Ruth, John L. *A Quiet and Peaceable Life.* Rev. ed. Intercourse, Pa.: Good Books, 1985. 59–60.

Ryden, Kent. "Ethics and Environment in New England Coastal Fiction." Paper presented at the New England American Studies Association, Mystic, Conn., May 9, 1998.

———. *Mapping the Invisible Landscape: Folklore, Writing, and the Sense of Place.* Iowa City: U of Iowa P, 1993.

Said, Edward W. *Orientalism.* New York: Vintage, 1979.

Savory, Allan. "Holistic Resource Management." In *Holistic Ranch Management Workshop Proceedings,* ed. J. Powell. Casper: Wyoming Agricultural Extension Service, 1985. 1–10.

Scheick, William J. "Mary Austin's Disfigurement of the Southwest in *The Land of Little Rain.*" *Western American Literature* 27 (1992): 37–46.

Schlenz, Mark. "Rhetorics of Region in *Starry Adventure* and *Death Comes for the Archbishop.*" In *Regionalism Reconsidered: New Approaches to the Field.* New York: Garland, 1994. 65–85.

Sessions, George. "Reinventing Nature: The End of Wilderness? A Response to William Cronon's *Uncommon Ground.*" *Wild Duck Review,* November 1995: 13–16.

Seton, Ernest Thompson. "Wully: The Story of a Yaller Dog." In *Wild Animals I Have Known.* 1898. Toronto: McClelland and Stewart, 1991. 189–208.

Shelton, Richard. "Creeping up on *Desert Solitaire.*" In Hepworth and McNamee 66–78.

Shepard, Paul. *The Tender Carnivore and the Sacred Game.* New York: Scribner's, 1973.

Silko, Leslie Marmon. *Ceremony.* New York: Penguin, 1977.

———. *Storyteller.* New York: Arcade, 1981.

Siringo, Charles A. *A Texas Cowboy, or Fifteen Years on the Hurricane Deck of a Spanish Pony, Taken from Real Life.* Biography and introduction by J. Frank Dobie. Lincoln: Bison, 1950.

Slotkin, Richard. *Regeneration through Violence: The Mythology of the American Frontier, 1600–1860.* Middletown, Conn.: Wesleyan U P, 1973.

Slovic, Scott, and Terrell Dixon, eds. *Being in the World: An Environmental Reader for Writers.* New York: Macmillan, 1993.

Smith, Adam. *The Wealth of Nations.* New York: E. P. Dutton, 1910.

Smith, Henry. "The Feel of Purposeful Earth: Mary Austin's Prophecy." 1931. In "Mary (Hunter) Austin, 1868–1934" 25–28.

Smith, Henry Nash. *Virgin Land: The American West as Symbol and Myth.* Cambridge: Harvard U P, 1970.

Snyder, Gary. *The Practice of the Wild.* San Francisco: North Point P, 1990.

Solheim, Dave, and Rob Levin. "The Bloomsbury Review: Interview." In Hepworth and McNamee 79–91.

Solnit, Rebecca. "Reclaiming History: Richard Misrach and the Politics of Landscape Photography." *Aperture,* midsummer 1990: 30–36.

———. *Savage Dreams: A Journey into the Landscape Wars of the American West.* New York: Vintage, 1994.

Soule, Michael E., and Gary Lease, eds. *Reinventing Nature? Responses to Postmodern Deconstruction.* Washington, D.C.: Island P, 1995.

Starr, Kevin. *Americans and the California Dream, 1850–1915.* New York: Oxford U P, 1973.

———. "Mary Austin: Mystic, Writer, Conservationist." *Sierra Bulletin* 61 (November–December 1976): 34.

Starrs, Paul F. " 'Cattle Free by '93' and the Imperatives of Environmental Radicalism." *Ubique: Notes from the American Geographical Society* 14.1 (1994): 2–4.

Stegner, Wallace. *The Sound of Mountain Water.* 1946. New York: Doubleday, 1969.

———. *Where the Bluebird Sings to the Lemonade Springs: Living and Writing in the West.* New York: Penguin, 1993.

Stelljes, Kathryn Barry. "Rangeland Can Improve with Grazing." *Agricultural Research* 43.9 (1995): 15–16.

Stewart, Frank. *A Natural History of Nature Writing.* Washington, D.C.: Island P, 1995.

Szynkiewicz, Slawoj. "Sheep Bone as a Sign of Human Descent: Tibia Symbolism among the Mongols." In Willis 74–84.

Taylor, Cynthia. "Claiming Female Space: Mary Austin's Western Landscape." In Engle 119–32.

Teale, Edwin Way, ed. Introduction to *The Wilderness World of John Muir*. 1954. New York: Houghton, 1982.

Temple, Eric, prod. and dir. *Edward Abbey: A Voice in the Wilderness*. 1993.

Terres, John K. *The Audubon Society Encyclopedia of North American Birds*. New York: Knopf, 1980.

Thoreau, Henry David. *The Portable Thoreau*. Ed. Carl Bode. New York: Penguin, 1975.

———. *Wild Apples*. 1862. Bedford, Mass.: Applewood Books, n.d.

Tompkins, Jane. *West of Everything: The Inner Life of Westerns*. New York: Oxford U P, 1992.

Tracy, Henry Chester. *The American Naturists*. New York: E. P. Dutton, 1930.

———. "Mary Austin." 1930. In "Mary (Hunter) Austin, 1868–1934" 24–25.

Trimble, Stephen, ed. *Words from the Land*. 1989. Exp. ed. Reno: U of Nevada P, 1995.

Trinh T. Minh-ha. *Woman Native Other: Writing Postcoloniality and Feminism*. Bloomington: Indiana U P, 1989.

Tuan, Yi-Fu. *Dominance and Affection: The Making of Pets*. New Haven: Yale U P, 1984.

———. "Topophilia, or, Sudden Encounter with the Landscape." *Landscape* 11.1 (1961): 29–32.

Turner, Frederick. "Cultivating the American Garden." In Glotfelty and Fromm 40–51.

Turner, Frederick Jackson. *The Significance of the Frontier in American History*. 1893. Introduction by John Alexander Carroll. El Paso: Texas Western College P for Academic Reports, 1960.

Twain, Mark. *Mississippi Writings*. New York: Viking, 1982.

Tyler, Moses. *A History of American Literature, 1607–1765*. 1878. Ithaca: Cornell U P, 1949.

Van Doren, Carl. "Mary Austin: Discoverer and Prophet." 1923. In "Mary (Hunter) Austin, 1868–1934" 22–24.

Van Dyke, John C. *The Desert*. 1901. Tucson: Arizona Historical Society, 1976.

Wallace, David Rains. *The Untamed Garden and Other Personal Essays*. Columbus: Ohio State U P, 1986.

Weaver, Bruce J. " 'What to Do with the Mountain People?': The Darker Side of the Successful Campaign to Establish the Great Smoky Mountains National Park." In *The Symbolic Earth: Discourse and Our Creation of the Environment*, ed. James C. Cantrill and Christine L. Oravec. Lexington: U P of Kentucky, 1996. 151–75.

West, Neil. "Biodiversity of Rangelands." *Journal of Range Management* 46 (1993): 2–13.

White, Lynn Jr. "The Historical Roots of Our Ecologic Crisis." In Glotfelty and Fromm 3–14.

White, Richard. " 'Are You an Environmentalist or Do You Work for a Living?': Work and Nature." In Cronon 171–85.

Whitehead, G. Kenneth. *The Ancient White Cattle of Britain and Their Descendants*. London: Faber and Faber, 1959.

Willis, Roy, ed. *Signifying Animals: Human Meaning in the Natural World*. London: Routledge, 1990.

Winkler, Karen J. "Inventing a New Field: The Study of Literature about the Environment." *Chronicle of Higher Education*, August 9, 1996: A1, A8–A9 + .

Work, James C. "The Moral in Austin's *The Land of Little Rain*." 1982. In "Mary (Hunter) Austin, 1868–1934" 41–44.

Worster, Donald. *The Wealth of Nature: Environmental History and the Ecological Imagination*. New York: Oxford U P, 1993.

Wyatt, David. "Mary Austin: Nature and Nurturance." In *The Fall into Eden: Landscape and Imagination in California*. New York: Cambridge U P, 1986. 67–95.

Wynn, Dudley. *A Critical Study of the Writings of Mary Hunter Austin, 1868–1934*. New York: Graduate School of Arts and Sciences, New York U, 1941.

———. "Mary Austin: Woman Alone." 1937. In "Mary (Hunter) Austin, 1868–1934" 46.

Young, Vernon. "Mary Austin and the Earth Performance." 1950. In "Mary (Hunter) Austin, 1868–1934" 29–32.

Acknowledgments

I am indebted to the Association for the Study of Literature and Environment (ASLE) and its organizers for providing me with the contacts and the lens through which to study literature in a manner I believe is tremendously important, both in the classroom and in the community. I was present as a charter member when Scott Slovic, Cheryll Glotfelty, and Michael Branch spearheaded a drive to form ASLE at the Western Literature Association conference in 1992. They inspired me to design and teach a course called "Environmental Literature" at Sul Ross State University in 1993. The following year, I headed to the University of Nevada, Reno, to study with Glotfelty. Dr. Glotfelty had been hired in 1990 when Nevada created the first academic position in literature and environment, and I became her first doctoral candidate. During the fall semester of 1995, Glotfelty offered a graduate seminar entitled "Representing the Other: Animals in Literature," which was known on campus, somewhat derisively, as "Critter Lit." This class sparked my ideas for what eventually became this book. A *New York Times Magazine* story entitled "The Greening of the Humanities" listed the course as one of the top six in the field, called Glotfelty one of the "gurus," and said: "Deconstruction is compost. Environmental Studies is the Academic Field of the 90's" (Parini). The new field was also featured in a front-page story in the *Chronicle of Higher Education* that included a two-page photograph of Glotfelty and called the University of Nevada, Reno, "a center for ecocentrism." Glotfelty has been a tremendous inspiration. I highly recommend both the program at Nevada and her tireless, gentle guidance.

While I studied at Nevada, both Slovic, ASLE's first president, and Branch, ASLE's third president, joined the environmental literature staff. I became Slovic's first graduate fellow and his administrative assistant in the Center for Environmental Arts and Humanities. As part of my duties, I served as assistant editor for the *American Nature Writing Newsletter* and for the journal *ISLE: Interdisciplinary Studies in Literature and Environment,* both of which Slovic was editing. I also served with Slovic as codirector for the Seventh North American Interdisciplinary Wilderness Conference. Therefore, I am also indebted to Slovic and Branch for guidance, inspiration, and their devil's advocacy.

At Nevada, I was further encouraged and inspired by Drs. Ann Ronald, a leading Edward Abbey scholar and the clout behind the environmental program at Nevada; Stephen Tchudi, a nationally recognized theorist who teaches an outstanding summer graduate seminar investigating the literature and rhetoric surrounding public land issues; Paul Starrs, a highly respected cultural geographer and expert on sagebrush rebellions; and Dale Holcombe, a female sheep production specialist deeply involved in grazing research who has won the respect of both rural and academic colleagues. Their combined perspectives further convinced me that our perception of domestic livestock, which is both reflected in and shaped by our literature, needed to be investigated.

I am also indebted to the administration at Sul Ross State University for allowing me to take a two-year leave of absence from teaching duties in order to pursue the research that eventually resulted in this book: President R. Vic Morgan Jr., Vice-President for Academic Affairs David Cockrum, and Languages and Literature Chair Sharon Hileman.

I would also like to thank the staff at the Huntington Library: Sue Hodson, Curator of Literary Manuscripts; and Sul Ross State University librarians, especially Eleanor Wilson and Mike Robinson, for their help and expertise. Although small, SRSU's library has an amazingly complete collection of Mary Austin's early work.

Thanks are also due to C. David Ankney, C. L. Rawlins, Kent Ryden, Roy McBride, and Hudson R. Glimp for allowing me to publish their works and words.

In addition, I thank those who read various parts of the manuscript and gave helpful corrections and advice: Dr. James Scudday, SRSU Professor Emeritus of Zoology; Roy McBride; Ron Goddard; Tommy Vaughn; Brian Larremore; Laurie Champion; Rhonda Austin; Melody Graulich; Peter Quigley; Richard Schneider; Andrea Purdy; Donna Cook; David Cockrum; and Bill Kittredge. Any remaining errors or awkward statements are my own fault, not theirs. I would also like to exonerate my copy editor, Mindy Conner, who did an excellent job of finding and fixing my grammar errors. Unfortunately, I asked her to change many of them back.

For emotional and personal support I am indebted to my daughter and son-in-law, Carla and Chris Spencer; my parents and brother, Dwain, Marge, and Richard DeGear; my colleagues at SRSU; my fellow graduate students at UNR, especially Gioia Woods; rural and small-town friends and neighbors; and the animals who have shared my life.

Index

Abbey, Edward: 56, 92–109, 110, 112, 149–53; *Beyond the Wall,* 93–94; *The Brave Cowboy,* 92; *Cactus Country,* 93–94, 98; *Desert Solitaire: A Season in the Wilderness,* 92, 98, 100, 105; *Down the River,* 100; *Fire on the Mountain,* 92, 100; *Good News,* 92; introduction to *The Land of Little Rain* by Mary Austin, 98–99; *The Journey Home,* 100, 109; *The Monkey Wrench Gang,* 92; *One Life at a Time, Please,* 107, 113; *Slickrock,* 93, 99, 149n1. *See also* gender; racism
Abram, David, 42–43, 137
adopting animals, 23, 27, 53, 56, 58–60, 86
Africa, 5, 10–11, 38, 105, 143n13, 152n21, 153n26
Allen, Caffilene, 146n14
Allen, Paula Gunn, 137
agribusiness, 11, 17, 100, 101, 108, 150n8, 151n18
American Rifle Association, 61
Amish, 11
animal rights, 1, 70, 102, 127
animism, 41–42, 99, 103, 131, 137, 144n15, 150n6
Ankney, C. Davison, 9–10, 142n11, 170
antelope, pronghorn, 12, 24, 38, 54–55, 69–71, 126, 127, 145n11–12
Antelope Hills, 70
anthropocentrism, 53, 77
anthropomorphism, 39–40, 43, 59–60, 68, 127, 145n3, 148n18, 149n5
apples, xiii, 6, 25, 105, 113, 119
Arizona, 27, 61, 65, 96–97, 104, 127
Arrivipa Canyon, 113

art, 33–34, 80, 105, 107, 150n6. *See also* music; work: men's art/crafts; work: women's art/crafts
Audubon, John James, 19
Audubon Society, National, 12, 153n23
Austin, Mary: on animals as teachers, 25–43, 137; *Children Sing in the Far West,* 32; critics hindered by concentrating on her life, 131, 149–50n5; *The Flock,* 23, 33; *The Flock* as reaction to Muir's denigration of sheep and shepherds, 74–91, 132; "The Folk Story in America," 43; *The Ford,* 20, 146n1; gendering animal stories, 44–57, 132; importance of sense of place, 133–35; importance of studying the animal stories of, 18–24, 130, 135, 137; as influence on Abbey, 94–109; *The Land of Journeys' Ending,* 25; *The Land of Little Rain,* 23, 31, 48, 57, 75, 94, 98–99, 103, 149n5, 150nn.7, 11, 151n15, 152n20; "A Lost Dog," 35–36; "Mamichee," 152n21; "Regionalism in American Fiction," 151n13; "A Shepherd of the Sierras," 149n20; *The Trail Book,* 27–36, 143n5; "When I Am Dead," 138–39. *See also* coyote; descent, line of; dogs; food; myth; Native American; sheep

badger, 36, 68, 99
Bakhtin, Mikhail, 76, 147n6
Barbary sheep, 38, 66
Basque, 76, 80
bear, 28, 54, 56, 61, 65, 71, 88, 90, 127, 148n19. *See also* grizzly bear
Berger, John, 16, 40, 42